BEHAVIOURAL FINANCE

A GUIDE FOR FINANCIAL ADVISERS

By
Simon Russell

First published in 2019 by Simon Christopher Russell as Trustee for the BCF Consulting Services Trust (trading as Behavioural Finance Australia)

www.behaviouralfinanceaustralia.com.au

Email: simon.russell@bfin.com.au
© Simon Russell 2019

National Library of Australia Cataloguing-in-Publication entry:
Creator: Russell, Simon Christopher, author.

Title: Behavioural Finance: A guide for financial advisers / Simon Russell.

Subjects: Wealth Management / Retirement Planning / Money Management / Investing / Budgeting / Portfolio Management / Analysis & Trading Strategies / Stocks

ISBN: 978-0-9946102-3-2 (paperback)

Simon is the founder of Behavioural Finance Australia (BFA). At BFA he provides specialist behavioural finance training and consulting to financial advisers, fund managers, major super funds and other investment professionals. His services help his clients to apply insights about investment decision-making to tailor their investment processes and client engagement strategies.

In addition to this book, Simon is the author of two other books on behavioural finance: *Applying Behavioural Finance in Australia* and *'Cyborg'*. He regularly speaks on client engagement and investment decision-making at industry and academic conferences. Some of Simon's articles on behavioural finance-related issues and videos of his conference presentations are available at behaviouralfinanceaustralia.com.au.

Simon's qualifications combine psychology and investments. He holds a Bachelor of Arts (Psychology) and a Bachelor of Commerce (Finance) both from the University of Adelaide, a Graduate Diploma in Applied Finance & Investments from the Securities Institute of Australia, a Master of Applied Finance from Macquarie University, a Diploma of Financial Planning from MLC Advice Education and a Graduate Certificate in Management from the Australian Institute of Management.

Simon lives in Melbourne with his partner, Leonora, and three children, Ben, Clare and Emma.

TABLE OF CONTENTS

What this Book is About   1

1. Behavioural Finance and the Subconscious Mind   9

2. Risk Tolerance, Perceptions & Profiling   31

3. Happiness, Motivation & Future Goals   49

4. The (Often Overstated) Role of Financial Literacy   65

5. Market Cycles & the Behavioural Roller-Coaster   81

6. Exploiting Behavioural Biases in Markets   101

7. Biases in Diversification & Asset Allocation   119

8. Advising Overconfident Investors   137

9. Residential Real Estate; the Most Biased Asset Class?   157

10. The Psychology of Saving & Retirement Planning   175

11. Client Engagement & Influence   195

12. Topical Issues: Ethics, Technology & Cognitive Diversity   221

13. Conclusions & Practical Challenges   241

Notes, References & Further Resources   249

Acknowledgements   281

WHAT THIS BOOK
IS ABOUT

Why do clients make silly decisions? Why do some of them acknowledge that they need to save for retirement, but continue to spend like there is no tomorrow? Why do some of them recognise that diversification can avoid unnecessary risks, but then invest in undiversified portfolios comprising only a handful of their favourite stocks? Why do some clients articulate goals that they say are important to them, but then later change their minds and pursue something entirely different? And why do some say they are long-term investors who understand and accept the risks associated with investing in growth assets, but then switch their investments to cash in response to short-term market fluctuations?

It is easy to conclude that these behaviours reflect foolishness, capriciousness, or a client's lack of discipline and fortitude. This interpretation suggests that these clients cannot be trusted to look after their own interests, and that they should therefore outsource all of their financial and investment decisions to their advisers.

This approach might work with some clients. However, advisers understand that for many clients they will need to take a more nuanced approach, one in which different aspects of decisions are shared between the client and their adviser. To do this, advisers need to be skilled at understanding why clients think and act as they do. In order to help them to make better financial decisions, advisers need to be able to influence clients to think and act differently. And, of course, advisers need to be able to convince clients about the value of their advice so that they are willing to pair a fair price for it.

This book is intended to help advisers to achieve these things. It discusses the psychological dynamics that underpin a range of common decision-making problems that advisers are likely to encounter with their clients. These dynamics run deep, often reflecting our evolutionary history as well as our neurological structures and functions. Rather than clients necessarily being foolish, the problems advisers encounter could simply be the result of them being human. By understanding the human failings that lead to clients' sometimes self-defeating financial decisions and behaviours, advisers can identify strategies to help clients overcome or circumvent these problems.

In many ways, advisers are ideally suited to understanding and influencing their clients. For an adviser with an eye for relevant psychological issues, their personal relationships potentially allow them to spot aspects of their clients' circumstances and experiences that can most heavily influence their decisions. Their client relationships can also allow them to employ influencing strategies at times and in ways that clients are likely to be most receptive to. And advisers' relationships also allow them to leverage the power of social influence to help keep their clients accountable and on-track in ways that would be difficult otherwise. If anyone can help these clients, psychologically savvy advisers can.

But the challenges advisers face should not be understated. While decision-making biases might mean that clients need advice, the very same biases can also mean that they don't see the need for assistance. Like how the submerged section of an iceberg remains hidden from view, psychological issues that reside in the subconscious are immune from introspection and awareness. Client behaviour that might appear to their adviser to be irrational, probably seems well considered to them. The powerful forces of self-deception that can influence people's decisions mean that sometimes those who need help the most are also those who are least amenable to receiving it. To them, the visible tip of the iceberg seems perfectly fine.

When problems lurk in the subconscious, an adviser trying to convince their client with 'rational' arguments, information, education and analysis is likely to be futile. For example, where they do not adequately account for the relevant psychological issues, some well-intentioned financial literacy campaigns merely provide false hope that they will make a meaningful difference. Similarly, where they neglect the true drivers of people's decisions, some poorly designed risk profiling tools can provide false confidence that advisers truly understand their clients. By aligning with the psychological evidence about how people think and behave, this book is intended to help advisers to focus on what works.

The insights provided in this book are drawn from a range of sources: psychological research from the laboratory, neurological research from brain scanners, behavioural finance research about investment decisions made in the real world, surveys of advisers and their clients, and the experiences of advisers and others from across the industry. In part, this book also reflects my personal experiences in applying behavioural finance concepts with my clients – financial advisers, major superannuation funds, fund managers and others.

While I now have several years of experience specifically focussed on the application of behavioural finance research, when I started, I didn't know what I was doing. I was aware of a wealth of psychological and behavioural finance research that showed that people didn't always act 'rationally' and that there was often a 'behavioural gap' between what people should do and what they actually did. And, as many advisers can probably attest, I knew that the gap could have important consequences, sometimes leading people to catastrophic financial and life outcomes. But what could I do about it?

It was in this context I decided to start a specialist behavioural finance business, with the aim of closing this behavioural gap, at least a little. I figured that my background in psychology, and expertise across various forms of financial and investment decision-making would be a fairly rare combination. In my experience, people with qualifications in psychology don't tend to have a deep understanding of investments, and vice versa.

To gather ideas for my new business I ran a few behavioural finance workshops. Fortunately, attendance of these early workshops was strong, otherwise my new business venture might have died in its infancy. About half of the workshop participants were financial advisers, with the rest from across the investment industry (from major super funds, asset managers, etc). Each workshop outlined psychological evidence demonstrating deficiencies with different aspects of financial decision-making, along with what we knew about their causes and consequences. Potential strategies to overcome, avoid or align with these decision-making biases were discussed.

In each workshop I sought feedback from participants on the practical challenges they could foresee and the areas in which they saw the biggest opportunities for improvement. It was evident that some participants were interested in technical aspects of investment decision-making and portfolio construction, but most were interested in practical strategies to better understand and engage with their clients.

Those workshops are now several years in the past. Since then I have learnt a lot about how behavioural finance can be applied to help advisers and their clients. My experience has taught me a few lessons; such as that some strategies that appear to make sense on the face of the psychological evidence are likely to encounter formidable barriers in the real world. Like a body rejecting an incompatible organ, psychological concepts cannot be directly transplanted from the university laboratory into an advice business. In part this is because the context in which a strategy is applied often makes a big difference. Nothing works for all clients all of the time.

When it comes to implementing behavioural strategies, I've also learnt that talking about someone else's biases is much easier than talking about your own; that aligning with decision-making biases is often more effective than trying to overcome them; and that small, simple and easy strategies can often be more effective than large, complex and difficult ones. Making things easy helps both clients and advisers.

Since my initial workshops behavioural finance has risen in prominence, particularly for Australian financial advisers. In an Australian context, the Financial Adviser Standards and Ethics Authority ('FASEA') has identified behavioural finance as one of the key topics in which advisers need to demonstrate their competence if they wish to continue delivering advice. As a result of FASEA's new requirements many advisers will need to complete a bridging subject in behavioural finance, and all advisers will need to complete an exam that incorporates some elements of behavioural finance.

As a consequence of these new requirements I was recently asked to design a behavioural finance bridging course for advisers. As part of that work I struggled to find a textbook to recommend to accompany the course materials; one that was practically applicable for advisers, relevant for an Australian context, and well-grounded in the academic literature. It needed to go beyond basic concepts, given that advisers often already have had some exposure to behavioural finance concepts and have high financial literacy. To fill the gap, I undertook to write a book about behavioural finance specifically for Australian financial advisers. This is that book.

Behavioural finance concepts are also being incorporated into the way other policy-makers and regulators are shaping the Australian investment and advice industries. For example, behavioural finance was a central part of the recent Productivity Commission report into the efficiency of the Australian superannuation system. The Productivity Commission report included 52 references to 'behavioural finance' and related terms.[1] Even had it wanted to, it would have been difficult for the Productivity Commission to have ignored behavioural finance, given that it was explicitly referred to in the terms of reference handed down to it by the then Treasurer.

The recent Royal Commission has added further weight to the use of behavioural finance in place of, or as a complement to, traditional approaches. The Royal Commission explored how both clients' and financial advisers' decision-making can be influenced in ways that go beyond their awareness.[2] Traditional approaches to regulation that aim to provide clients with more disclosure, more educational materials and more choice are ineffective when clients simply ignore the disclosure, fail to understand or respond to the educational materials, and become overwhelmed by too much choice. A behavioural approach is required.

Of particular relevance for advisers, the Australian Securities and Investments Commission ('ASIC'), the key regulatory body for financial advice, has been using behavioural insights for some time. Anecdotally, its focus on behavioural finance seems to have recently been heightened. This is evidenced by the fact that when ASIC recently required an Australian Financial Services License (AFSL) holder to send a letter to its clients, ASIC was reportedly not satisfied that the letter simply presented all the relevant facts so that clients could make an informed decision. In addition, it required the letter to be framed and presented in a way that aligned with the psychological evidence about how clients were likely to process the contents of the letter and respond to it. Advisers who are unaware of the psychological evidence about client decision-making now risk being blindsided by regulators who are a step in-front of them.

In addition to the behavioural finance 'stick' created by these regulatory changes, there is also a 'carrot'. For example, advisers who understand behavioural finance can benefit from the increased opportunities left behind by those who fail to satisfy the new education requirements. And as existing revenue models are disrupted by regulatory changes, advisers who can use behavioural insights to help clients appreciate the value in their services and trust their advice stand to benefit.

Other industry changes also create headwinds for some advisers but opportunities for those who are versed in the use of psychological insights. For example, as the ubiquity of information creates increasing challenges for some advice propositions, advisers who are adept at understanding and influencing their clients can continue to deliver value by helping to coach their clients and to guide their decision-making. And as new technologies are introduced, advisers who are able to use digital technologies and data to better influence and engage with clients will thrive, while others fail to compete with cheaper 'robo-advice' services.

Beyond these commercial benefits, hopefully advisers who are better able to understand and influence their clients will experience less stress and frustration, and will enjoy their work more. This book is intended to assist advisers who are interested in the carrot, the stick, or both.

Three broad perspectives, or 'lenses', are woven together throughout this book. Firstly, there is an outward-looking lens. This lens is intended to help advisers to better understand and influence clients; including how clients think about risks, set goals, respond to financial literacy initiatives and to market cycles, save for retirement, build portfolios and choose properties to buy and to live in. This outward-looking lens also helps advisers to understand how people's decision-making biases can influence markets, leading to systematic distortions that savvy investors can potentially exploit.

Secondly, there is an inward-looking lens. That lens examines how decision-making biases can influence advisers too. Sophisticated financial professionals might not necessarily be impacted by the same decision-making biases as are their clients, but that is not to say they are immune. To believe that they are beyond the reach of bias is to fall foul of 'blind-spot bias' (thinking that biases only apply to others).

And finally, a third lens focuses on the interaction between the client and their adviser. This lens examines the psychological factors that can mean clients fail to trust their adviser or to value their advice, even when their adviser is trustworthy and their advice is valuable. In turn, in their client interactions advisers can sometimes fail to check the assumptions that they implicitly make about clients and fail to ensure that their communications are received as they were intended.

In summary, just as there are many ways decision-making can go wrong, there are also many strategies advisers can use to improve engagement, decision-making and outcomes. Hopefully these strategies are articulated in sufficient detail throughout the book. However, readers seeking further information are referred to the references and further resources included at the end of the book, and are invited to visit my website: behaviouralfinanceaustralia.com.au.

1

BEHAVIOURAL FINANCE AND THE SUBCONSCIOUS MIND

Probably for most financial advisers, behavioural finance is not entirely new. Many have read at least one book describing experiments that demonstrate humans' money-related fallibilities. Some have attended workshops and conferences that have discussed aspects of behavioural finance and decision-making biases. And if they haven't read the books or attended the conferences, they have almost certainly witnessed firsthand examples of apparently irrational financial decisions made by their clients.

Despite this, I sometimes find that advisers' knowledge of behavioural finance is patchy, with many being familiar with some core concepts from the field, but not with others. In addition, some advisers lack a conceptual framework to integrate behavioural finance into the way they think about investment issues, and into the way they work with clients.

The purpose of this chapter is to fill these gaps, by outlining the key themes and concepts from behavioural finance that are relevant in the context of financial advice. For example, how does behavioural finance differ from traditional approaches to investment decision-making? From what perspective and evidence base are insights drawn? What are some of the ways that people's decisions can be made or influenced beyond their complete conscious awareness or control? And what are the potential implications for advisers and their clients? In answering these questions, this chapter lays the groundwork for the strategies and applications that are discussed throughout the remainder of the book.

THREE VIEWS

Financial decision-making can be viewed broadly in three ways. These are the *'normative view'*, the *'descriptive view'* and the *'prescriptive view'*. The normative view represents what people theoretically *should do*, and it forms the basis for traditional finance theory. The descriptive view challenges this theory by describing what people *actually do* when faced with various financial and investment decisions. In turn, the prescriptive view combines finance theory with insights about actual behaviour. In doing so, it seeks to identify practical strategies that can lead to people achieving better outcomes. What follows is a whistle-stop tour of the three views, how they differ, why each is useful for advisers to understand, and some of the strengths and limitations of each.

The normative view

The normative view refers to what people should do if they were fully 'rational'; that is, if they were able to process all available information perfectly and free from any cognitive or emotional limitations. This view forms the basis for the often elegant and sophisticated models that underpin traditional economic and finance theories, some of which are discussed below.

According to these traditional models and theories, people should make decisions that maximize their *'utility'* (or happiness) across their lifetimes. In doing so, there are assumed to be diminishing marginal returns to consumption. This means that people are assumed to get more pleasure from the first dollar they spend at each point in time, compared with the pleasure from spending their second dollar or their hundredth dollar.

As a result of these diminishing marginal returns, maintaining a relatively stable level of spending across a person's lifetime is likely to create greater utility than alternative spending patterns that involve periods of relative feast and famine. Put differently, we should expect 'rational' people to engage in *'consumption smoothing'* (ie saving during periods of relatively high income, and dissaving or borrowing during other periods). This is referred to as the *'Life Cycle Hypothesis'*.

With the wealth they accumulate from their savings, theoretically rational people are assumed to invest in a way that maximises their expected return for a given level of risk, or minimises their risk for a given return. To achieve this, they undertake a process of *'mean-variance optimisation'* in accordance with *'Modern Portfolio Theory'* (MPT). This process involves calculating the expected returns and co-variances of different investments and building an *'efficient frontier'* of *'optimal portfolios'*. From these portfolios individuals then select one that suits their preferences for risk and return.

In this rational world, because it is suboptimal to accept risks that can be avoided through diversification, everyone holds a broadly diversified portfolio. And because everyone is holding diversified portfolios, nobody cares about *'idiosyncratic risks'* (ie risks related only to specific investments, rather than to broad market or economic factors).

Theoretically, the only risk that these rational investors care about is how much each investment contributes to the overall risk profile of their portfolios. This risk contribution is referred to as an investment's *'beta'*. According to the *'Capital Asset Pricing Model'* (CAPM), this beta can then be used, in combination with the risk-free rate of return and the market risk premium, to value individual investments.

Finally, because these theoretically rational investors process information immediately and perfectly, there is no point anyone trying to beat the market. Rational investors will still face uncertainty in this theoretical world, but there would be no pricing anomalies or inefficiencies for them to systematically exploit, at least not by using publicly available information. This, of course, is known as (one form of) the *'Efficient Markets Hypothesis'* (EMH).

The descriptive view

In contrast to the normative view, which suggests what fully rational investors theoretically should do, the descriptive view examines how people actually behave and make decisions. Psychologists, neuroscientists, behavioural finance researchers and others have used a range of techniques to learn about the financial choices people make. In controlled laboratory experiments they have analysed the impact on people's choices of slight variations in the way those choices are framed. They have studied people's brains while they make decisions from inside neuroimaging devices. They have collected saliva samples and assessed changes in people's hormone levels after they encounter stressful decisions. They have tracked people's eye movements to see what parts of a decision they most focus on. They have explored links between people's behaviour and patterns in their DNA. And, importantly, they have measured people's financial choices and outcomes in the real world, both with and without the benefits of financial advice.

What this research shows is that often people don't conform with *'rational'* models and theories.[1] Rather, they are subject to a range of decision-making *'biases'*. These biases are often deeply rooted in the way people think, in the structures and functions of their brains, in their shared evolutionary histories, in their social environments and cultures, in the lessons they have learnt from past experiences, and sometimes even in their genetic codes. While the evidence from these studies is often stark, because many biases operate at a subconscious level, their influence on people's decisions can often remain hidden.

The descriptive view challenges a number of traditional financial theories and models. For example, rather than methodically engaging in consumption smoothing, in the real-world people struggle to resist the urge to consume in the present and to save for retirement. Lifetime consumption can also be far from smooth for people who fail to appropriately insure for life-changing events, such as the risk of them suffering an injury that leaves them permanently incapacitated. As advisers would be well aware, these risks can result in substantial hardship for individuals and their families.

Not even Harry Markowitz himself, the founder of MPT, tries to calculate co-variances when choosing portfolios, at least not all of the time. When asked how he determined his initial pension fund asset allocation, he reportedly said: *'I should have computed the historical co-variances of the asset classes and drawn an efficient frontier. Instead, I visualised my grief if the stock market went way up and I wasn't in it – or if it went way down and I was completely in it. My intention was to minimise my future regret. So I split my contributions 50/50 between bonds and equities.'*[2] If Nobel Laureates don't conform to the rational models they themselves developed, what hope is there for mere mortals?

Similarly, flaws have been found with the assumptions, behaviours and outcomes relating to other traditional financial theories. For example, counter to the CAPM, beta does not appear to be the only measure, or even a very good one in some cases, that is relevant for calculating expected returns. Several other measures have also been found to be important. These are often referred to as 'risk-factors', and include value, quality and momentum. Each can be at least partially explained using psychological research. And, counter to the EMH, arguably some of these types of anomalies can be exploited by savvy investors to earn additional returns, without requiring them to accept additional risk. Traditional financial models and theories might be elegant, but the real world is messy.

The prescriptive view

Given the challenges to traditional models and theories, should financial advisers discard the normative view, replace it with the descriptive view, and spend their time hunting for market anomalies? Not so fast! Both the normative and descriptive views have strengths and weaknesses; neither of them is definitively superior. While there are flaws in some of the assumptions on which traditional models are based, these models can still provide useful frameworks to work from. Just because people don't undertake mean-variance optimisation doesn't mean that they shouldn't diversify, for example. Advisers clearly shouldn't throw out the diversification-benefits-baby with the incorrect-theoretical-assumptions-bathwater.

And just as there are strengths with the normative view that mean it shouldn't be entirely discarded, there are also weaknesses with the descriptive view that mean it shouldn't be entirely adopted. What works in a relatively simple, controlled laboratory environment might not work in the relatively complex, uncontrolled real world. The real world is different from what is assumed by theoretical financial models, but it is also different from the artificial world created in universities' psychology departments.

The prescriptive view is a compromise. Rather than adopting either the normative or the descriptive views, the prescriptive view seeks to take the best of both approaches and combine it with a large dose of practical reality. In doing so, it attempts to answer the all-important question: *given what we know, what should real people do in the real world?'* Answering that question in the context of financial advice is the purpose of this book.

The realities of the real world that the prescriptive view seeks to incorporate can sometimes make a big difference. For example, while decision-making biases might lead to market anomalies, the practical reality is that arbitragers could eliminate those anomalies or transaction costs could make them uneconomic to exploit. Despite the apparent flaws with the EMH, if active managers are unable to effectively exploit market anomalies then arguably investors should invest as if the EMH were true.

This would also be the case if some active managers could systematically exploit market anomalies but investors and their advisers were unable to reliably identify those successful active managers ahead of time. In this case, determining what investors should do requires understanding the issues and opportunities created by several layers of decision-making – how investor behaviour creates market anomalies, how asset managers exploit those anomalies, and how investors and advisers select asset managers. These topics are addressed in subsequent chapters.

What about MPT? Even if advisers can reliably create an efficient frontier of optimal portfolios, choosing between them can be difficult. Selecting the most appropriate portfolio requires understanding each client's preferences for risk versus return. The normative view assumes that these preferences are known, but psychological research shows that if not carefully measured, a client's risk tolerance can be easily obscured by their recent experiences, or by the way risk profiling questions are framed. And determining a client's financial goals is not straightforward either. The psychological challenges advisers face in understanding clients' risk tolerances and in identifying their goals are discussed in Chapters 2 and 3, respectively.

The traditional theories and models of the normative view, and much of the psychological evidence of the descriptive view are now well established. In contrast, the prescriptive view is at the bleeding edge of behavioural finance. In building upon the normative and descriptive views, the prescriptive view incorporates the results of initial attempts to apply psychological insights to improve people's financial decisions.

Some of these initiatives have been well-designed, have had their results rigorously recorded and analysed, and ultimately have had papers about them published in peer-reviewed academic journals. While the results of initiatives that fail to meet these lofty academic criteria need to be viewed with some scepticism, they can nevertheless be informative for advisers too. They can reveal where psychological insights interface with practical challenges and commercial realities, for example. Lessons from both published academic research and unpublished industry initiatives are discussed throughout this book.

KEY DECISION-MAKING CONCEPTS

The remainder of this chapter provides a short summary of six of the important decision-making biases that are relevant in the context of financial advice. While each is separate, the key theme that connects them is that they often occur beyond people's conscious awareness. When people introspect they might find apparently rational, considered explanations for their decisions. However, the psychological research shows that conscious processes often play a smaller role in people's decisions than they imagine. As a result, some of the reasons that clients provide advisers to explain their decisions are likely to be merely post-decision rationalisations. These explanations are constructed to cover the real reasons for clients' decisions, reasons that lie beyond the reach of their conscious experience.

1) People are too sensitive to losses

That people dislike losses is unlikely to be news to many financial advisers; of course, people would rather have gains than losses. However, behavioural finance research provides a deeper and richer understanding of people's relationship with losses. This allows advisers to better understand their clients' tolerance for accepting risk. Psychological insights can also assist advisers to better understand and influence the way clients respond to the losses that they experience.

One of the key psychological insights about losses is that people's dislike of them can be disproportionately large. Psychological research typically demonstrates that the prospect of suffering losses impacts people's decisions roughly twice as much as does the prospect of achieving equivalent sized gains. This is referred to as 'loss aversion', and uncovering it contributed to Daniel Kahneman winning a Nobel Prize in Economics.

There are a number of reasons why loss aversion can be important in the context of financial advice. For example, seeking to recoup their losses might contribute to a client making things worse by 'throwing good money after bad'. Ironically, as in this example, some attempts to avoid losses can actually increase the risk of a client experiencing them. This problem, in part, underpins the 'disposition effect' and short-term momentum, both of which are discussed in Chapter 6.

Another example of how loss aversion can cause a problem is if an investment gains $15k, followed by a loss of $10k. While the total return in this case is positive, if people are twice as sensitive to losses as gains, the psychological impact for an investor experiencing these returns could be negative. A loss-averse investor might therefore forgo this otherwise profitable investment.

This relatively simple example belies some of the complexity inherent in it, not least of which is whether the expected return is adequate given the investor's goals, their risk tolerance and the alternatives that are available to them. However, it does highlight one of the perennial challenges facing financial advisers: how to help clients to reduce their fear of losses and be able to sleep at night, while still benefiting from the higher expected long-term returns that come from investing in risky assets. Finding the cheapest, easiest and most effective ways to help clients achieve this mix of financial and psychological benefits is a focus of this book.

One of the strategies advisers can use to mitigate the impact of a client's fear of losses is derived from the fact that the way information is framed can change how people respond to it. In the preceding example, one of the complexities that was glossed over was how the client actually experienced the gain and the loss. On the face of it, it seems simple: $15k was the gain and $10k was the loss. However, if the client didn't check their investments after the $15k gain and only did so following the subsequent $10k loss, then they might have only observed a single $5k gain. While the investment outcome is the same, the psychological impact might be quite different. Like a proverbial tree falling in a forest, if they weren't observed, did losses actually happen? From a psychological perspective at least, the answer is 'no'.

More than this, investment returns create opportunities that fallen trees do not. Whereas fallen trees remain fallen, in a sense, losses don't always remain losses. As in this example, when viewed over longer time frames, losses can be more than offset by typically larger gains. Similarly, when the returns from the many different investments that clients might hold in their portfolios are combined, the gains and losses that each individual investment achieves can also offset.

The broad conclusion from this is that advisers should typically frame investment information in ways that focus their clients' attention on long-term returns and on total portfolio outcomes. The way investment information is presented in reports, on web sites and in Statements of Advice should align with these principles.

While there are good examples of investment professionals using these insights appropriately, it is also not difficult to find cases of those who don't. For example, while I was writing this chapter, I logged onto my superannuation fund's web site where I was invited to create a graph of the returns achieved from my investment option. Despite having been invested in the same superannuation fund and same investment option for more than 5 years, the time frames that I was able to choose from to create the graph were all short-term: 1 year, 1 month, or 1 week. Showing investors a chart of the 1-week return they have achieved unnecessarily exposes them to the adverse psychological impact of losses. In addition, by being provided as an option at all, a 1-week timeframe implicitly suggests to fund members that this is a useful period for them to consider.

What this example shows is that there is still some low hanging fruit in the application of behavioural insights to improve client engagement and decision-making across the investment landscape. It also shows the importance of advisers being able to reframe the decisions for clients who might have been exposed to this type of information.

2) People's level of confidence can be misleading

People use their sense of confidence to guide their decision-making. Anxiety and uncertainty can understandably lead people to reconsider, defer or avoid making a decision, and to seek more information or advice. This is likely to describe many financial advice clients, particularly those with relatively low financial literacy.

For these clients, taking no action can seem like the safe option. This is because people often regret acts of commission (ie things they do) more than they regret otherwise equivalent acts of omission (ie things they fail to do). But while inaction can have psychological benefits, unfortunately, in the context of financial advice this sense of safety can sometimes be illusory. This can happen, for example, where a client's inaction leads to a misalignment of their investment strategy with, say, their goals and aspirations. If their goals change but their investments don't, or vice versa, some action is likely to be required to bring them back into alignment. In this case, by allowing the misalignment to persist, inaction provides clients a false sense of safety.

At the other end of the spectrum, confidence can embolden people to make decisions and to take actions. There would be no problem with this if decisions made with confidence were always good ones. Unfortunately, psychological research shows that people's sense of confidence is often a poor guide to the efficacy of their decision-making. In an investment context, risks arise when people become overconfident, such as when the confidence they have in their investment decisions surpasses the accuracy of those decisions.

Overconfidence has a number of facets that are relevant in the context of investing and financial advice.[3] Firstly, overconfident investors might believe their judgments are more precise than they actually are. Psychologists refer to this form of overconfidence as 'over-precision'. When considering an investment issue, were an overconfidently over-precise investor to articulate a range of possibilities, then the actual outcome would fall outside that range more often than they expect. Put differently, these investors underestimate the amount of risk and uncertainty in their decisions.

Given how central dealing with risk and uncertainty is to effective investment decision-making, the implications of over-precision are broad and important. They impact decisions about the construction of portfolios, the timing of markets and the selection of asset managers. A number of these implications are discussed in subsequent chapters.

Secondly, overconfident investors might believe the investment results they achieve are better than they actually are. Psychologists refer to this form of overconfidence as 'over-estimation'. In the context of financial advice, this is reflected in advisers' common lament that they rarely find self-directed investors who claim to have underperformed the market, despite evidence showing that most do. It is also reflected in financial literacy tests in which people rate their literacy as 'high' but then achieve low scores on objective tests of their actual literacy.[4]

When clients believe they are better than they are it can create a barrier to them perceiving the need for financial advice. In turn, when advisers have this belief, it can create a barrier to them outsourcing aspects of their investment decision-making when there are better alternatives available elsewhere. And when asset managers have the same belief, it can lead them to taking unnecessary risks on the basis of their overstated expertise.

Thirdly, overconfident investors might believe that they are better than average. Psychologists refer to this form of overconfidence as 'over-placement'. This tendency is consistent with the well-known finding that most people think they are above average drivers. While it's theoretically possible that most people are actually above average drivers, just as the vast majority of people have an above average number of legs, this finding is probably indicative of people systematically over-estimating their driving skills relative to others.

In an investment context, arguably many decisions involve an implicit assumption that the decision-maker is above average. For example, to buy a stock that an investor believes has good prospects often requires being wiser or better informed than the seller who is on the other side of the trade.[5] However, unseen to the buyer, the apparently ill-informed seller might have undertaken a comparably rigorous analysis that has led them to an opposing view. As a result, the seller is happy to find what they consider to be an apparently foolish buyer to offload their shares onto. By fostering a sense that they are wiser than their counterpart, overconfidence can lead investors to make these choices too frequently, or in amounts that are too large relative to the risks, costs and benefits involved.

The problems caused by overconfidence are not trivial. In fact, overconfidence has been referred to by some psychologists as *'the mother of all decision-making biases'*. Moore, Tenney and Haran (2016) argue that it deserves this title on account of its durability and ubiquity, and also because it *'gives other decision-making biases teeth.'* By this they mean *'if we were appropriately humble about our vulnerabilities then we might be able to better protect ourselves from the errors to which human judgment is prone.'* The challenges and opportunities for advisers in working with clients with varying levels of confidence, as well as in managing and communicating their own confidence, are discussed in subsequent chapters.

3) People have limited cognitive capacities

The human brain's capacity is amazing, but it comes at a cost. Whereas the brain comprises about 2% of an average person's body weight, it has been estimated to consume about 20% of a person's total energy requirements. Until very recently (in evolutionary terms) energy was scarce; conserving it was paramount. As a result, people have inherited an in-built toolkit of cognitive strategies to conserve their mental energy. Those strategies help people to selectively pay attention to information and to simplify decisions where there is a risk of being overwhelmed by information overload or complexity.

I recently undertook a survey that demonstrated how individual investors choose to pay attention to, or ignore, information. In conjunction with Livewire, a leading Australian on-line investment content platform, I surveyed around 400 individual investors who subscribe to its service. One of the questions I asked these investors was how they would describe their attention to detail. The results showed that, of those who answered this question, around three in every four described their attention to detail as either *very good - I almost always read things thoroughly* or *good – I read most things thoroughly*.

While on the face of it these investors' self-assessments could be correct, that interpretation appears optimistic given the instructions that were provided to them immediately before they answered the question. Under the heading 'Important Information' those instructions were as follows:

> *'Collection of survey information can be an effective way to gather empirical evidence into people's decision-making. Surveys can sometimes show results that do not accord with our initial expectations, thereby creating an opportunity to learn more about how the human mind works, and to find ways to apply that knowledge to benefit individuals who are likely to make similar decisions in a real-world context. Survey design is an important consideration, because often people do not pay attention to relevant information. When they ignore relevant information they can make mistakes that, were they aware of the relevant information, those mistakes would not have been made, mistakes that can create real economic costs for individuals, industries and countries. To test whether you are still paying attention, please ignore the first question below and skip straight to the second question.*

These instructions were deliberately long-winded and prosaic. As readers who waded through the text might have noticed, it included only one important phrase: *please ignore the first question below and skip straight to the second question*. But would investors read these instructions and, if so, would they notice this critical phrase?

The result was that most didn't; the proportion of investors who read and responded to these instructions was only 27%. The other 73% ignored the instructions and completed the first question. Ironically, it was this inattentive 73% who then mostly described themselves as having either 'very good' or 'good' attention to detail.

The point of this demonstration was not to be critical of these investors. In a fast-paced world with an increasing abundance of information it can be entirely rational to ignore information that appears to be irrelevant. Without doing this, investors would risk becoming bogged down in minutia. Rather, the point is that people often use mental short-cuts or *'heuristics'* to avoid being overwhelmed by information overload and complexity. In this case, the short-cut investors used might have been: *'things labelled as important information are important to someone's legal team, but not to me as the reader. I can therefore ignore it.'* Given their experiences reading various investment-related documents, it is understandable how they might have reached this conclusion.

While these types of short-cuts can often be effective, they can also cause problems. For example, what if people systematically skip information that turns out to be important? And what if they skip information without realising that's what they're doing – as appeared to be the case with many of the investors in my survey? Or on the flip side, what if these shortcuts lead them to systematically pay attention to information that is not important or is simply misleading?

The results of my investor survey are perhaps not surprising. But given the result, what is more surprising is that there is no shortage of investment-related information that is presented to clients in ways they are likely to ignore. The lesson for financial advisers is that if they want to influence clients' decisions, they should align their communications with the way that clients pay attention to information, and with the psychological strategies that they are likely to use to cut through complexity and information overload. A number of these strategies are discussed throughout this book and, in particular, in Chapter 11.

But the psychological challenges of dealing with information overload and complexity don't just apply to clients; they are also directly relevant for advisers' decisions. They are relevant for determining how advisers manage their own workflows, their sources and uses of information, and their scarce cognitive resources more generally. Ideally, cognitively demanding and effortful tasks, such as deep thinking or difficult client conversations perhaps, should not coincide with periods in which advisers suffer diminished mental capacities, such as when they are tired, hungry or in need of a break. In this regard, what helps replenish the body, such as exercise, food and rest, can also work for the brain.

4) People don't appropriately adjust their beliefs

Theoretically, when people receive new information and new advice they should take the opportunity to update their beliefs. They should discard beliefs that the new information and advice shows to be false. They should modify beliefs where the new information and advice shows that more nuance is required. They should downgrade the confidence they have in beliefs over which new information and advice casts doubt. And they should maintain existing beliefs in the face of unreliable, invalid, incorrect or irrelevant information and advice.

To some extent each of these things happens. But in many cases psychological research shows that there are systematic flaws in the way people update their beliefs in the face of new information and advice.

One problem occurs when people fail to update their beliefs sufficiently, in spite of receiving relevant and reliable new information and advice. A range of psychological mechanisms might cause this. One such mechanism is 'anchoring'. For example, when assessing the value of a share, the purchase price can serve as a powerful anchor. When something fundamentally changes with the company an investor owns shares in, their expectations can nonetheless be wedded to the now largely irrelevant historical price at which they purchased their shares.[6]

Relatedly, 'confirmation bias' means that investors disproportionately seek and respond to information that confirms their original beliefs and expectations, while tending to disregard or discredit disconfirming information and advice. These effects can contribute to the reluctance an investor feels when considering whether to sell a poorly performing stock. Anchoring makes the stock appear cheap relative to the original purchase price, while confirmation bias makes the factors that caused its poor performance seem insubstantial.

In addition, some psychological mechanisms can contribute to investors failing to respond to input from other people. Generally, advice received from other people suffers from 'egocentric discounting'; people discount the value of others' input simply because they didn't think of it themselves. In fact, research shows that when there is no basis to distinguish between the accuracy of other people's views and their own judgment, such as when both parties have equivalent information and expertise, people tend to place a 70% weight on their own views and only 30% on the input of others. In many cases they don't adjust their own opinions at all.[7]

This is similar to the 'Ikea effect', which refers to the fact that people tend to value things more if they have contributed to the creation of those things. Together these psychological effects emphasise the importance of advisers ensuring that they offer sufficient opportunities for clients to provide their input throughout the advice process. These effects also underscore the importance of strategies to help clients appreciate advisers' expertise and the value of their advice, topics that are explored in Chapter 11.

While people can fail to update their beliefs sufficiently there are also circumstances in which, by reacting too much, they can do the opposite. This overreaction is likely to occur where new information is mostly just 'noise'.

Many advisers will be well versed in trying to assist their clients to ignore different forms of noise, such as short-term market movements, short-term fund manager performance, or daily news cycles. Simple reframing strategies, such as changing the order in which investment returns are presented in a table, can help reduce the impact of noise on clients. Obtaining pre-commitments from clients is another behavioural strategy aimed at avoiding noise and nudging clients towards better decisions. Both of these strategies are discussed in subsequent chapters.

Like clients, financial professionals can sometimes find it difficult to escape the impact of noise on their decisions. The single most popular in-house workshop that I run for a range of investment professionals, including listed equity managers, private equity funds, and corporate M&A teams, is titled: 'Turning down the decibels: how to deal with noise in a noisy world'. This session outlines the psychological evidence pertaining to how and when people erroneously find patterns in the noise. It also discusses how noise can impact people at a subconscious level, and therefore be difficult to overcome, and how professional investors can recognise the circumstances in which noise is likely to be most damaging.

The workshop also provides potential strategies for limiting the negative impacts of noise on sophisticated investment decision-making processes, and discusses the practical challenges in using these strategies. The strategies include the use of filters, framing techniques, checklists and decision-weighting systems. The practical challenges include the fact that team-mates and clients often equate the relative simplicity of approaches that cut through the noise, with a lack of sophistication. The popularity of this session suggests that financial professionals also find it challenging to deal with noise.

5) People are social creatures
In addition to being influenced by their adviser, clients' decisions are likely to be impacted by the actions and statements of other people in their social context. The psychological evidence shows that social influence can sometimes be both powerful and subconscious.

I recently demonstrated how social factors can influence investment decisions by providing a hypothetical investment scenario to the same group of 400 individual investors who had previously been tormented with the wordy 'important information'. This time I asked them, *"Based only on the following information, on a scale of 1 to 10, where 1 is 'very unlikely' and 10 is 'very likely', how likely would you be to consider the following as a potentially suitable investment opportunity."* They were then provided the following table of information about a hypothetical fund.

Period since inception	7 years 5 months
Fund size	$595m
Since inception performance	+1.6% pa versus benchmark
Asset class	Australian equities (Large/mid-cap)
Approach	Invests in companies with sustainable and growing cashflows
Investor sentiment	At a recent workshop that was designed for novice investors to learn the basics of investing, 80% rated the fund as 'above average'

My intention with this question was to test the extent that survey participants were influenced by the views of the novice investors who were referred to in the table. Because these novice investors were attending a seminar to learn the basics of investing, they were unlikely to be investment experts. On that basis, survey participants should have ignored the fact that the novice investors rated the hypothetical fund as 'above average'. Arguably, if anything, the views of these novice investors should serve as a contra-indicator for a good investment.

To test whether the novice investors had an impact on people's decisions, half of the survey participants were shown an alternative version of the hypothetical scenario. In the alternative version all of the details were the same except that, rather than 'above average', 80% of the novice investors rated the fund as being 'below average'.

The results showed that the investors who viewed the first version (in which the novice investors regarded the fund as 'above average') rated the hypothetical fund more favourably than did those who saw the second version. This demonstrates how even clearly irrelevant social cues can influence investors' decisions.

In the context of a financial advice relationship, social influence is likely to be more important than in the artificially constructed world of surveys. In the survey it would have been relatively easy for participants to mostly ignore the hypothetical novice investors whom they had never met, whom they probably saw as being different from them, and whom they probably did not aspire to be like.

In contrast, in the context of an advice relationship advisers can design social influencing strategies that are salient, personally relevant and meaningful for clients. They can weave relevant 'social norms' (what other people do) and 'injunctive norms' (what others say or agree is the right thing to do) into the case studies, anecdotes and data they discuss with clients. When used by advisers, the power of social influence can be harnessed to nudge clients toward decisions that are in their best interests.

As is discussed in subsequent chapters, advisers can use insights from social psychology across a range of other contexts too. For example, they can leverage mutual self-disclosure, reciprocity and commitment to build trusting relationships with their clients. They can help clients identify and guard against the adverse effects of social influencing strategies that they might encounter when bidding at a property auction. And within their own organisations, advisers can use insights about group dynamics to improve the functioning of their teams, committees and boards.

6) People don't think it's about them

If you've read the decision-making concepts discussed so far and thought, 'that applies to my clients, but not to me', then this last one is for you. Sometimes called the 'blind-spot bias', it refers to the fact that people often recognise the impact of biases on other people, but fail to see the impact on themselves.

Of course, much of the preceding discussion was couched in terms of clients' decisions. However, many of the same concepts apply to sophisticated financial professionals too, just not necessarily in exactly the same ways or to the same extent.

The blind-spot bias is somewhat self-serving, as it allows people to think of themselves as being entirely unbiased and objective. It is also consistent with broader psychological research that shows that people tend to be poor at understanding the real drivers of their own decisions and actions. When researchers query participants about the potential role of various biases on their choices, people often proclaim there to be none, sometimes in the face of irrefutable evidence to the contrary. The same effect is evident among some of the financial professionals who participate in my workshop exercises.

In overcoming the blind-spot bias, advisers should be particularly careful of assuming that awareness of different decision-making biases is sufficient to overcome them. It is not. For example, in one workshop of financial professionals, when I asked how many of them were aware that I had used an anchor in an exercise that they had just completed, every participant raised their hand. Despite this, the anchor was still effective at roughly doubling the responses of the group who had seen the high anchor, relative to the group who had seen the lower one. Awareness of biases is a good start, but is far from sufficient to overcome them. Appropriate actions have to be taken too.

As I said in my first book: *'Daniel Kahneman, Nobel Prize winning psychologist and founder (with Amos Tversky) of much of the thinking about decision-making biases, openly acknowledges that he is unable to escape biased decision-making. For anyone else to think they can, at least where those decisions incorporate an element of subjectivity, is likely to be overconfident folly.'* In reading the remainder of the book, advisers should try to think about the implications for both clients and for themselves.

CONCLUSIONS

This chapter has described some of the key psychological concepts that are relevant in the context of financial advice. They include how people think about losses, how having high or low confidence can affect people's decisions and actions, the impact of information overload and complexity, how people adjust their beliefs to reflect new information and advice, and the role of social context. Because each of these concepts can influence people beyond their awareness, both clients and advisers are likely to feel that they are unaffected. Part of the psychological iceberg is hidden from view, but it's there nonetheless.

The brief overview provided in this chapter is somewhat dangerous. Broadly speaking, advisers should combine the psychological concepts discussed in this chapter with traditional financial models and with relevant practical considerations. However, this chapter has necessarily omitted much nuance that is required to understand how the concepts apply to different clients and advisers across different contexts. It has so far only alluded to the potential strategies that advisers can use with clients, with themselves and with their teams. These strategies and the associated nuances are discussed in the chapters that follow.

2

RISK TOLERANCE, PERCEPTIONS & PROFILING

Risk and return are two fundamental building blocks upon which investment decisions are founded. In many cases clients need to make a trade-off; if they wish to achieve higher returns, they need to accept higher risk. Helping clients to understand this trade-off, and to choose investments that align with their risk profile, is a core part of many advice conversations. For Australian advisers at least, it is also a legal requirement.[1]

However, risk is a difficult concept for many clients to grasp and to think about objectively. Rather, what people perceive as risky is subject to a range of distortions and can be quite subjective. To some extent, clients with different experiences, personalities, genders and ages, or who are presented with risk-related decisions in different contexts, are likely to think about and respond to risks quite differently.

This chapter examines the psychological challenges advisers face in communicating risk-related issues, in understanding and measuring their clients' risk profiles, and in translating them into investment portfolios. If these challenges are not appropriately addressed advisers can inadvertently recommend investments that are misaligned with clients' preferences, and which expose clients to risks that those clients don't really understand or accept.

BIASES IN RISK-RELATED DECISIONS

The psychological evidence shows that a number of factors can distort how people think about risk. Some risks receive greater prominence in people's decisions than their associated probabilities and consequences suggest they should, while other risks tend to be overlooked. This section outlines the psychological factors that can influence people's risk-related decisions, including the role of loss aversion, salience, familiarity and emotions.

Loss aversion

The idea of loss aversion, being that people respond more to losses than to equivalent gains, was introduced in Chapter 1. Loss aversion means that if a $50 note irretrievably fell from your pocket, perhaps down a nearby drain, then you would probably feel more psychological pain than the pleasure you would feel from finding a $50 note lying unattended. This is shown diagrammatically below. The primacy of losses over gains is represented by the part of the curve that represents losses (to the left of the origin) being steeper than the part representing gains (to the right of origin). In the diagram, y units of pleasure are received from a gain of $x, while 2y units of displeasure are suffered from a loss of the same magnitude.

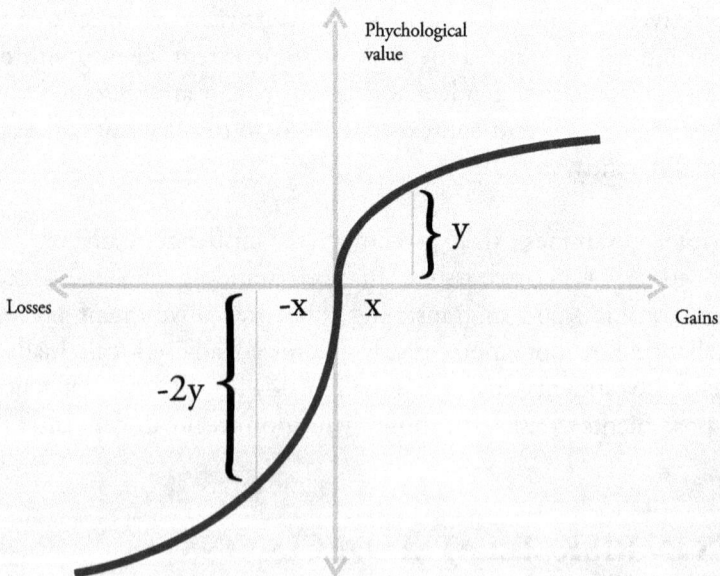

Losses are more impactful than gains, and separate small gains and losses are more important than equivalent gains and losses experienced together.

The other important insight in the diagram is that the total psychological impact of several separate small gains is greater than from a single larger gain. This means that you would probably feel more pleasure from finding a $50 note today and then finding another tomorrow, than were you to find a $100 note once. This is represented in the diagram by the curve flattening as it moves further away from the origin to the right. The same concept also applies to losses, with the curve flattening as it moves to the left.

Implicit in the diagram is that gains and losses are measured relative to a reference point. When the $50 note was lost down the drain in the previous example, the reference point was how much money you had in your pocket immediately prior to your misfortune. Relative to that reference point you suffered a loss of $50.

Because people can sometimes have different reference points, two nearly identical clients can perceive the same risks quite differently. For example, for an investor who has only recently purchased some shares, the risk of a share price decline would probably be perceived as a loss. Contrast this with an otherwise identical investor who happened to purchase their shares earlier, and who has already profited from some share price appreciation. For them, rather than being seen as a loss, the prospect of the same share price decline might be perceived as a reduction in their gains. While theoretically the risk both investors face is the same, the prospect of reduced gains is less psychologically impactful than the prospect of incurring losses.[2]

What this example demonstrates is that advisers need to understand how their clients' personal contexts and mindsets *frame* their risk-related decisions as being either gains or losses. Understanding the reference points clients use can be a big part of this. An investor's original purchase price is an obvious reference point, as was the case with the two hypothetical share investors discussed above. Clients might also think about other salient reference points, such as recent share price highs or lows. Among other things, which reference points are relevant will depend on the time periods over which a client thinks about their investments, and whether they focus on their total portfolio or on their individual investments separately.

Once discovered, advisers need not take their clients' reference points as immutable. As alluded to in Chapter 1, part of how an adviser can help influence clients to make better risk-related choices is by framing those choices relative to appropriate reference points. What is a loss over one year might be reframed as a gain relative to a market average, and what is a loss and a gain on two separate investments might be reframed as a gain for a total portfolio. By choosing appropriate reference points in their conversations and in their communication materials, advisers can reframe the oxygen away from their clients' loss aversion fires.

Problems with probabilities

When thinking about risks, some low-probability future events weigh too heavily on people's decisions. People don't tend to think about risks in probabilistic terms. How psychological research reveals people actually incorporate probabilities into their decisions is represented in the diagram shown on the next page. In that diagram the 45-degree line shows how people should think about future events, while the curved line shows how they actually think.

The relationship shown in diagram reveals three important things that are relevant for how clients perceive risk. Firstly, people tend to place too much importance on low probability events. This is reflected towards the bottom left-hand corner of the diagram by the curved line (how people perceive probabilities) being above the 45-degree line (which represents actual probabilities). Lotteries and plane crashes fall into this category.

Secondly, people tend to place too little importance on things that are almost certain to happen, but not quite. This is reflected towards the top right-hand corner of the diagram by the curved line being below the 45-degree line. Giving people the certainty they desire is one of the reasons that some people value guaranteed income products and insurance; both can potentially translate a likely outcome into a certain one.

And thirdly, when responding to uncertainty, people tend to be insufficiently sensitive to differences in intermediate probabilities. People tend to have a relatively undifferentiated 'maybe' bucket into which they place all the things

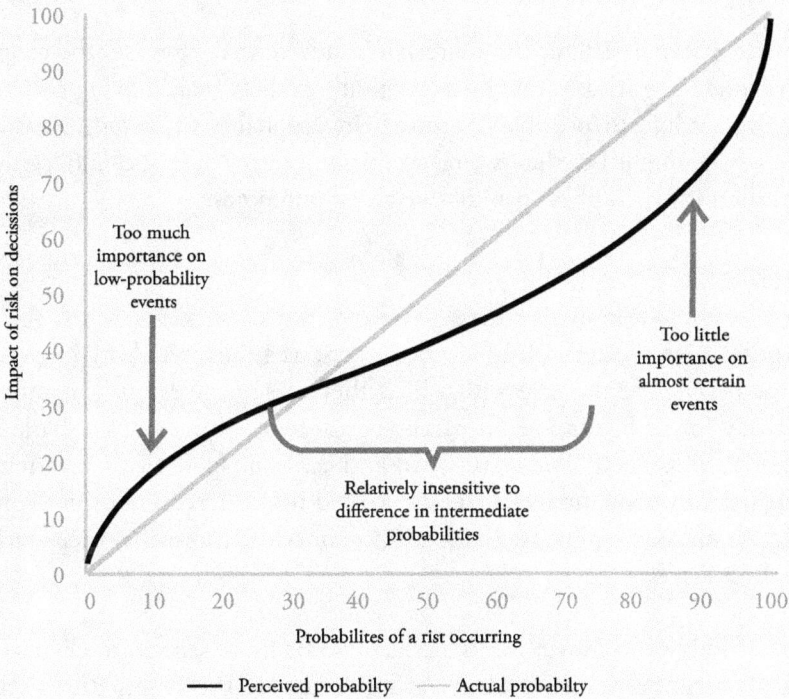

People place too much importance on low probability events, not enough on almost certain events and are relatively insensitive to differences in intermediate probabilities.

that might happen. Research suggests that they can do this without having sufficient regard for the fact that these events could have very different likelihoods of occurring. This is reflected in the middle section of the diagram by the curved line being flatter than the 45-degree line.

The broad conclusion from these insights is that advisers need to be sensitive to how clients' perceptions can deviate from more objective probabilities. One way to do this is by advisers tailoring their engagement to align with how clients think about probabilities. For example, at one extreme, advisers should expect that clients who have no chance of reaching a particular goal would be particularly grateful for advice that results in them having at least a small chance of success. At the other extreme, clients could also appreciate advice that results in goals they are already likely to achieve becoming certain.

What clients are less likely to appreciate is advice that increases the chance of them achieving goals but that does not result in their goals moving either from being 'impossible' to 'possible', or from being 'probable' to 'certain'. As valuable as the advice might be, clients tend to think in terms of 'hope' and 'certainty', rather than in terms of probability-weighted outcomes.

Salience

Why do people fear shark attacks more than car crashes, when it is the latter that pose a far greater risk of death or serious injury? At least in part it is because people use the ease with which they can imagine a risk materialising as a proxy for its likelihood. In psychological terms, the risk of a shark attack is referred to as being *'salient'* (ie vivid and easily imagined). By creating high salience, Hollywood images of giant, jagged-tooth creatures rising from the murky depths help to elevate shark attacks above the threat that their statistical likelihood justifies.

Beyond Hollywood movies, risks are likely to be more salient for clients where there is a recent example of them having occurred. This is sometimes referred to as the *'recency effect'*. The recency effect can be accentuated by a client's personal experiences. A client having had a recent personal experience with a risk will make that risk particularly salient for them. On the flip-side are the low-salience risks for which clients are unable to bring to mind recent examples and for which they have no direct personal experience. These risks tend to be overlooked.

Unfortunately, people don't learn from other people's experiences nearly as well as from their own. This is doubly so if other people's experiences are reflected in statistical averages, rather than in individual case studies and anecdotes. One person's story of personal hardship is a tragedy, and one that might motivate a client to acquire adequate insurance, say, whereas a million people's hardship is merely a statistic that is easily ignored.

The way that salience impacts clients' risk perceptions therefore has implications for how advisers assess clients' risk profiles, as well as for how they communicate risk-related issues. It also reinforces the need for advisers to adequately explore clients' personal experiences. For example, clients could neglect important personal risks, such as the risk of a serious injury or death, when they have no direct experience of a similar incident among their circle of friends and family.

In these cases, advisers could help their clients to appreciate the risks they are exposed to by increasing the salience of those risks. A good example I have seen of how to do this used a visual representation of the causes of people losing their homes. Every home lost through fire, a salient risk against which many people insure, was represented as the peak of a pyramid. The larger body of the pyramid showed the much greater number of homes lost due to less salient risks, such as due to marital breakdowns, loss of employment, or unforeseen medical conditions. By representing it this way, the pyramid neatly raised the profile of less salient risks, by representing them visually, as well as by connecting them with risks that were already salient for clients.[3]

Familiarity

In what is referred to as the *familiarity effect*, people tend to prefer things with which they are already familiar. Familiar things can seem less risky. And while in life generally it might be better to stick with the devil you know, in the context of investment decisions there are important exceptions. For example, investors who are unfamiliar with shares might miss the long-term returns that they can provide. And those who are only familiar with a selection of Australian blue-chip shares might miss the diversification benefits that can come from investing in less well-known small-caps and global equities. These less-familiar investments are not as devilish as they might seem.

The role of familiarity suggests that to understand clients' risk profiles, as many advisers currently do, they should pay particular attention to which investments clients are already familiar with. It also suggests that advisers can use familiarity as an engagement tool; by making things more familiar for clients they can help clients feel more comfortable investing in them. To achieve this, in addition to providing education, advisers could link foreign concepts to those with which clients are already familiar. One approach that many advisers use to achieve this is by highlighting the well-known brand names, such as Apple or Microsoft, within an international equities portfolio. In doing so, foreign investments can seem less foreign.

The investments that clients are familiar with can also be used as a guide to build portfolios that satisfy both clients' investment objectives and their risk profiles. For example, a client who needs to invest in growth assets, such as equities or property, might be more amenable to choosing property if they happen to be already familiar with it. Investing in a diversified portfolio that includes equities might be theoretically optimal from a mean-variance perspective, but when subjective risk assessments are applied, investing more in property could be an appropriate behavioural compromise.

Hot states

Psychologists refer to *'hot states'* as contexts in which there are strong emotional influences on people's decisions and actions. As the name suggests, they contrast with *'cold states'*, in which emotional influences are less pronounced. As can be attested by anyone who has written an angry email in the heat of the moment and later regretted sending it, decisions made in the two contexts can sometimes differ dramatically.

What can create an additional challenge for advisers is that, when viewed from a cold state, clients are likely to under-estimate the impact emotions will have on the subsequent decisions that they make in hot states. For example, in one study, when faced with a choice between chocolate and bananas a week in advance, only a quarter of participants said they would choose the chocolate. However, one week later, when given the choice on the spot, nearly three quarters succumbed to temptation. These participants' earlier cold-state choices did not sufficiently account for the way that their decisions were influenced by the hot-states they subsequently experienced.[4]

Applying this concept in the context of assessing a client's risk profile, if an adviser asks their client how they would respond if the market were to suffer a significant decline, it is easy for the client to say they would be unconcerned. After all, in a cold state they might see themselves as being a sensible long-term investor who recognises that market volatility is an unavoidable part of investing in growth assets. However, when the hypothetical event materialises and emotions run high, the client nonetheless runs for the exits along with everyone else.

One approach to overcoming the disconnect between clients' stated preferences and what is revealed by their behaviour is for advisers to simply ask about clients' actual past behaviour.[5] Unless something important has changed, how a client responded during the last bear market could be a more reliable indicator of their future behaviour. Of course, this approach creates additional challenges, such as how to allow for the effects of clients' potentially fallible and self-serving recollections of their past behaviours. This is a topic that is discussed in more detail in Chapter 11.

A broad conclusion from this section is that clients' predictions about their own future behaviours, decisions and preferences can be unreliable. They can be unreliable because people often don't understand the real drivers of their own decisions. However, advisers who probe a little deeper can uncover some of those hidden drivers, such as how clients frame their choices as gains or losses, or how they might have been impacted by recent personal experiences. Advisers can then use these insights to better communicate risk-related issues and to build clients' confidence around unfamiliar concepts. And, importantly, they can recommend portfolios than incorporate the risks that clients are most comfortable accepting.

DRIVERS OF RISK-TAKING BEHAVIOUR

The previous section discussed many of the contextual factors that can influence how clients think about risk. This section considers how more permanent client characteristics, such as their personality and gender, relate to their risk-related decisions and behaviours.

Personality

While many different personality tests exist, personality researchers tend to focus on what are referred to as the 'Big 5' personality characteristics. These characteristics can be remembered with the acronym 'OCEAN', which stands for Openness, Conscientiousness, Extraversion, Agreeableness and Neuroticism. Clients can be high, low or average on each of these traits, so that one client could be an agreeable extravert, say, who is neither high nor low on the other three traits. This particular client would probably be more warm, friendly and trusting, and less cynical or suspicious than other clients, reflected by their high agreeableness. And, being an extravert, they would probably also be more sociable and talkative than other clients.

However, this agreeable extravert would not be especially imaginative, curious of new information and experiences, or open to unconventional ideas, given they are not high on the trait of openness. Neither would they be especially diligent, persistent or motivated, or have a particularly high level of self-control, given they are not high on conscientiousness. And finally, they wouldn't be especially emotionally unstable, given they don't have high neuroticism. But, by being average on openness, conscientiousness and neuroticism, neither would they be especially low in these qualities.

Researchers have found links between personality traits and different aspects of decision-making, as well as with the underlying neurological processes that drive them. More specifically, different types of risk-taking have been found to be positively associated with extraversion and openness, and negatively associated with neuroticism, agreeableness and conscientiousness.[6]

Some of these findings intuitively make sense in the context of financial decisions. For example, taking risks is one way that extraverts could seek excitement and stimulation. It is also easy to draw a connection between being high on openness, and therefore being open to new and unconventional ideas, and being willing to accept more risk. But these two traits do not lead to the same risks. While openness is associated with higher risk-taking, it also tends to be associated with higher intelligence, knowledge and performance. Therefore, compared with excitement-seeking extraverts, the greater risks taken by people who are high on openness are more likely be well-considered and appropriate.

In contrast to open extraverts, fewer risks would be expected to be taken by people prone to suffering emotional distress when things go wrong, or by people who prefer to maintain self-control. These characteristics describe people high on neuroticism and conscientiousness, respectively.

If they understand their clients' personalities, advisers can potentially tailor their engagement to align with the different drivers of clients' risk-related preferences, decisions and actions. For example, risk-averse clients who are high on neuroticism would probably benefit the most from strategies that help to mute their emotional reactions across market cycles. Clients with high conscientiousness might prefer a rules-based, policy-driven investment strategy. And because of their higher social information processing, risk-averse clients who are high on agreeableness might be most influenced by engagement strategies that leverage the power of social influence.

In each case, by aligning with clients' personalities advisers can potentially allow their clients to become more comfortable investing in higher risk/return assets than they otherwise would be. As part of an advice process that appropriately explains risks to clients, the result could be clients achieving higher returns but without them feeling higher anxiety.

Despite the potential benefits, the role of personality-related strategies should not be overstated. The differences between clients based on their Big 5 personality traits are merely tendencies, broad averages around which advisers should expect much variability. A further complication comes from the fact that clients are likely to possess a combination of each of the Big 5 traits to differing degrees. Advisers who use personality profiling will therefore need to contemplate how their clients' personality traits might interact, offset or compound in different contexts. For example, a client who is high in neuroticism might feel strong emotions when markets fall, but this might not matter if they are also high on conscientiousness, and therefore diligently stick with their long-term plans nonetheless. With this in mind, while personality profiling can provide a useful lens to better understand and engage with clients, advisers should also be careful not to over-rely on it.

Gender

Apparently, men are from Mars and women are from Venus. But does the psychological evidence support this interplanetary disparity in the context of their risk profiles? In some ways, it does. For example, men tend to be more confident investors than women. One of the most well-known pieces of research that supports this assertion was undertaken by Brad Barber and Terrance Odean. Using a large database of individual investors, these researchers found that men took bigger risks and traded more frequently than did women. Unfortunately for men, they also found that the female investors in their study achieved higher returns.[7]

But just as being an over-confident male can cause problems if it leads to making unwise share investments, being an under-confident female can also be a problem. By women tending to have both lower investment balances and higher life expectancies they typically need to accept higher risks in order to achieve their financial objectives. As a result, women can suffer significant adverse consequences if having a low risk tolerance translates into them having low exposure to growth assets. Within the context of superannuation, this tends to be the case, with women tending to make lower-risk investment choices than men.[8] As a generalisation, the challenge for advisers therefore is to prevent over-confident male clients taking too much risk in the active choices they make, while helping under-confident female clients to invest more aggressively in growth assets.

But while it might be easy to bring to mind examples of over-confident men and under-confident women, the psychological evidence is more nuanced. For example, men's greater risk-taking is *'domain-specific'*, meaning that while men are generally more confident with their investments, advisers should not expect this confidence to necessarily translate into men's non-financial decisions. In some domains of life, such as when making social decisions, women are no more risk-averse than men.[9] A male client's propensity to accept investment risk could therefore be quite different from the risks he is comfortable accepting in his estate-planning arrangements, for example.

Even where research finds significant gender differences, often there still remains a substantial overlap between men and women's risk profiles and behaviours. This means that a confident female can be more confident than a risk-averse male. Because gender is likely to be one of the most obvious and salient characteristics of a new client, it is easy to focus on it and to overstate its role. Broad gender differences in risk profiles can provide a guide to the types of issues and opportunities that might apply differently for men and women. However, of course, that guide should not get in the way of advisers responding to their clients' specific circumstances and requirements.

Other demographic variables

In terms of their risk profile, other client characteristics can often be more important than their gender. For example, female board directors are just as confident as their male peers.[10] In terms of their level of confidence, in this example it is being a board director that is significant, not their gender. Other characteristics that have been found to relate to risk tolerance include people's marital status and their education. Generally, single people and those with higher levels of education are willing to accept greater financial risks than are married people and those with lower education attainment.[11]

Risk tolerance also tends to decrease amongst the elderly. For example, in one study nearly half of the retirees said that they would refuse a gamble with a 50% chance of winning $100 and a 50% chance of losing as little as $10. This suggests that these retirees felt the risk of loss about 10 times more heavily than gains.[12] This extreme response has been referred to as 'hyper risk aversion'. As discussed further in Chapter 10, it can sometimes have unexpected and important consequences for clients as they approach and move through retirement.

And while younger people tend to be more risk-tolerant than the elderly, the impact of the global financial crisis on the current cohort of young people has also resulted in a 'new normal for younger investors, involving more prudence and a lower asset allocation to stocks'.[13] Consistent with this, researchers have found a humped shape age-profile for the asset allocations chosen by superannuation fund members, with equity allocations peaking at age 34 and declining thereafter.[14] Early investment experience can have a disproportionate long-term impact on clients' psyches and, as a consequence, on their investment outcomes.

MEASURING AND USING RISK PROFILES

This section discussed some of the practical challenges advisers face in appropriately measuring clients' risk profiles and incorporating them into investment strategies. In particular, it leverages insights from a review of advisers' risk-profiling practices that was undertaken by the then UK financial regulator, the Financial Services Authority.[15]

Risk means different things to different people

When discussing risk, advisers and clients can sometimes be talking at cross-purposes. Volatility, downside volatility, maximum drawdown, the proportion of years in which losses are expected, and risk labels each attempt to communicate different aspects of investment risk. However, abstract statistical concepts are likely to be difficult for many clients to fully understand and appreciate the implications of, while vague labels (like 'medium risk') convey little meaningful information.

In decision-making research, broader *frames* (ie broader ways of thinking about problems) tend to be preferred to narrower ones. Broader frames encourage more aspects of a decision to be considered together, thereby allowing creative solutions to be identified, solutions that would be invisible if the problem was assessed in a more piecemeal way. Focusing on the risk that a client does not achieve their goals is one such broader frame. Arguably, this is also the risk that is ultimately most relevant for clients.

Focussing on the risk that clients do not achieve their goals provides advisers with a number of potential ways to help their clients. These include changing the profile of the client's investments, influencing the client's behaviour during the investment journey, or helping the client to consider more realistic goals and expectations. While statistical concepts have a role to play in understanding aspects of risk, framing risk in terms of clients' goals not only aligns with what is meaningful for clients, but also creates more opportunities for advisers to provide valuable advice.

Different types of risk

Even when risk is framed in terms of a client's goals, rather than being a single measure, a client's risk profile is multi-faceted. One component of a client's risk profile is their 'risk capacity'. This can be thought of as the extent a client's ability to meet their goals is sensitive to possible adverse scenarios. As advisers will be aware, an assessment of a client's risk capacity should incorporate a consideration of their financial position (wealth, income, debt, etc), as well as their capacity to respond to adverse scenarios, such as by deferring goals, finding alternative employment, or relying on family members. While clients' risk capacities are clearly important, the FSA review found that they were insufficiently incorporated into the advice provided by some advisers.

A second component of a client's risk profile is their 'risk perceptions': to what extent do clients feel that certain risks are likely to occur and with what consequences? As was discussed in this chapter, these perceptions can be subject to a range of decision-making biases that make them highly context dependent and unstable over time. Because clients' risk perceptions are likely to rise and fall with markets, advisers who over-react to these changing perceptions risk making correspondingly pro-cyclical investment recommendations. Because they are unstable, clients' risk perceptions are unlikely to form a sound basis upon which an adviser could construct a long-term investment strategy. However, despite its drawbacks as a tool for recommending appropriate investments, understanding clients' changing risk perceptions could still be useful in helping advisers to predict and influence their clients' decisions across market cycles.

A third component of a client's risk profile is their 'risk tolerance'. Risk tolerance can be conceptualised as a stable personality trait, akin to the Big 5 discussed above, but that specifically relates to a client's long-term comfort with risk. Personality traits tend to be relatively stable over people's lifetimes, although some age-related decreases in risk tolerance should be anticipated. If risk tolerance is appropriately measured, it could be a valid input into the advice process.[16]

But measuring a client's risk tolerance appropriately is not straightforward. One of the challenges is ensuring that risk tolerance is not confounded with a client's risk capacity or with their risk perceptions. For example, risk-profiling questionnaires that ask about clients' preferences for investing in different asset classes might inadvertently blend a client's risk tolerance with their risk perceptions. A client's stated preference for investing in shares could reflect the fact that they have a high risk tolerance. But their response could also be because they currently have low risk perceptions, perhaps following a period of strong share market returns. This ambiguity can make it difficult to provide appropriate advice.

Other challenges in assessing clients' risk profiles

Another challenge for risk-profiling questionnaires is ensuring that clients and their advisers have a consistent understanding of the questions and their responses. Of course, the use of technical or complex terms and concepts as well as unclear language are likely to be unhelpful. In these cases, the adviser might be the only one who knows what the risk-profiling questions were supposed to mean, while the client is the only one who knows what they had in mind when they provided responses to them.

Perhaps less obviously, vague terms (such as 'some', rather than a specific number or amount) invite different subjective interpretations, even among sophisticated financial professionals. Response options that do not distinguish between 'don't care' and 'not applicable' can also lead to a disconnect between clients' intentions and advisers' interpretations. And both clients and advisers can be blindsided by the significant impacts that apparently small changes in the way questions are framed can sometimes have on the responses that those questions solicit.

Given that each individual question on its own is likely to be a noisy measure of the underlying psychological trait that it seeks to measure, risk questionnaires need to have enough questions to allow this noise to cancel out. Having fewer questions might make it more likely that clients complete the questionnaire at all, but if not well managed, this can lead to results that are more prone to error and misinterpretation.

Given these types of challenges, even the best risk profiling tools will never create a perfect representation of clients' tolerance for risk. Psychological concepts are rarely that precise. This suggests a role for advisers to identify the weaknesses and limitations of the tools they use and to improve upon their outputs where required. However, one of the concerns the FSA raised in its review was that that *many firms do not understand how the tools they use work, including what they are (and are not) designed to do.'* To help overcome this they suggested that *'tools need processes for advisers to validate answers and resolve conflicts.'*

Despite their potential flaws, risk-profiling questionnaires can play an important role in an advice process, compared with simply relying on advisers' subjective assessments of their clients' risk profiles. As is discussed in Chapter 7, one of the problems in relying solely on advisers' subjective assessments is that advisers can project their own risk profiles onto their clients. Another potential problem is that in face-to-face conversations clients can provide responses that they think their adviser hopes for or expects. In contrast, clients can sometimes be more honest when providing responses in the relatively less personal context of a questionnaire. Given their different strengths and weaknesses, a combination of approaches is likely to be best. Advisers could combine the strengths of their own insight and client engagement skills with the reliability, consistency and scalability of well-designed risk profiling questionnaires.

CONCLUSIONS
This chapter has discussed how decision-making research can help advisers to better understand and engage with their clients about risk. It has shown how clients' responses to risk can be subject to a number of important biases, such as loss aversion, salience, familiarity and emotion. These effects have broad implications for how clients perceive risk in different contexts. In addition, advisers should anticipate differences in the way clients with different personalities think about risk and, to some extent, differences based on clients' demographic characteristics.

The research discussed in this chapter challenges how some advisers conceptualise, measure and communicate risk. Any adviser who does not account for these psychological challenges in the way they assess and use a client's risk profile is creating a house of cards. Even if nothing meaningful changes, altering the way a few risk-profiling questions are framed could lead to significant changes to a client's apparent risk profile, and therefore also to the advice they receive. Recommending investments on this basis and hoping they are in the client's best interest is risky, for both the client and the adviser. Clients understandably wouldn't want to jeopardise their financial futures by relying on the haphazard responses they provide to risk-profiling questions whose significance they don't appreciate, that are communicated in a way that they might not fully understand, and where their responses are influenced by psychological factors that are beyond their awareness.

But this research also highlights opportunities for advisers. Advisers can identify and help manage the risks that their clients are blindsided by, they can communicate risk-related issues in ways that are meaningful for clients, they can recommend investments that incorporate the risks that clients are most comfortable accepting, and they can influence their clients' risk-related decision-making across market cycles. Given that risk is the foundation of much investment decision-making, it is difficult to over-state the importance for both clients and their advisers of getting these things right.

3

HAPPINESS, MOTIVATION & FUTURE GOALS

In addition to their risk profile, a client's goals should be another key driver of the decisions they make and the advice they receive. Among other things, a client's goals form the basis of their required investment returns and liquidity. However, for clients, predicting their future wants and needs can be difficult. As a result, clients can set goals that they think they want but subsequently change their minds. In this case the returns and liquidity they apparently required might not be required after all. Or clients can achieve their goals but find that they don't result in the happiness and satisfaction that they hoped for or expected. Or they can set goals but fail to take the actions required to achieve them, relegating their goals to being no more than wishful thinking.

These problems create challenges for advisers. If they believe that their clients' goals will not make them happy, or that clients are unlikely to stick to their goals, should advisers help their clients to set different goals? There are arguments both ways. On the one hand, some clients might not expect to receive this type of advice and, correspondingly, some advisers might not see it as their role to provide it. Understandably, advisers will also be cautious about ensuring they don't railroad clients into choosing goals that aren't genuinely theirs. But on the other hand, to not help clients in these circumstances risks undermining the benefits of advice. What is the point of advice that helps clients travel to a destination they ultimately will not want to reach?

This chapter is intended for advisers who would like to assist their clients to set more appropriate goals, and who seek to better align their advice with those goals. How can advisers help clients create goals that will make them happy, are meaningful for them and that they feel motivated to achieve? And what advice can they provide to help clients achieve their goals if those goals are likely to change? This chapter discusses how behavioural finance research can be used by advisers to help answer these questions.

SETTING GOALS THAT LEAD TO HAPPINESS

If the ultimate purpose of a client's goals is happiness (their own, and perhaps the happiness of their family and other people), then providing appropriate financial advice requires understanding the connection between money and happiness. This section covers psychological research about happiness, including how happiness relates to income and wealth. Whether a client is happy is, in part, genetically determined. But while advisers can't change their clients' genes, they can do other things to influence their clients' happiness. However, as is discussed below, those things are not necessarily what people expect.

What is happiness?

To be able to increase a client's happiness, a useful place to start is with a more precise understanding of what happiness is. There isn't a single definition of happiness; happiness comes in many forms. Happiness researchers often refer to a broad concept of subjective wellbeing. Depending on how it is measured, subjective wellbeing could comprise the experience of various positive emotions, the absence of experienced negative emotions, or an overall sense of satisfaction with one's life.

Importantly these elements are not equivalent. In fact, in some cases they can be very different. These differences can lead people to make different choices depending on which aspects of their subjective wellbeing they focus on. The implication of this is that advisers can better understand and potentially influence a client's choice of goals by identifying, and perhaps constructively challenging, the aspects of happiness on which they most focus their attention.

For clients who focus on the present, positive or negative emotions are likely to be most important, as these emotions are experienced in the moment. In contrast, a sense of satisfaction comes when someone abstracts themselves from their present reality and reflects on their life more generally. Importantly, as anyone who has binged on chocolate, alcohol, shopping or a TV series can attest, maintaining a surplus of in-the-moment positive emotions over negative ones does not reliably equate to the type of satisfaction one feels on reflection. Rather, it can be diametrically opposed.

Even when people engage in more wholesome activities, their post-hoc reflections do not represent a simple time-weighted average of the positive and negative emotions they have experienced. Instead, people tend to focus on both the peak and the end of an experience. Daniel Kahneman refers to this as the 'peak-end rule'.[1] An implication is that clients whose goals include holidays should plan for a single stand-out experience. In the years to come they will think less about the 7 days they spent lying on the beach, and more about the 60 seconds they spent sky-diving from a plane high above it.

The counter-examples to binging have a poor balance of experienced emotions in the present but lead to greater life satisfaction on reflection. For some people, education and spending time with small children are examples.[2] The in-the-moment unpleasantness of exams and of changing dirty nappies is offset by the life satisfaction that comes from reflecting on one's academic achievements and offspring. The type of happiness a client values most will help determine whether they should pursue further education and/or raise a family.

The relationship between income and happiness

Should clients' personal goals include achieving higher incomes? Greater income does lead to greater happiness, but the relationship between money and happiness is not straightforward. Because being dirt-poor is unpleasant, achieving a comfortable income matters. However, beyond that, higher incomes have little impact on people's happiness, at least when measured in terms of one's in-the-moment emotional experiences.[3]

This is somewhat paradoxical: people with higher incomes should have fewer financial constraints on their choices, which should allow them to choose things that make them happier. Clients would be justified in feeling sceptical if told that having more income wouldn't make them happier. However, the evidence suggests that, in general, something prevents this from occurring.

One way that having more income might not lead to greater happiness is if it also comes with offsetting negative consequences. These consequences could include longer working hours, feeling more stress, or having a poor job fit. One study found that optimal wellbeing was observed for people working between 35 and 44 hours per week and who also had high perceived '*job fit*'.[4] It's easy to focus on the benefits of having a higher income, but if clients want to maximise their happiness, even if they don't express it in this way, then their goals need to also have sufficient regard for these offsetting effects.

What more reliably contributes to someone's happiness is not their income per-se, but changes in their income. People whose incomes rise experience greater happiness as a result of being better able to move towards and meet their goals and aspirations. However, over time people adapt to their higher income levels, raising their aspirations beyond their then higher incomes. As a result, without further pay rises their increased happiness is temporary.[5] What this suggests is that clients would be right to think that they would feel happier if they got a pay rise, but they would be wrong to think that that increased happiness would persist.

What also contributes to happiness more than people's absolute incomes are their relative incomes. Earning $100k might be perfectly acceptable until someone realises that their colleagues all earn $150k. A study of Olympic medallists showed a similar effect: those who won bronze were rated as appearing happier than those who won silver. It was not the colour of their medal that mattered for their happiness, rather it was each competitor's point of comparison. Whereas bronze medallists felt fortunate for avoiding 4th position and making it to the podium at all, silver medallists felt disappointed that they missed out on gold.[6]

A related problem occurs when people compare their own feelings with others' apparent happiness. A difficulty with doing this is that because people often mask their internal states, they can appear happier than they actually are. As a demonstration of this effect, Seth Stephens-Davidowitz compared the terms people used to refer to their husbands on Facebook with those used on Google.[7] A key difference between the two platforms, of course, is that what people post on Facebook is seen by others, whereas whatever is typed into Google remains anonymous. The top terms used on Facebook to describe husbands were all positive: 'the best', 'my best friend', 'amazing', 'the greatest' and 'so cute'. In contrast, the terms used on Google were, with the exception of 'amazing', much less effusive: 'gay', 'a jerk', 'annoying' and 'mean'. People's public image was quite different from their private thoughts. Just as comparing incomes can lead to unhappiness, if advisers want to help clients be happy they could counsel them to *'not compare their insides to other people's outsides.'*

What these examples demonstrate is that, as has been discussed in previous chapters, the reference points that people choose can significantly impact the conclusions that they draw. Advisers can positively influence clients' goals and happiness by assisting them to find helpful comparisons and to avoid unhelpful ones. For example, perhaps a client's unhappiness-inducing higher previous salary is now irrelevant given a substantial change in their role. Or greater happiness might be derived by a client thinking about their old school buddies who have followed less well-paid careers, rather than about the new BMWs owned by their mates from law school. Research shows that what people choose or are prompted to think about can significantly impact their assessed level of happiness. If a client's ultimate goal is happiness, then changing the way they think could be an easier and more reliable path to success than changing their income.

Smarter spending

Another strategy to improve clients' happiness is to help them spend their money more wisely. By aligning their goals more closely with the psychological research, clients can create greater happiness from the same level of wealth and expenditure. The reason people don't do this already is that they make errors in *'affective forecasting'* (ie in predicting their future emotional states). They *'mispredict what will make them happy, how happy it will make them, and how long that happiness will last'.*[8] When they mispredict, they spend money on things that they think will make them happy, but for various reasons do not.

One of the misprediction problems occurs when people don't sufficiently account for the fact that they habituate to the parts of their lives that don't change over time. For example, the impact of a new car is greatest initially, but it can fade into the background of one's life thereafter. It's hard for something to make a client happy if they no longer pay much attention to it. For it to continue to capture attention it has to remain at least somewhat novel.

This is one of the reasons why experiences have been found to trump material items as a path to happiness. Whereas material items largely remain the same, or perhaps diminish with age, experiences tend to be more varied. As a result, experiences can continue to attract people's attention in ways that material items sometimes cannot. Therefore, when thinking about their goals, advisers could suggest their clients focus their spending more on positive experiences, and on the avoidance of negative ones, and less on material items.

For even greater impact, clients should try to separate their positive experiences. This is because while people tend to habituate less to experiences than to material items, habitation can play a role with experiences too. Breaking experiences into smaller chunks allows for the habituation to subside and for those experiences to regain some of their initial novelty.

A popular example of this is an experiment in which participants were asked to sit in a chair equipped with a massage cushion. Those who experienced two shorter massages found the overall experience more pleasurable than did those who had a single, longer massage of equivalent total length.[9] Just as finding $50 twice was better than finding $100 once, two shorter massages are better than one longer one. In the context of setting financial goals, this means that where practicable, two shorter holidays might lead to greater happiness than one longer one, or the more varied experience of working part-time might be preferred to transitioning directly from full-time employment to retirement.

Another way that people can spend money in ways that are likely to make them happy is to buy time. Expenditures that make people more *time affluent* have been shown to make them happier. According to Assistant Professor Ashley Whillans, *'people who feel time-poor experience lower levels of happiness and higher levels of anxiety, depression and stress. They experience less joy and laugh less. They exercise less and are less healthy. Their productivity at work diminishes'* and *'they are more likely to get divorced.'* [10]

Whillans concludes that people's belief that spending time to get money, thinking that money will lead to happiness, is backwards. Rather, she suggests that the happiest people use their money to buy time, such as by hiring help to avoid disliked chores, or by paying for more convenient transport to cut their travel times. This means that while there can be a dollar cost to taking sabbaticals or leave without pay, in order to have more time to pursue external interests or to tend to family commitments, say, it could also come with an under-appreciated happiness dividend.

SETTING MEANINGFUL AND MOTIVATIONAL GOALS
People are motivated by more than just income and expenditure of course. This section discusses how advisers can help their clients set meaningful goals and goals that give them a sense of purpose. They can do this by ensuring that a client's goals 'make sense' in the context of their personal narrative and align with their higher-level values. To motivate clients to act on them, these goals need to strike a balance between aspiration and achievability, and need to be broken into bite-size actions.

Goals with meaning and purpose
A client's goals don't exist in a vacuum; they are constructed within the context of the client's past experiences. When a client interprets and makes sense of those past experiences, they create meaningful narratives about their lives that they tell themselves and others. The narratives clients create help to reframe their past memories, and can provide a sense of comprehension. In this context, a client's goals represent the unwritten next chapter of their life stories. A client's life and their goals can be considered meaningful when they have an underlying coherence. As many advisers are already aware, by understanding their clients' life stories they can help them to set goals that are meaningful for them.

To do this, advisers need to know more than just their clients' experiences, they also need to know how their clients interpret those experiences. Big differences can result from essentially the same experiences, depending on the meaning clients draw from them. For example, was a client being overlooked for a promotion an indication of their low value as an employee, or perhaps an indication of the presence of a strong alternative candidate? Was suffering a loss a sign that investing in shares is generally unprofitable, or an expected set-back on the long-term road to wealth? In each of these cases, more conservative goals are more consistent with the pessimistic narrative.

In addition to simply understanding these narratives, advisers can potentially also help clients to interpret their life events in ways that are constructive and optimistic. As the organisation Action for Happiness suggests, people should *'see life as it is, but focus on the good bits'*.

A related concept to 'meaning' is 'purpose'. Whereas meaning can be thought of as backward-looking and seeking to aid comprehension, purpose is forward-looking and drives action towards a goal. Clients and advisers who find it difficult to connect with the idea of having a purpose could interpret it as *'voluntarily assumed, important, higher-level life goals or values that motivate behaviour towards achieving or obtaining them'*.[11] While not everyone experiences or even desires to experience a purpose in life, those who feel their life has a purpose enjoy a range of benefits. Having a sense of purpose is associated with higher happiness, life satisfaction and general wellbeing, plus better health outcomes and longevity.[12]

How might having a sense of purpose deliver these benefits? For a start, it can keep people doing things that are difficult but rewarding. For example, *'self-regulation'*, such as self-talk to keep yourself going during mentally and physically challenging activities, has been found to increase when those activities align with someone's sense of purpose. And for some challenging activities self-regulation is not even required, as purposeful activity can feel relatively effortless and enjoyable, and less stressful.[13] This research suggests that there could be a substantial benefit for clients if advisers can help them to articulate goals that align with their sense of purpose.

Where can clients find their purpose? Some people gain a sense of purpose from their employment, and their employment can in turn influence their overall happiness. In terms of their employment, younger and older workers (relative to those of intermediate ages) and the self-employed (relative to employees) tend to be most satisfied.[14] An important gap can be created when a client's employment ceases. In the case of retirees, advisers could potentially assist their clients by helping them to rediscover a sense of purpose, such as through continuing part-time work, mentoring or volunteering.

Some clients might find their purpose in helping others. People who devote more money to 'pro-social' spending (ie spending money on other people, giving to charities, etc) have been found to be happier, even after controlling for their income.[15] Also, in an experimental context, when people were given money and randomly assigned to spend it either on themselves or on someone else, on average those who spent it on others subsequently reported being happier. This is an average however, meaning that within an adviser's clients there are likely to be many who are focused on various pro-social endeavours (philanthropy, socially responsible investing, etc), but others who are not. Adviser would obviously need to ensure they understood these individual differences.

Another place clients might find their purpose is in achieving difficult, effortful goals. Achieving these types of goals benefits from 'cognitive dissonance', which refers to the psychological discomfort people feel when they have conflicting thoughts. In the context of achieving a difficult goal, a conflict can arise from thinking 'I have invested a lot of time and energy into achieving X' while also thinking 'X is not worthwhile'. The conflict can be simply resolved by believing that X is, in fact, worthwhile. And because this deft reinterpretation typically happens beyond people's awareness, a client's subjective experience is likely to be that the difficult goal was inherently worthwhile.

As a result of increasing cognitive dissonance, the more time and energy that a client invests and the fewer financial and other benefits that they receive, the more worthwhile something is likely to feel. This suggests that mountain trekking will feel more worthwhile than a beach holiday, and volunteering will feel more worthwhile than the equivalent activities performed as part of one's paid employment.

While clients having a sense of purpose can have benefits, not having a sense of purpose but wanting one can create anxiety, something that is referred to as 'purpose anxiety'. Purpose anxiety might be a fitting description for some midlife crises. Arguably, when people's basic needs are already fulfilled, they have too many options. When there are too many options there is more reason to be anxious about choosing the wrong one, thereby contributing to an apparent crisis.

And finally, for those who manage to find their purpose there is the constant challenge of living in accordance with that purpose, given the constraints of time, money and other obligations. It is with these challenges that advisers can potentially assist, by helping clients to articulate goals that balance their sense of purpose with these practical considerations.

Goals that motivate action

Setting goals is one thing, achieving them can be quite another. Not all goals are equally effective at motivating clients to do the things required to achieve them. Some research favours setting harder goals. *'So long as a person is committed to a goal, has the requisite ability to attain it, and does not have conflicting goals, there is a positive linear relationship between goal difficulty and task performance.'* This was the conclusion drawn from a review of goal-setting research undertaken by Professors Edwin Locke and Gary Latham.[16] These researchers found that across a range of contexts (not specific to financial planning), having higher goals leads to greater effort and persistence than do moderately difficult, easy or vague goals.

However, while higher goals generally lead to higher outcomes, that doesn't necessarily mean they also lead to greater happiness. Kahneman argues that because goals set the primary standard for self-assessing one's performance, and because difficult goals create a greater risk of failure, *'one recipe for a dissatisfied adulthood is setting goals that are especially difficult to attain'.* [17]

Especially difficult goals are arguably also a recipe for clients' dissatisfaction with their adviser. As a result, difficult goals can potentially come with both a psychological cost for the client and a commercial cost for the adviser. Therefore, for both the client's and adviser's sake, goals should balance being challenging and aspirational with being reasonably achievable.

Where goals create this balance, advisers can assist to motivate clients to undertake the necessary actions by providing them feedback on their progress towards their goals. This could involve establishing a series of smaller goals that ultimately lead to the end objective. To motivate clients to take a journey of 1,000 miles, the psychological evidence suggests that advisers should focus them on the single next step. While the ultimate goal might be large and difficult, each step can be specific, simple and easy. Focusing on the end goal can create inspiration, while focussing on each step is what makes it happen.

It also helps if clients have a sense of their own 'self-efficacy', a sense that through their actions they can control whether they achieve their goals. Why bother trying if you can't see the connection between your action and the intended outcome? An advice tool that shows the impact of a client's current savings on their future retirement outcomes is one way to help clients make this connection. Other ways are discussed in Chapter 10.

DEALING WITH CHANGING GOALS
As has been discussed, it can sometimes be difficult for clients to articulate appropriate goals. For clients who experience this difficulty, advisers can help them to explore some of the issues covered in the preceding sections: the types of happiness that they value most, the possible trade-offs between their income and their happiness, their spending priorities, their life narrative, and their sense of purpose. Each topic is intended to help clients to focus on the things that are meaningful to them and that are important for their future happiness.

But what about clients at the other end of the spectrum, those who are able to confidently articulate their goals and aspirations? For these clients the problem is more likely to be that the crystal ball through which they view their future is more opaque than they imagine; their future desires could be quite different from how they currently envisage them.

One of the reasons people's future desires can be hard to predict is due to the role played by context. One of the key findings of decision-making research is the surprisingly strong influence of the context in which people make their decisions. People typically fail to anticipate how different their choices are when made in hot emotional states, or in different social contexts, for example. While some aspects of people's personalities endure over time, this does not mean that their preferences will necessarily be stable or ubiquitous across time and in different contexts. In simple terms, this is why some people who drink beer at the pub with their mates, prefer wine while dining at a restaurant with their spouse. Rather than having a fixed preference for beer or wine, their preferences depend on the context.

The changeability of people's preferences is particularly important when a client's life context changes significantly. In these cases, advisers should expect that the client's preferences will also change, potentially in ways and to extents that the client does not fully anticipate. A major life transition, such as from having no children to being a parent, can mean that a '20-something' who desires a sportscar can easily find themselves becoming a '30-something' who is shopping for a 7-seater. And similarly, the relaxing unstructured free time that is so highly valued by a full-time employee can become depressing and isolating for a client who has recently retired. Clients' expressed goals might unexpectedly and significantly change across these transitions, even if the transitions themselves are expected.

So, how can advisers work with clients whose goals are likely to change? One approach is for advisers to explicitly discuss with clients the uncertainty related to each of their goals. Clients might be able to articulate each goal's relative priority, the relationships between their goals, and the various contingencies to which each goal is subject.[18] This elaboration could be a useful starting point to understanding each goal's changeability.

However, as discussed in Chapter 1, clients' subjective assessments of their own certainty can be a poor guide to their actual accuracy. Psychological research shows that it is easy for people to feel certain about something and yet still be wrong. As a general rule, the greater a client's expectations diverge from the experiences of other people in similar situations, the more advisers would have grounds to be concerned that their client's expectations might not be realistic. Ignoring others' experiences is a form of 'base-rate neglect', a bias that is discussed in subsequent chapters. Of course, it is possible the client and their circumstances are unique.

Another approach to dealing with the uncertainty inherent in a client predicting their future desires is for them to set *fuzzy goals*. These are goals that are specified only at a high level, and that are imprecise and flexible as to the specific details, including their magnitude and timing.[19] The less precise the forecast, the more likely it will be right. Fuzzy goals stand a better chance of remaining relevant in the context of a client's changing reality. They are likely to be approximately right, rather than being precisely wrong.[20]

Flexible goals have other benefits too. A client having a flexible target retirement age or flexible holiday plans, say, can allow them to absorb additional investment risk. When markets inevitably fall, it matters less to achieving the client's goals if those goals can be satisfied at different times, in different amounts or in different ways. As a result of having flexible goals, clients are able to accept more risk, thereby creating the opportunity for higher returns. When clients are flexible about their retirement date, a client's contingent human capital (ie their willingness and ability to continue to work) can be translated into additional investment capital (as a result of them being able to earn higher expected returns). Flexible goals can therefore have real financial value.

When clients have difficulty predicting their future preferences, advisers should try to avoid complexity. If an adviser were to create a complex investment strategy to precisely match a complex set of client goals, then they would be failing to appreciate the spurious accuracy that this would entail. From the perspective of effective decision-making, when dealing with a combination of complexity and uncertainty, relatively simple approaches are often best. This is doubly so if these strategies must then be communicated to the client in an intelligible way. With these considerations in mind, Brooks, Davies and Smith recommend that advisers only focus on a client's important and large goals, the ones that meet their client's key needs, with an overarching aim of having enough money to spend on all of the goals, as and when required.[21] Unimportant secondary goals risk becoming a distraction.

And finally, clients' goals need to be updated to reflect changes over time, creating a series of 'successive approximations' towards clients' end objectives. As advisers would already be aware, updating is particularly important as clients traverse significant life events.

However, there are psychological issues to consider with updating too. Having placed their hand on their heart and declared a particular goal to be important, for a client to return to their adviser the following year with a change of plan might make them feel uncomfortable. Some psychologists refer to this as a *'consistency effect'* (ie the fact that people feel the need to be consistent with their past statements and behaviours). To assuage their sense of inconsistency, clients might need to be reassured that changes in their preferences are to be expected, and are not an indication of their capriciousness or tenderness of mind. As Nobel Prize winning economist Dr Paul Samuelson reportedly said: *'when events change, I change my mind. What do you do?'* [22]

CONCLUSIONS

A client's goals are fundamental to financial advice. However, as has been discussed in this chapter, clients' goals can have a range of psychological problems associated with them. These problems can mean that clients can change their minds before they reach their goals. Or they can reach their goals but be disappointed that the goals fail to lead to the happiness and satisfaction that they desire. Alternatively, clients can fail to do the things needed to achieve their goals at all. These problems can create significant challenges for advisers in providing appropriate advice.

Underlying these problems is the fact that people are often blindsided by what makes them happy. Short-term pleasures don't equate to long-term satisfaction, higher incomes don't lead to sustained increases in happiness, people tend to habituate to both good and bad things over time, and people's changing life circumstances can significantly impact what they desire.

To counter these problems advisers can employ strategies that help to better align clients' goals with the psychological research. They can recommend clients find ways to spend their money on shorter experiences, and to pursue goals that are meaningful for them. They can help ensure that these goals balance being aspirational with being achievable. And, when faced with major life transitions, advisers can recommend their clients set fuzzy/flexible goals, paired with more concrete, short-term actions needed to achieve them.

This chapter has highlighted that non-financial strategies could play a substantial role in helping clients. Clients who already have their basic needs satisfied and are looking to increase their happiness might achieve a benefit by simply focusing their attention on the good things in their lives. For example, research shows that people can reap substantial enjoyment from anticipating an upcoming event, and that people who devote time to anticipating enjoyable experiences report being happier in general. Another study found that individuals who had a strong capacity to savour the mundane joys of daily life were happier than those who did not.[23] Anticipation costs nothing, and neither does expressing gratitude for, savouring or reflecting on the positive things in one's life. Arguably developing these skills should be every client's goal.

4

THE (OFTEN OVERSTATED) ROLE OF FINANCIAL LITERACY

Financial decision-making can be complex. It is therefore understandable that people with low financial literacy often make poor financial choices. People with lower financial literacy tend to be less likely to plan for retirement, less likely to hold equities, more likely to hold undiversified portfolios, less able to estimate the time needed to pay off a credit card balance, more likely to incur fees for late payment and exceeding borrowing limits, and more likely to pay higher interest rates on their mortgage.

Because people with low financial literacy often fail to understand fundamental investment concepts, such as compound interest, it appears that greater financial literacy education would be helpful. However, financial literacy presents an apparent paradox: while people with low financial literacy often make poor financial decisions, providing them financial education commonly provides little or no benefit. *'What degree of effectiveness should appropriately be claimed for the current model of financial literacy education? As yet, none,'* pessimistically concludes Professor Willis, in a review of financial literacy research.[1]

This chapter discusses the role of financial education and financial literacy in improving people's financial decisions and outcomes. More specifically it discusses the potential applications of financial literacy education in the context of a financial adviser's client engagement. Advisers can recommend certain decisions and actions, but often rely on clients to make the final call. When educating clients about making appropriate choices, advisers need to avoid the minefield of well-intentioned but failed financial literacy initiatives. These initiatives are often ignored by clients, or are misunderstood or forgotten. Advisers need to educate clients in ways that they will actually understand and respond to. Given their personal relationship with clients and their face-to-face engagement, advisers are well suited to fulfil this role.

WHAT IS FINANCIAL LITERACY?

Most advisers probably have a general conception of financial literacy. However, to measure and study its effects requires a more precise definition. One approach is to equate financial literacy with financial knowledge; doing so means that it can then be tested by asking people questions such as *'if you put $100 in a bank account earning 2% per annum and left the interest to accumulate, how much would you have at the end of 2 years?'* Being able to select the correct multiple-choice answer of *'more than $104'* requires knowing about compound interest.

However, one of the drawbacks of focusing on an individual's level of financial knowledge is that it doesn't necessarily lead to decisions, actions and outcomes. Among other things, translating knowledge of the benefits of compound interest into a financially rewarding action requires additional skills, such as being able to access relevant information and to make appropriate comparisons. It also requires having certain attitudes, such as motivation and a sense of self-efficacy. And behaviours matter too; if they don't shop around, set up an account and transfer funds, a person who understands compound interest still won't benefit from investing in a higher-yielding savings account.

Reflecting these additional factors, an alternative view of financial literacy conceptualises it as also incorporating a set of financial skills, attitudes and behaviours that help people to make effective decisions, take action and achieve improved financial outcomes.[2] As in the example of a person who understands compound interest but then fails to benefit from it, these skills, attitudes and behaviours can be quite different from financial knowledge; they can even use different parts of the brain. If advisers want their clients to achieve their financial objectives, it is this broader concept of financial literacy that is most relevant.

By tailoring financial literacy education to account for these additional factors, advisers can potentially improve the effectiveness of the education that they provide. For example, for a compulsive spender, as well as education about the benefits of saving, advisers could teach planning skills and strategies to manage self-control problems. Similarly, for clients nervous about investing in growth assets, as well as educating them about risk and return, advisers could help build their confidence by providing case studies about how others have overcome their fear of investing. To a theoretically rational investor, the historical choices made by other clients that appear in these case studies should be irrelevant. However, theoretically rational investors are easier to find in theory than in practice.

WHAT DO FINANCIAL LITERACY ASSESSMENTS TELL US?

Why do financially literate people tend to make better financial decisions than do those with lower literacy? Is it because of their financial literacy, or are there other plausible explanations? In answering these questions, this section examines how financial literacy varies across socio-economic groups, between genders and across different age groups. It also considers the links between financial literacy and other psychological measures. Advisers can use these insights to identify and engage with clients with different levels of financial literacy. They can also use them to help overcome the barriers to learning that are relevant for different clients, and to ascertain for which clients financial literacy education is likely to be most important.

Lower socio-economic groups have lower financial literacy

Perhaps unsurprisingly, financial literacy correlates with socio-economic status. This means that people with more education, income and wealth tend to have higher financial literacy. There could be a number of reasons for this. Firstly, there is some evidence that financial literacy is transferred from parents with greater education and investment experience to their children. Some of the efforts people put into teaching their children about money appear to work.

Another possible explanation is that people with lower income and wealth arguably stand to gain the least from investing in their own financial literacy.

Given the costs of one's time and energy, if the benefits are small or expected to be in the distant future, then it could be rational for a person of low financial literacy to remain financially illiterate. As with other forms of human capital, there will be an optimal amount of financial literacy education that each person will invest in, with that amount depending on each person's circumstances.

If advisers seek to provide financial literacy education to people from lower socio-economic groups, it could help to improve this cost/benefit equation. Advisers can potentially do this by reducing the financial or non-financial costs of the education they provide, or by linking it with meaningful, tangible and not too-distant benefits. Of course, there could be advantages in improving this equation for other clients too.

Women have lower financial literacy

On average, women have lower financial literacy than men, at least in terms of their financial knowledge. For example, ANZ's survey of adult financial literacy in Australia found that *'women had lower scores on average than men on financial knowledge and numeracy from 28 years of age on.'* They reported that women were less likely to believe that investments with higher returns probably also had higher than average risks, and were less likely to consider diversification to be 'very' or 'quite' important.[3] Similarly, the Australian 'HILDA' survey reported *'a clear gender divide in financial literacy'.* In particular, this survey found that women were less able to correctly answer questions involving calculating simple interest, adjusting for inflation, as well as understanding diversification and the trade-off between risk and return.[4]

However, lower financial literacy scores are not consistent across all groups of women; among other things, the results vary based on women's marital status. Some evidence shows that women who are married or in a long-term relationship tend to have lower financial literacy than other women or equivalent men. This suggests that women might cede financial responsibilities to their husbands and partners, leading to an increasing gap in their relative levels of financial literacy over time. In contrast, women who are divorced or widowed, and therefore no longer able to delegate financial decision-making to their husbands, appear to increase their financial knowledge. At least in part, women's lower financial knowledge appears to reflect the nature of their relationships.[5]

In addition, when a broader view of financial literacy is taken, women's lower levels of financial knowledge can obscure other important differences between the genders. For example, in relation to financial attitudes, ANZ's survey found that compared with men, women tended to more commonly report that dealing with money was stressful. They also tended to have lower financial aspirations than men, particularly during their child-rearing years. And they were also less impulsive in both their spending and risk-taking. In terms of their behaviours, the survey found that women were more likely to keep track of finances, but were less likely to choose financial products or to stay informed.

While each individual and couple is likely to be different in some ways, these findings reinforce the need for advisers of married couples to be sensitive to potential differences in the financial knowledge, attitudes and behaviours of husbands and wives. They also suggest that financial advisers can potentially play a role in helping newly divorced or widowed women on their journey to financial literacy and financial independence.

Lower financial literacy among the young and old
The relationship between age and financial literacy follows an inverse U-shape, with financial literacy being lowest among the young and old. Correspondingly, financial mistakes tend to decline with age until people reach their early 50s, before increasing again.[6] This pattern is consistent with an increasing accumulation of financial skills and knowledge throughout adulthood, eventually offset by cognitive decline in old age.

There is an obvious conclusion from the relationship between age and financial literacy. It is that advisers could target both younger and older client segments with strategies aimed at overcoming the poor decisions that are particularly relevant for each age cohort. For younger groups, education about managing spending and credit card debt might be relevant, say, while older cohorts could benefit from learning strategies for identifying and avoiding investment scams.

One of the challenges in working with people with lower financial literacy is engaging with those who don't recognise the poor quality of their own knowledge and decisions. There can be a marked disparity between someone's actual and perceived financial abilities. Among older people this can result in their reluctance to recognise their increasing need for assistance as they age. This problem is discussed in more detail in Chapter 10 in the context of retirement planning.

Cognitive skills & other psychological traits

Financial literacy tends to be higher among people with better numeracy and with greater cognitive ability generally. Does this mean that those who lack strong cognitive or numerical capabilities are doomed to poor financial literacy? Maybe, but less pessimistic interpretations are also plausible. For example, if people with higher cognitive and numerical abilities find acquiring financial knowledge and skills easier, then they could simply be more likely to seek financial education. Lower cognitive and numerical skills create greater, but not necessarily insurmountable, barriers to people seeking and acquiring financial skills and knowledge. This suggests that advisers making financial education more psychologically accessible might allow more people to improve their financial literacy. Strategies to achieve this are discussed below.

The relationship between cognitive ability and financial literacy could have other underlying causes too. For example, people with lower cognitive abilities tend to have higher 'discount rates' (ie lower willingness to delay gratification), as well as lower tolerance for risk. Not only do these characteristics mean they are less likely to make good long-term financial decisions, it could also mean they are less likely to invest in financial literacy education. Like saving and investing, education typically has short-term costs and provides longer-term benefits. The more certain and closer to the present the benefits of financial education can be made, the less problematic this becomes.

Differences in time preferences and risk-profiles can have important implications for people with lower cognitive abilities. For example, one US study found that a 'present-biased' time orientation (ie having a higher discount rate) had a stronger impact on the likelihood that people participated in a retirement savings plan than did their financial literacy.[7] This demonstrates how having lower financial literacy can potentially mask more important issues facing people with lower cognitive and numerical abilities. For advisers, this suggests that an easier path to helping these clients might not be by trying to increase their financial knowledge, but by finding more direct ways to, say, help them prioritise the long term.

DOES FINANCIAL LITERACY EDUCATION HELP?

What can advisers learn from the numerous attempts that have been made to provide financial literacy education? Have they been successful? The results to date have been disappointing. For example, a meta-analysis of 201 financial literacy studies showed that financial literacy education realised little benefit. In fact, the authors concluded that *'interventions to improve financial literacy explain only 0.1% of the variance in the financial behaviours studied'*.[8] Across these studies, differences in people's financial behaviours were typically not the result of whether they had been provided financial literacy education. Similarly, in an Australian context, ANZ's 2018 Financial Wellbeing Report found that *'detailed knowledge and experience of financial products or services had only limited direct influence on financial wellbeing.'*[9]

These results can feel counter-intuitive, particularly given that people who partake in financial literacy programs often review them positively. However, while people might report positive feelings towards particular financial literacy initiatives, there is so far little empirical evidence that they have had a meaningful impact on improving financial decisions and outcomes. Unfortunately, what seems to be beneficial and what actually helps can be two quite different things.

This is not to say that financial literacy education is a lost cause; merely that the initial attempts to impart financial literacy education, to change financial decisions and behaviour, and to measure positive impacts from them, have largely been unsuccessful. However, these studies provide a clear warning about the potentially limited benefits of financial literacy initiatives that focus solely on improving participants' financial knowledge. Other factors are likely to be more important, include the roles of people's skills, attitudes and behaviours, their socio-economic status, their cognitive and numerical capabilities, as well as the context in which their decisions are made. Advisers who seek to improve their clients' financial literacy need to build on the lessons from these initial failures. Financial literacy initiatives founded on good intentions, but that are naïve to the psychology of financial decision-making, will probably not succeed.

OVERCOMING BARRIERS TO EFFECTIVE FINANCIAL LITERACY EDUCATION

For financial literacy education to be effective it needs to ensure that recipients actually learn from the education, that they can recall the lessons they learn, and that they apply those lessons. There are a number of barriers to overcome to achieve these outcomes. For example, knowledge imparted through financial literacy education tends to decay quickly; people quickly start forgetting. To help their clients, advisers should try to tailor their financial literacy education so that it is delivered in easily digestible amounts, at times when people are most receptive to it, in ways that facilitate actions, and in formats that clients prefer to receive.

Barriers to learning

One challenge in providing effective financial education is that it can yield surprisingly weak changes in financial knowledge. For example, a review of a number of studies of financial literacy initiatives found that *the interventions only explained about 0.44% of the variance in financial knowledge*.[10] In other words, leaving aside whether it changed people's behaviours or outcomes, the financial education made almost no difference to participants' financial knowledge itself!

What is it about financial literacy education that means that people don't absorb the knowledge that the education is intended to impart? There are a number of potential explanations. One is that, in contrast to fields like science and maths that are more successful in changing people's knowledge, with financial literacy it is can be difficult to be definitive. Whereas the speed of light in a vacuum is constant, what constitutes an optimal financial decision can be significantly different depending on a client's individual circumstances and preferences.

Those circumstances and preferences can vary in ways that transform what is a good decision for one client, into a poor one for another.

If what clients learn from financial literacy education is that 'it depends', this rather unhelpful conclusion is understandably quickly forgotten. To translate this conclusion into something more meaningful, useful and memorable the dependencies need to be identified and elaborated. If the dependencies are sufficiently simple and standard they could potentially be articulated and incorporated into a short burst of financial literacy education, a rule-of-thumb or a decision-making tool. However, if this becomes complex there is a chance of it backfiring. Revealing all of the complexities risks clients becoming overwhelmed, particularly for people with low cognitive or numerical capabilities.

Knowledge decay

Even if knowledge is gained, another problem is that it decays over time, typically quite quickly. For example, 1 hour of instruction tends to be of no benefit after 5 months. As you would expect, more education produces larger initial benefits. However, this is offset by the fact that it also suffers a stronger decay over time. For example, to double the period of the benefit from 9 to 18 months requires quadrupling the amount of instruction (from 6 to 24 hours). Researchers have concluded that *'even initiatives with many hours of instruction have been found to have negligible effects on behaviour 20 months or more from the time of intervention.'*[11]

Given the diminishing marginal benefits from larger initiatives, clients are likely to get the most benefit from multiple short bursts of financial literacy education. As Ulrich Boser puts it, *'we learn better in small doses'.*[12] And given how rapidly knowledge decays over time, where possible advisers should provide this financial literacy education shortly prior to or, better still, at the point when clients actually need to use it. Otherwise the lessons will be long forgotten when it comes time for clients to make a decision.

As well as minimising the potential for knowledge decay, there is some evidence of the effectiveness of this *'just-in-time'* financial literacy in improving clients' decisions and behaviours. For example, counselling provided to people applying for (probably inappropriate) complex mortgage products led less sophisticated consumers to either abandon their search or to select more competitive products.[13] Arguably greater benefits should be anticipated in the context of a financial advice relationship, where more support can be provided.

To align with the broader behavioural finance research, just-in-time financial literacy should provide concise, specific, action-oriented, high quality information that is tied to a particular decision or action that is immediately relevant for the client. As Benartzi notes, *'information becomes vastly more valuable if it is accompanied by the means to take action right now.'* [14] Together, these characteristics maximise the likelihood of influencing clients' decisions and behaviours. They achieve this by limiting clients' knowledge decay, by providing them an immediate benefit, and by removing *'frictions'* that could impede them taking action.

The right timing

In addition to providing financial literacy education just prior to clients making a decision, there are other times when they are likely to be receptive to it too. As it happens, I am writing this sentence on New Year's Eve, at a time when my inbox is full of articles about how to keep my New Year's resolutions. And while most people's resolutions are likely to be broken, the New Year is actually a time when people are more receptive to changing their habits. For example, more people prefer January to increase their savings rate than any other month. Similarly, people search for the word 'diet' on 1 January about 80% more than on other days, and gym visits tend to increase at the start of a new year. People are also more receptive to these types of habit-changing behaviours at the start of a new week or month, or following their birthday.[15] Daniel Pink argues that these dates are *'temporal landmarks [that] interrupt attention to day-to-day minutiae, causing people to take a big picture view of their lives and thus focus on achieving their goals'.*[16]

Financial advisers who are aware of their clients' landmark dates can target financial literacy initiatives to those times. To do this, advisers need to be aware not just of clients' birthdays, but also of other events in clients' lives that could make them change their focus, such as changing jobs, changing residence, starting a family, or receiving an inheritance. It is during these times that clients are both more likely to be receptive to financial literacy education and, in many cases, also most in need of advice.

Use multiple approaches to financial literacy education

Advisers are likely to have clients with different knowledge, skills, behaviours and attitudes, and who need to make decisions across a number of different circumstances. Determining which approach is best for each client can be difficult. This is, at least in part, because clients can be an unreliable guide to their own financial literacy requirements. People's self-reported financial knowledge, skills and behaviours can be quite different from reality. For example, when recounting their financial decisions and actions, those that are considered socially desirable, such as saving and budgeting, are likely to be over-remembered, compared with, say, borrowing for consumption. This is not necessarily the result of clients deliberately fabricating their responses; it can result simply from the operation of people's faulty, self-serving memories.

To at least partially cover clients' diverse but somewhat uncertain requirements, advisers can provide financial literacy education covering a range of content and formats. It can be delivered as part of a face-to-face advice conversation; through group seminars and workshops; through the provision of reading material, videos and podcasts; or with the use of interactive tools and calculators. When an adviser is not completely sure how to unlock a client's financial understanding, it pays to be armed with several different keys.

Advisers can also help clients to learn from their own personal experiences. Learning from past experiences is one of the primary ways that many people state that they learn about personal finance.[17] However, this approach carries the risk of people simply learning the wrong lessons. While clients' personal experiences can have high salience, they can also have poor statistical validity. This means that while these experiences effectively attract clients' attention, they can also be unrepresentative. A client's experience of winning the lottery, say, does not mean that lottery tickets are a good investment.

One of the key criteria for effectively learning from one's experiences is that people have the opportunity to receive timely and accurate feedback about their past decisions. The problem is that some financial decisions, such as buying a house or investing for retirement, occur infrequently. And the feedback about whether and why these decisions were successful is noisy and ad-hoc. On top of this, people tend to recall and to attribute meaning to their experiences in self-serving ways, crediting good outcomes to their skill, and poor ones to their bad luck. By helping clients to understand their experiences in a broader context, advisers can potentially assist their clients to learn the right lessons.

REDUCE THE NEED FOR FINANCIAL LITERACY

Increasing financial literacy is only one approach to improve the decisions made by clients who have a poor understanding of financial concepts. Other approaches can play a role too. One is to make it simpler and easier for people with limited financial literacy to make decisions. Another is to ensure that simple decision-making shortcuts, or rules-of-thumb, lead most of these clients to good outcomes most of the time.

Simpler and easier decisions

Financial decisions can be complex, and the products, information and disclosure that goes with them correspondingly so. But need it necessarily be this way? For clients with similar needs, a limited number of relatively simple products and strategies could suffice. While these strategies might still need to be tailored to some degree to suit each client's requirements, increased tailoring can come with a trade-off. If more tailoring means more complexity and, in turn, more complexity means clients with low financial literacy fail to understand or follow their adviser's advice, then simpler solutions could be preferable. A simple strategy that is accepted can be superior to a more complex one that is ignored.

In contrast, clients with higher financial literacy or with particularly complex or unusual requirements could still benefit from more nuanced advice. For these clients, the burden of more difficult decision-making would be more than offset by the value of receiving advice that was finely calibrated to their specific needs and preferences.

As simple as an adviser might try to make it, to some extent complexity is unavoidable. When this is the case, advisers can at least make their clients' subjective experience less complex. As many advisers are already aware, providing graphical representations of complex points and limiting the use of unfamiliar language can assist.

Also, in advisers' face-to-face or written communications, information can be *'layered'*. This means the adviser presents concepts and decisions in a way that exposes clients to only the highest-level, most important points first. Increasing detail is then progressively revealed, only as and when clients are ready. So, for example, a decision about whether to invest in growth assets versus defensive assets precedes a decision about Australian shares versus international shares. In turn, this precedes the choice of an asset manager.

It is understandable that people recoil from making any decision about their superannuation when they are presented with choices that conflate complex decisions, such as by jumping straight to the choice of asset manager. Effectively asking clients to make three decisions at once makes this choice unnecessarily difficult. By reducing clients' perceived and experienced complexity they are less likely to become overwhelmed and more likely to understand and accept the most important aspects of the advice they receive.

Effective decision-making shortcuts

While advisers are obliged to make a proper assessment of whether a strategy is in a client's best interest, clients are under no such obligation. Whether they do so consciously or not, when faced with difficult financial decisions clients tend to use a number of decision-making shortcuts. In place of a complex financial analysis, a client who uses one of these shortcuts might simply choose the default option, or the same option as everybody else. Alternatively, they might choose the option they have heard of, or the cheapest option, or the middle option. Or they could simply choose to stick with the status quo. Behavioural finance research shows the ubiquity of these decision-making shortcuts.

Given that clients are likely to use these types of shortcuts, advisers can frame their recommendations so that they are presented as being the default option, the middle option or the popular option, for example. Advisers can also create their own rules-of-thumb for clients to follow, such as *'this is the best option for people with young families'*, or *'this suits people who don't need to access their money at short notice'*. Despite their advice potentially having been based on a complex and detailed analysis, it is often simple decision-making shortcuts like these that clients actually rely on.

CONCLUSIONS

It's easy to point the finger at inadequate financial literacy for some people's poor financial choices. Those from lower socio-economic groups, some women, the young and the elderly, and people with poor cognitive capabilities are particularly at risk. These problems are relevant for advisers if they want their clients to understand, accept and act on their advice.

As has been discussed in this chapter, more financial literacy training is not the solution, at least not the types of financial literacy education that have typically been used to date. They don't work. To be effective, financial literacy training must overcome a number of barriers, such as rapid knowledge decay and the fact that increased knowledge often doesn't translate into improved decisions, action and outcomes. As Professor Tahira Hira puts it, *'we must exercise caution when expecting financial education to result in behavioural change. We must not lose sight of the fact that changing human behaviour is a very challenging job.'* [18]

To overcome these barriers, financial literacy education should be delivered in easily digestible amounts, at times when people are most receptive to it, in ways that facilitate actions, and in formats that clients prefer to receive. And it should focus on more than just financial knowledge, by also considering clients' relevant skills, attitudes and behaviours. If there is a lesson that behavioural finance has taught it is that we have historically paid too much attention to the types of conscious cognitive processes for which financial knowledge might be useful, and we have not paid enough attention to the other psychological mechanisms that can powerfully drive financial decisions, behaviours and outcomes.

The good news is that given their personal relationships with clients, advisers are well suited to delivering effective financial literacy education. Advisers can deliver it at times it is most relevant for each client, in multiple formats, and in ways that align with the decisions and actions that each client can most benefit from. And through their personal relationships they can help keep clients accountable for achieving positive outcomes.

For clients and advisers, engaging in financial literacy education has both costs and benefits. For clients who don't have the time, inclination or skills, it might not be worth their effort. In these cases, there could be easier ways for advisers to help clients who have low financial literacy. Simplifying advice and nudging clients towards better choices might be possible without needing clients to understand complex financial concepts. A client might not know about compound interest, but if they have learnt some simple rules of thumb to control their spending habits, have paid off their credit cards and have started saving for retirement, is their lack of financial knowledge really a problem?

Even if advisers make few inroads into improving their clients' financial knowledge, in the context of an advice relationship there could be important indirect benefits. As a result of receiving support to improve their financial literacy a client might trust their adviser more, or feel more confident in investing in otherwise unfamiliar assets. When combined with other strategies discussed throughout this book, efforts to improve their clients' financial knowledge could be merely the small tip of the much larger iceberg.

5

MARKET CYCLES & THE BEHAVIOURAL ROLLER-COASTER

Investing successfully should be relatively straightforward; much can be gained from simply holding investments over long periods and benefiting from the wonders of compounding. However, while this might be simple, it isn't necessarily easy. Investing across market cycles can create a behavioural roller-coaster: excitement, euphoria and risk-taking when things go well, and anxiety, uncertainty and conservatism when they don't. As a result of poor decisions, clients can achieve lower returns and incur higher taxes, costs and risks. And for advisers, the challenge of influencing clients throughout market cycles can create stress, frustration and anxiety. It can sometimes also mean losing clients.

This chapter reviews the psychological drivers of clients' decisions throughout investment cycles. There is much more involved than just emotions. Social dynamics, mental accounting and plausible-sounding mental shortcuts also play a role, among other things.

Reducing the risk profile of a client's investment portfolio might solve their behavioural problems. However, it can come at a high cost if it also lowers their expected returns. As an alternative, this chapter discusses a number of relatively simple behavioural strategies, each of which is designed to enhance clients' decisions without sacrificing their returns. While for advisers, using these strategies can make their difficult client conversations easier.

WHAT IS THE PROBLEM?

The decisions made across market cycles can have adverse consequences for clients. As the market falls they get depressed and anxious and sell at the bottom. As the market rises they get excited and buy at the top, or so it would seem. In my first book (*'Applying Behavioural Finance in Australia'*) I provided a critique of the thinking and statistics that are commonly relied on to support this conception of investor behaviour. I argued that individual investors are probably not quite as systematically wrong as this simple representation of their behaviour suggests.

But even if investors aren't necessarily buying right at the top and selling right at the bottom, it is beyond doubt that they are doing some form of ill-advised transacting across market cycles. Selling out of equities and investing in cash in response to market movements has a cost, even if it is done haphazardly over a market cycle. The cost represents a failure to capture the equity risk-premium – the difference between the average return the investor would get from equities and from the cash they hold instead.

The consequences of being out of the market can be devastating where the investor maintains their cash position over an extended period. A decision to divest risky assets during a market decline might then be followed by a long period before the investor overcomes their psychological scars and inertia to reinvest in risky assets.

Of course, this problem can be particularly important for younger investors. For these investors, at the time they suffer a substantial loss they are likely to have had a relatively narrow set of investment experiences to compare it with. This means that a substantial loss can have a disproportionate and enduring impact on their financial decisions and outcomes. As a result, some argue that the *'financial crisis may have created an entire lost generation of younger, more risk-averse investors'.*[1] For advisers working with younger clients, there is an opportunity to shape the beliefs that they derive from their early investment experiences in a way that will set them up for long-term investment success, rather than for perpetual risk-aversion.

In addition to investors who miss out on some of the equity risk premium, clients who respond to market cycles by buying and selling can incur higher costs and taxes than those who don't. And they can also suffer greater risks as their asset allocations vary across a cycle, accepting too much risk at the top of the cycle and too little at the bottom.

Advisers can also be impacted by their clients' decisions across market cycles. I ran a workshop for a team of financial advisers recently in which they related their experiences in working with clients during the depths of the global financial crisis. Conversations that they had with clients who were angry or upset were understandably difficult. Some clients blamed their advisers for failing to foresee the extent of the market rout. The advisers also expressed frustration at not being able to convince some clients to do what they thought was in their best interest at the time. In some cases, clients even terminated their advice relationship.

These experiences reflect both a psychological and a commercial cost on advisers and their businesses as a result of clients' behaviour during difficult market conditions. They suggest the need for strategies to better work with clients, for both the sake of the client and their adviser.

CAUSES OF CLIENT DECISION-MAKING PROBLEMS

There is a number of psychological factors that drive faulty investment decision-making across market cycles. Some operate at an emotional level and result in people following a cycle of 'fear and greed'. Others relate more to conscious decision-making processes, resulting in them following what appears to be more sophisticated and 'rational' approaches but that are, nonetheless, still detrimental to their wealth. Unfortunately, the fact that a strategy for investing across market cycles comes with an apparently plausible explanation does not mean it is correct.

Emotionally-driven decision-making

Perhaps the most obvious culprit for the poor decisions made by unsophisticated investors across market cycles is emotion. In response to news of sharp falls in investment markets people become more fearful. This is accentuated by the fact that the stress investors experience reduces their use of the areas of their brains that are responsible for more rational decision-making. Losses heighten investors' expectations and anxiety about there being further losses to come. As a result, their appetite for risky assets is diminished. When this happens, selling feels like the right thing to do.[2]

Subconscious emotional effects are deeply rooted in people's neurology and physiology; they create both a brain and body experience.[3] And because these emotional effects sometimes helped our ancestors to survive life-and-death encounters, they were not designed to be easily resisted. Strategies that require clients to exercise will-power are unlikely to succeed in the face of such a formidable psycho/physiological adversary.

Part of the challenge is that emotional responses operate largely beyond people's conscious awareness. As a result, they can be immune to introspection. Somewhat comically, it is not uncommon that when people who participate in psychological studies are asked why they made a particular decision, unbeknownst to them, their espoused rationale is in fact a complete fabrication. Clients might have reasoned explanations for their actions, but these should not necessarily be taken at face value. They could simply be a post-hoc rationalisation for what are actually emotion-laden decisions.

While market movements can create strong emotions, emotions don't necessarily need to be derived from markets to impact a client's investment decisions. A client's mood might significantly influence their investment decisions whether their mood was caused by them thinking about their investments, or from a recent row they had with their spouse. Advisers therefore might find it helpful to keep in mind a client's broader life context when thinking about their investment decisions.

Changing expectations
Past returns can be a poor guide for future returns; however, they can provide a more reliable guide to people's return expectations. A 1% decrease in investors' experienced returns typically produces a 50bps decline in the future returns that

those investors expect thereafter.[4] People tend to think, or at least feel, that past market rises or falls are a harbinger for further rises of falls, respectively. In part this reflects a *recency bias*, whereby recent events are extrapolated into the near future.

When people's beliefs change in response to market movements, their subsequent behaviour makes sense. If more losses are expected to follow after initial losses, then it is logical to sell and wait for the market to start rising again before buying back in. Unfortunately, this expectation doesn't fit with the reality of largely unpredictable short-term market movements, juxtaposed with the more predictable long-term benefits from owning risky assets. Behavioural strategies need to allow long-term thinking to regain the ascendency.

Following the crowd

Another contributor to investors' decisions across investment cycles is the power of social influence. In rising markets, when everyone else seems to be making money, it can be hard to resist the urge to take more risk in order to do the same. Clients are likely to anticipate regret if they stick to their guns. The same applies in reverse when everyone else appears to be running for the exits.

The behaviour of the herd creates a new reference point against which gains and losses are judged. Using everyone else as a benchmark, a loss that is also suffered by other investors seems not nearly as bad. While the dollar impact remains the same, at least it allows clients to be comforted by the regret-reducing rationalisation of doing no worse than other investors.

But it can sometimes be logical to follow the crowd. If other people know something that you don't, you would be foolish not to pay attention to them. For example, if the driver of the car in front sees the lane ahead is blocked, slows and indicates to change lanes, there can be benefits in the trailing drivers preparing to do the same. If these trailing drivers' views are obscured, then the lead car's actions could be their best guide to the road ahead.

However, while following the car ahead can make sense, as was demonstrated in the example with the 'novice investors' in Chapter 1, what others do or say can influence people's decisions even when those actions and statements are logically irrelevant. In the case of investing across market cycles, 'logical irrelevance' describes other investors' behaviour quite well. Other investors provide a very poor guide to future market returns. They also provide a poor guide to the decisions that are appropriate for people who have their own specific investment objectives and circumstances. To mimic these other investors is akin to following a blind driver who is on their way to the wrong destination.

The house money effect

In the case of rising markets, another decision-making bias can also have an impact: the 'house money effect'. This bias takes its name from the way in which some gamblers account for their winnings. Imagine you started a night at the casino with $100. After a few winning hands, you now have $200 in your pocket. Applying a common mental accounting strategy, this $200 can be thought of as $100 of your own money, plus $100 of 'house money' (ie money won from the casino). While this logic makes some sense, it obscures the fact that the entire $200 is now yours, regardless of its source; every dollar in your pocket is entirely fungible with every other dollar.

Why this gambler's logic is important is that by thinking of the additional $100 as 'house money' it assumes a different risk profile from the initial $100; it would feel less bad for the gambler to lose the $100 of house money than to lose their original cash. Whereas each dollar should logically be treated the same, as a result of the way they mentally account for their winnings, the gambler feels comfortable taking riskier bets with the house money.

The same idea can apply to the profits from a client's past investment successes. Thinking of their past investment successes as 'house money' can result in clients being willing to take increased risks. The implication is that if advisers want to understand their clients' decision-making across market cycles, they need to know not only their clients' past track record of investment successes, but also the way they mentally account for them.

Dollar cost averaging

As has been discussed already, when faced with complex decisions, one strategy people use to conserve their scarce cognitive resources is to use simple mental shortcuts. Some of these shortcuts can be useful when it comes to investing, such as *'don't put all your eggs in one basket'*. But others can lead investors astray. One example is dollar cost averaging (DCA), the strategy of progressively investing a lump sum over time, rather than investing it all at once. For clarity, this is different from the strategy of simply investing progressively over time as and when funds are available to do so.

The DCA strategy provides a few plausible-sounding simple mental shortcuts. One of these is *'diversification is good and, by having multiple investment dates, DCA is a form of diversification'*. This is one of many ways that investors can misunderstand diversification. Another is *'you can't lose with DCA: if the market goes up, you win, while if it falls, you get to invest at a lower price'*. The reality is more nuanced and less favourable. Another is *'nobody can tell where the market is going, so why implicitly predict that now is the best time by investing all at once?'* Again, this contains a grain of truth while still being fallacious. Each of the DCA mental shortcuts sounds plausible, but none withstands scrutiny.[5]

The reality is that DCA is an implicit market timing bet – it is a bet that the market will be lower at some time in the future. If investors were able to reliably predict market movements then using DCA would be profitable. However, if they can't, then it pays to go with the odds that markets will rise. Because markets tend to rise more than they fall, for an investor using DCA the opportunity cost of not being fully invested when markets rise typically outweighs the benefit of not being fully invested when they fall.

Buying the dips

Another investment strategy that is grounded in simple mental shortcuts is *'buying the dips'* (BTD). This is the idea that, given markets display short-term volatility, people are better-off investing only at the times in which markets temporarily dip below their long-term trend.

Like with DCA, the BTD strategy is supported by its own plausible-sounding decision-making shortcut: *'investing only when the market is lower will increase my return by lowering my purchase price'*. This is true, but only so long as the investor can predict market movements. If they can't, they need to think through various alternative scenarios that could eventuate. One of these scenarios is that, while they wait for the market to fall, the market actually rises to well above where they could have previously invested. Like with DCA, this adverse scenario includes a foregone opportunity cost. But as opportunity costs lack salience, they are easily overlooked.

The DCA and BTD strategies both demonstrate the power of simple mental shortcuts to drive investor behaviour. In both cases, by investors ignoring important but less salient complexities, these shortcuts can result in worse investment outcomes.

But the reality of an adviser's client relationships is not as black and white as this analysis suggests. Theoretically sub-optimal strategies like DCA and BTD can become optimal when viewed in the context of a client's broader circumstances and decision-making. For example, DCA could potentially reduce a client's anxiety about picking the perfect day to invest. In doing so it could leave a risk-averse client better off by helping them to invest in equities at all, even if they sacrifice a bit of return on the way.

Also, by creating multiple purchase prices an investor who uses DCA has a less salient anchor around which loss aversion will apply. The disproportionate impact of losses is diffused if a client is not easily able to work out whether they have, in fact, made a gain or loss. Given these considerations, as I said in my first book *'if I were to pick my battles on the road to building trust with a client and helping them achieve their financial goals, trying to eliminate DCA and BTD wouldn't be top of my list'*.

Finding patters in the noise

The most popular workshop that I run for professional investors relates to dealing with noise. At these workshops I give participants a jumble of 10 blue and green squares. Their job is to predict the colours of as many of the next 10 squares as they can. To more clearly define success, I ask them to imagine that they will receive $10 for each square they guess correctly. To make the task more realistic, I tell them that the sequences of coloured squares that I have given them is not entirely random, but neither is it entirely systematic. In doing this I try to establish the task as being akin to many investment decisions; somewhat predictable, but far from certain.

What I don't reveal to participants until later is that the coloured squares were generated by my daughter rolling a die. Rolling a 1, 2, 3 or 4 translated into a blue square, and 5s and 6s became green squares. In effect, the unpredictability of the sequence was determined by the chaotic bounce of the die, whereas the predictable element was determined by the fact that there were more likely to be blue squares than green ones. This was reflected in the sequence of 10 squares participants saw, of which 6 were blue.

To maximise their profits in this game, participants need to ignore the noise (the precise sequence of coloured squares) and find the signal (that there were more blues than greens). Without knowing precisely when green squares will occur, the most profitable strategy is to predict 10 more blue ones. This is akin to investing across market cycles: if you can't predict when markets will rise and fall (the precise sequences of blue and green squares), then your best bet is to be always invested (choose all blue). You're unlikely to get all 10 correct using this strategy, but you are likely to make more money than if you were to follow any other strategy.

Do participants predict 10 blue squares? Occasionally, but fairly rarely. Mostly they find a pattern in the sequence and apply that pattern to predict the next 10 squares. Finding these types of patterns is often easy and automatic; the patterns are beguiling. It can be challenging to ignore them and to instead follow statistical averages. Given this tendency to find patterns in the noise, some clients will understandably question why they should remain fully invested across a cycle when short-term returns appear to be demonstrably predictable.

The power of narratives
Outside of simplified workshop exercises, in the real-world the human capacity for pattern recognition is reinforced by the presence of narratives. In the

workshop exercise discussed above I provided no story about why a blue square was in position 4, for example. In contrast, investment commentators typically have no difficulty explaining why the market behaved as it did. This is important because psychological research confirms that people are more impacted by information that is presented in the form of a narrative than when the same information is presented in a non-narrative form.

Narratives can be a great way for advisers to communicate and engage with their clients. However, where these narratives lead clients to rely on specious explanations for essentially unpredictable events, they can do more harm than good. Ideally, narratives that explain yesterday's (essentially unpredictable) market movements should be replaced with narratives about long-term investors who followed sound investment principles to meet their retirement goals.

Paying attention to the wrong things

If there is one psychological factor that can accentuate or mitigate all of those discussed so far, it relates to how people pay attention. If investors didn't pay attention to what the market was doing, they wouldn't have an emotional response to it. Neither would they have changing expectations about it. They wouldn't notice what other investors were saying or doing, or think about the 'house money' they had made. They wouldn't know whether they happened to mistime the market by investing all of their capital at once, and they wouldn't notice the dips that they might want to 'buy'. They wouldn't have the information required to find patterns in the noise, and they wouldn't know about the narratives that appear to explain those patterns. If investors had been trapped on a desert island, none of these problems would apply.

But in the modern world these things can be hard to avoid. Stock market reports are pervasive and they are often presented in a way that draws attention to the least helpful things. But while the deleterious impacts of the financial media are bemoaned by many advisers and are difficult to control, there are some things advisers can do. At the very least they can use psychological insights in the way they communicate with their clients to direct clients' attention to what matters most. In doing so they can nudge their clients towards better investment decisions. Some strategies to do this are discussed next.

BEHAVIOURAL SOLUTIONS TO CLIENT PROBLEMS

This section turns to the potential solutions to clients' decision-making problems as they invest across market cycles. Traditional approaches can offer some value, but often have either substantial costs or limited efficacy. Behavioural strategies, on the other hand, typically have low cost and, in some cases, have been shown to significantly influence clients' decisions.

Reduce risk

If investors are unable to cope with market downturns, one obvious solution is to reduce their exposure to risk. Having a smaller exposure to risky assets should reduce the size and/or frequency of the inevitable draw-downs clients suffer. But while this is likely to have a positive impact on investors' behaviour, it typically comes with a cost in terms of lower expected returns.

Balancing these offsetting effects can be tricky, particularly for younger investors. Their longer investment horizons make them suited to investing in portfolios with relatively high risk/return characteristics. However, if their portfolios suffer large drawdowns, those early adverse experiences could have an enduring negative impact on their investment decisions thereafter. Reducing their investments' risk/return profiles could mitigate these behavioural problems. However, it could also come at a heavy cost if it means that these young investors fail to benefit from the compounded effects of years of higher investment returns. This suggests that advisers should consider alternative approaches to achieve the same behavioural outcomes, ones that come at a more reasonable cost to their clients.

Change reference points

As discussed previously, gains and losses are only seen as such as a result of people comparing an investment outcome to a reference point. The reference points that clients use to do this may or may not be relevant or helpful. Clients might use reference points that are too short-term, they might fail to apply appropriate benchmarks, and they might fail to adjust for important factors, like the amount of risk or the timing of cashflows.

In their client conversations and in the written reports they provide clients, advisers should be careful to choose reference points that are relevant and helpful, but that also positively influence clients' behaviour. A client who has suffered a loss over the past year might also be a client who has achieved a gain over the past three years, or a gain relative to the market return, or a gain relative to an alternative investment strategy they could otherwise have selected. By choosing appropriate reference points, an adviser can transform a difficult client conversation about a loss into a much easier one about a gain.

Ultimately the reference points that should matter most are a client's goals. How did an investment outcome impact their achievability? While for some clients the link between investment outcomes and their goals might be quite strong, this is less likely to be the case for younger investors. This is because their lower investment balances mean the dollar impact of any loss is likely to be small. Also, their longer investment horizons mean that their losses are likely to be recovered if they continue to invest in growth assets. And their greater years of paid employment ahead of them means they have more opportunities to offset losses with increased savings. What seems like a catastrophic loss in percentage terms could be relatively benign in terms of a younger client's income in retirement.

Change the order of returns

Where investment returns are shown to clients, another strategy is to simply change the order in which they are presented. When showing a table of returns achieved over different periods, the traditional approach is to present the shortest period on the left, with increasingly longer periods shown progressively to the right.

Because people tend to read from left to right, with the traditional approach they see the short-term returns first. The problem with this is that what people see first tends to attract the most attention. It can also colour how people interpret what they read subsequently. This matters because returns over shorter periods are more likely to be negative than are returns over longer periods. As a result, presenting short-term returns on the left can adversely affect how clients subsequently respond to more meaningful longer-term returns, if and when they scroll their eyes to the right.

As an alternative, the order of returns could be reversed, with the longest-term returns shown on the left. I recently tested this approach by presenting around 400 individual investors with the choice of two hypothetical asset managers. As part of an on-line survey they were asked *'if you had $100,000 to allocate to the following two Australian equity managers (based solely on their past investment performance relative to the benchmark), how much would you allocate to each of Manager A and Manager B?'*

The investors were then shown the following table, which shows the investment performance of the two managers relative to the benchmark. From the table it can be observed that Manager A has a better long-term track record than Manager B, but has suffered some short-term under-performance.

	3 months	6 months	1 year	3 years (pa)	5 years (pa)
Manager A	-2.1%	-3.4%	1.0%	1.5%	1.7%
Manager B	1.0%	2.5%	1.2%	0.5%	0.9%

To determine whether the order in which the returns were presented made a difference, that order was reversed for half of the participants, as shown below.

	5 years (pa)	3 years (pa)	1 year	6 months	3 months
Manager A	1.7%	1.5%	1.0%	-3.4%	-2.1%
Manager B	0.9%	0.5%	1.2%	2.5%	1.0%

The results accorded with expectations. The investors who saw the first version of the table of returns were more influenced by Manager A's short-term under-performance. They chose to allocate less of their hypothetical $100,000 to Manager A than did those investors who saw Manager A's good long-term returns on the left.

Changing the order of returns won't change everyone's decisions all of the time, but it will change some people's decisions some of the time. It is a simple and easy way for financial advisers to help reduce the adverse impact of losses on their clients' decisions across market cycles, and to help them focus on the long-term. It is also a strategy that is starting to become more commonly accepted across parts of the Australian investment community. Whether it be in their communications to their clients or to their own trustee boards, some super funds and asset managers have now started reversing the way they display their returns. Australia's largest investor, the Future Fund, now does it this way too.

Focus on less frequent, total portfolio returns

Related to the order that returns are presented is the frequency of their presentation. Every time an investment return is checked is another chance for clients to experience an emotion-inducing short-term gain or loss. Where practicable, advisers should consider ways to limit the frequency with which they provide unsolicited investment return-related information. This is particularly relevant for clients with high neuroticism, who are more likely to respond emotionally to the investment returns they see. There are plenty of other ways to engage with clients about their investments and broader advice requirements.

Another way to reduce clients' exposure to more volatile return information is to focus their attention on the returns from their portfolios in total, rather than from their portfolios' constituent investments. Just as how short-term gains and losses tend to average out to become longer-term gains, the gains and losses on constituent investments should tend to average out to become gains at a portfolio level. By providing less frequent, portfolio-level return information advisers are not reducing the investment risks clients are exposed to, but they are reducing clients' emotional responses to those risks.

Of course, some clients will understandably want to be able to check their investments returns whenever they wish and to regularly see how the constituent parts of their portfolios have performed. Therefore, in addition to more high-level reporting of pertinent information, advisers need to make this detail available. The challenge then becomes how to give clients what they want, without adversely impacting their decisions across market cycles.

To do this, more frequent or more detailed return information could be provided to a limited set of clients who consider it particularly important and who have opted-in to receive it. Or it could be provided via a portal that clients have to proactively log-in to view, rather than via a report that they receive automatically. Or if it is part of a report they receive, it could be an appendix to that report.

In each case the detailed information is not being withheld from clients; it is merely a small step away. But while opting-in, logging-on or turning to an appendix are not difficult, small behavioural barriers like these can sometimes make an important difference to people's decisions. It has been estimated that 90% of the impact of investment reports comes from what is presented on the first page.[6]

Get pre-commitments

Many of the problems of making investments decisions across market cycles stem from the context in which those decisions are made. As has been discussed throughout this chapter, the investment decision-making context can be laden with emotion, social cues, and with seemingly compelling, but often misleading, investment narratives and patterns. One way to help avoid the adverse influence of these factors is by clients pre-committing to a course of action before they encounter market turbulence.

Pre-commitment strategies are often related to the fable of Ulysses. According to Greek mythology, Ulysses wanted to hear the Sirens' song, although he knew that doing so would render him incapable of rational thought. This would ultimately lead to his ship being sunk and to him and his sailors being drowned, as he was lured towards the Sirens. His solution was to put wax in his sailors' ears so that they could not hear, and to have them tie him to the ship's mast so that he could not jump into the sea. He ordered them not to change course under any circumstances and to keep their swords upon him and to attack him if he should break free of his bonds. In doing this, Ulysses was able to expose himself to a stimulus that he knew would otherwise lead him to make poor choices.

The same concept also applies to investors; they should make decisions ahead of time if they expect that their future decisions will be impaired. An adviser can help their clients to do this by establishing a set of pre-agreed investment policies. Those policies might specify asset allocation ranges, such as a client's minimum and maximum allocations to cash. They could also specify the maximum amount of time that the client will remain out of the market, and minimum levels of portfolio diversification that they will accept. And they could specify the circumstances under which the client will rebalance their portfolio, including *if … then*' rules such as *if the market falls by 25%, then I will rebalance*'.

These policies could also incorporate a cooling off period for big and important decisions. Doing so allows time for the power of the context to weaken. Long-term professional investors can have lengthy investment processes, committees and reviews, helping to at least partially immunise them from some decision-making problems. Advisers can help their clients capture the same benefit when it matters most.

Pre-commitment strategies can benefit advisers too. As discussed earlier, when feeling anxiety about falls in the value of their investments, clients might blame their adviser. This can be perpetuated by a client's *hindsight bias*', which make adverse market outcomes seem predictable with the benefit of hindsight, even if they were entirely unpredictable ahead of time. With this in mind, advisers could potentially solicit pre-commitment statements that presage this eventuality.

The types of pre-commitment strategies discussed above leverage a number of psychological insights. They recognise the powerful influence that the context can have on people's decisions, and allow clients to make choices at a time that is more conducive to long-term decision-making. They establish an expectation for future market declines, recognising that expected losses are less psychologically impactful than unexpected ones. They apply broad framing, by using rules about successful investing that apply in a range of similar situations. And because these rules can be relatively simple, pre-committed strategies can also reduce the difficulties associated with advisers communicating complexity.

Pre-commitment strategies can influence clients' future behaviour because of the urge people have to remain consistent with their past statements and actions. People don't like to see themselves as being inconsistent and capricious in their decision-making, nor do they like others to see them as such. Pre-commitment strategies are therefore a powerful way that advisers can help their clients improve their decision-making across market cycles.

Asking clients to pre-commit to future decisions and actions creates an additional burden on the advice process at a time when market volatility might not be a problem. However, these pre-commitments represent an investment in the future that will benefit both the client and the adviser. A behavioural stitch in time saves the proverbial nine.

Use social norms

As discussed earlier, what other people do and say can be one of the contributors to poor client decisions across market cycles. However, advisers can also use the power of social influence to help nudge clients in the right direction. Social norms can be presented in the form of case studies, client testimonials or statistics. For example: *'did you know that 88% of our clients have decided to rebalance in response to the recent market falls'*. If people are going to follow the crowd, advisers can help ensure that the crowd provides a helpful guide.

When using social influencing strategies, the more apparently similar to the client the case study protagonists or the reference group from which the statistics are drawn, the more powerful the positive influence is likely to be. This can be true even if the nature of the similarity should not, logically, be relevant.

One popular experiment that demonstrates this involved the willingness of hotel guests to re-use their towels. When a hotel room contained a sign that asked people to reuse their towels to help save the environment, 35% did so. When the sign also used a social norm, by informing occupants that most guests at the hotel reused their towels, 44% complied. And when the sign mentioned that most previous occupants of that particular room had reused their towels, it rose to 49%. While in each case saving the environment should have been the reason to reuse their towels, the social norms made a difference; the more apparently relevant the social comparison group, the stronger the effect.[7]

Where relevant social norms are not available, perhaps because the data is not available, or because people don't actually demonstrate the desired behaviour, injunctive norms can potentially be used instead. An injunctive norm provides an indication about what other people say or think is the right thing to do, even if they don't actually do it.

Injunctive norms can be solicited from client surveys that ask, for example, *'what do you think is the best thing to do following a market decline of 20%?'* Or they can be reflected through the use of quotes from well-known authoritative sources. Warren Buffet is often used as a good example, with his well-known statement about how investors *'should try to be fearful when others are greedy and greedy when others are fearful'*. The power of social influence can be part of the problem for clients making decisions across market cycles, but when advisers can align it with good investment decision-making, it can also be part of the solution.

CONCLUSIONS

This chapter has detailed some of the causes of clients' sub-optimal decision-making across investment cycles, as well as some potential solutions. How investors respond to losses can be countered by changing reference points and by focussing investors' attention on longer-term, portfolio-level returns. The influence of emotions during periods of market volatility can be countered by pre-commitment strategies that are established in calmer times. The destabilising influence of the herd can be countered with the use of appropriate social and injunctive norms. And the patterns people find in the short-term noise can be countered with simple long-term investment policies, like periodic portfolio rebalancing. While no single approach is likely to work for all clients in all circumstances, behavioural finance provides a kit-bag of alternatives that advisers can select from.

Higher returns, lower taxes and lower risks are all potential outcomes for clients from overcoming their ill-advised decisions across market cycles. For advisers, there are benefits too, both commercial and psychological. When clients focus on their gains instead of their losses, and when they feel that their losses were entirely expected, difficult client conversations can be made easier before they even begin.

6

EXPLOITING BEHAVIOURAL BIASES IN MARKETS

If investors suffer from predictable decision-making biases, do those biases impact markets? Do they create opportunities for savvy investors to exploit? If they do, what are the barriers that advisers must help their clients to overcome in order to capture those opportunities? These are the questions that are addressed in this chapter.

There are a number of systematic distortions from the predictions of the Capital Asset Pricing Model (CAPM) and the Efficient Markets Hypothesis (EMH). According to these models, the only characteristic of a share investment that should matter is its undiversifiable risk (ie its 'beta'). However, in conflict with this, the long-term evidence shows that some other characteristics have predictably provided share investors with excess returns. These apparent market anomalies shouldn't exist in a rational world, but do in a world populated by human beings.

The value effect, momentum, the quality effect and the low-volatility effect are some of the major anomalies that researchers have identified. As is discussed in this chapter, each has causal explanations linked with investor psychology and with specific decision-making biases. The biases that are the DNA for each of these effects are different, so each has its own characteristic finger-print.

But if predictable ways to make money exist, why isn't everyone doing it already? This chapter also discusses the behavioural and practical barriers that can make it difficult or uncomfortable for investors to capture the benefits of these apparent anomalies. The anomalies exist because they go against the behavioural-grain. The good news is that these difficulties suggest that the opportunities will continue to persist for behaviourally-savvy investors and advisers to exploit.

THE VALUE EFFECT

The value effect refers to the fact that *'value stocks'* tend to outperform in the long term. Different measures are used to describe value stocks, but typically they have below average PE or P/B ratios, lower earnings growth and above average dividend yields. *'Growth stocks'*, against which value stocks are often compared, tend to have the opposite profile.

The value effect was first documented several decades ago. One of the original long-term studies was published in 1977 and showed a portfolio comprising the deepest value stocks outperformed growth stocks by 7% pa, and the broader market by 4% pa.[1] Subsequent research in Australia has shown the value effect is relevant in our market too. For example, Basu & O'Shea (2014) found that a portfolio comprising value stocks outperformed growth stocks by 18% pa. They remarked *'it seems that the Australian market has shown a stronger P/E effect in the short run [1 year periods] than other international markets,'* and that *'investing in a portfolio of low P/E stocks would have yielded, on average, a cumulative return [over 5 years] 132% greater than the market portfolio.'* While the value effect certainly isn't evident in all periods, based on theoretical rational models, it shouldn't exist at all.

What decision-making biases can contribute to the value effect? As is discussed below, forecasting errors, probability effects and subconscious emotional cues can each play a role. These decision-making biases predispose investors to favour growth stocks relative to value stocks.

Forecasting errors

The fact that growth stocks have higher prices relative to their earnings shouldn't necessarily be a problem. Their relatively higher prices could be justified if the higher future earnings that was forecast for these companies was realised. However, on average it is not. As Basu & O'Shea comment, investors *'seem to overestimate the growth potential of certain firms resulting in bidding up of their prices and subsequent disappointment.'*

One reason that this could occur is that investors over-estimate the likelihood that growth companies' higher historical growth rates will continue. This is, at least in part, due to investors favouring causal and intentional narratives for growth companies' high historical growth. As a result, investors can too readily assume that growth companies have performed well historically because of their visionary management, customer-centric products, or because of their engaging marketing campaigns, for example. These things are likely to be true to some extent, but luck often plays a bigger role than investors imagine. Why this is important is because luck doesn't tend to persist. The more luck that is involved, the more we should expect the reversion of historically high growth towards a less favourable mean.

The tendency for even professional investors to overlook the power of mean reversion is easy to demonstrate. To do this I sometimes ask professional investment teams this question: *'if a mother and father's height are both on the 90th percentile relative to their peer groups, what is the best guess for the height percentile of their child, relative to the child's peer group?'*

It is true the child will probably also be tall relative to the child's peers, but the best guess for the child's height is not the 90th percentile, it's less. The reason is that height is not perfectly genetically determined. There are other, less predictable variables at work. Being particularly tall involves a combination of 'tall person genes' plus some 'tall person luck'. As the luck is less likely to be passed on to the next generation, the child's height tends to revert towards the mean. Responses to the height question demonstrate that professional investors, like other humans, often overlook the power of mean reversion.

Mean reversion isn't just relevant for abstract questions about height. With one of my asset management clients I confirmed how mean reversion impacted the growth forecasts that they used as an input to their investment process. A failure to sufficiently account for mean reversion was revealed by comparing historical earnings forecasts with the actual earnings that companies subsequently reported. What this analysis showed was that for companies that had experienced high growth historically, the forecasts for subsequent growth were too optimistic. Across the 7 years for which data was available, the forecasts assumed that the growth for these high growth companies would slow. However, the companies' subsequent results revealed earnings growth that was, on average, lower than these forecasts. The forecasts had accounted for some mean reversion, but not enough.

Value companies, by contrast, do not present the same problem, at least not to the same extent. For a start, the role of luck is lessened because the level of uncertainty associated a value stock's future earnings is often lower. An archetypal value company is an established business in a mature industry, with existing products and customers, and relatively low growth. While there is still uncertainty in forecasting the future earnings of value stocks, compared with growth stocks, the future expectations for value stocks are more grounded in their current reality.[2]

In fact, the mean reversion story might be a little stronger than this. If value companies have suffered below average EPS growth historically, then they might actually benefit from mean reversion. This was born out by the asset manager's forecasts that I analysed. It wasn't simply that the forecasts were too optimistic overall; by not sufficiently accounting for mean reversion, the forecasts for companies with below-average EPS growth were too pessimistic. What this showed was that not only were the high expectations for growth stocks too high, but the low expectations for value stocks were too low.[3]

Probability effects

Another contributor to the value effect is the way people think about probabilities. In a theoretical rational world, an event which has a 50% chance of occurring would be given a 'weight' of 50% in an investor's decisions. However, this is not how people tend to process uncertainty. In particular, as was discussed in Chapter 2, some low probability future events are weighed too heavily in people's decisions. There may only be a 1% chance that a new drug will be a blockbuster, but on average people tend to make decisions as if the chances were higher. For events which are stated as having a 1% probability, people tend to make decisions as if the chance was actually 5.5%.[4]

The result of this distortion in the way people respond to probabilities is that stocks with *'lottery'* style characteristics (ie with a low probability of the investor making a fortune), can become overvalued. With potentially large payoffs from new products, new technologies and new business models, these lottery characteristics are more often associated with growth stocks.

Emotions

Finally, emotions can play a role in the value effect too. Kahneman characterises the way emotions can impact decisions in terms of substitution; an emotion-laden and simplified question is substituted in place of complex analytical one.[5] For example, *'what do I think about BHP as a potential investment?'* becomes *'what do I feel about BHP as a potential investment?'* If something about BHP generates positive feelings, those positive feelings will lead the investor towards a decision to buy its shares. As Kahneman argues, this substitution can happen imperceptibly, and can be masked by seemingly rational explanations for decisions in which investors deny the influence of the subconscious.

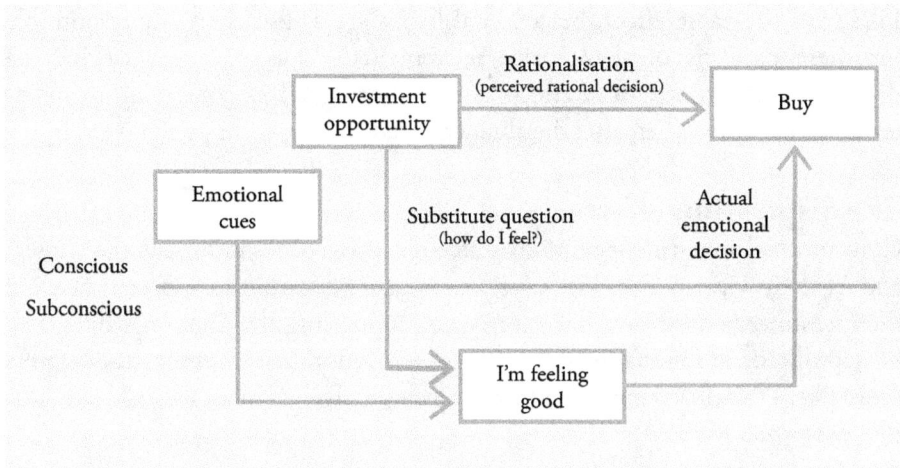

Emotive features (cues) about an investment can trigger a sub-conscious emotional response which can then drive investment decisions.

So, what emotional cues might impact growth companies more than value companies? The possibilities are numerous, including excitement about high growth itself, or perhaps about the new technologies and products growth companies are developing. Value companies can be the opposite: boring, or worse. Value companies need to financially compensate investors for the meagre emotional benefits that they provide.

SHORT-TERM MOMENTUM & LONG-TERM REVERSION

According to the weakest form of the Efficient Markets Hypothesis, past price movements should not be predictive of future returns. But to some extent they are. Stocks that have risen in the recent past (typically the past 3 to 12 months) tend to continue rising in the near future. This is short-term momentum. In the longer term (3 to 5 years), the pattern changes; companies that have risen over this period tend to go on to have lower returns. The equivalent pattern applies to falling stocks – they tend to continue to fall in the short term, but recover in the longer term.

Like with the value effect, behavioural biases are at least partially responsible for these patterns of share price movements. As is discussed below, the disposition effect, attention effects and anchoring biases contribute to short-term momentum. Thereafter, herding can lead to long-term price reversals.

The disposition effect

Conventional investment wisdom states that investors should cut their losers and let their winners run. However, investors tend to do the opposite: holding the investments they have lost money on, and selling the ones on which they have profited. Individual investors have been found to be approximately 50% more likely to sell a winner than a losing stock. This tendency is referred to as the *'disposition effect'*. [6]

To see how the disposition effect can create short-term momentum, consider a rising stock – for one reason or another, winning a major new customer, say, the share price has risen from $1 to $2. As it rises, the stock becomes a 'winner' for existing shareholders. Unfortunately, because investors prefer to sell their winners, this can result in increased selling pressure. The stock reaches $2, but had it not been for the biased selling decisions of its shareholders, perhaps it would have reached a fair value of, say, $3.

Importantly, the impact of the disposition effect is not permanent. Over time, shareholders who have invested at historically lower prices are progressively replaced with new investors who do not carry the same emotional baggage. As a result, the bias towards selling is reduced. As it reduces, the encumbrance that has beset the stock is lifted and it is allowed to rise to its fair value of $3. As is shown in the diagram below, short-term momentum is thereby created: an initial share price increase is followed by more increases. The equivalent mechanism works to create negative momentum too.

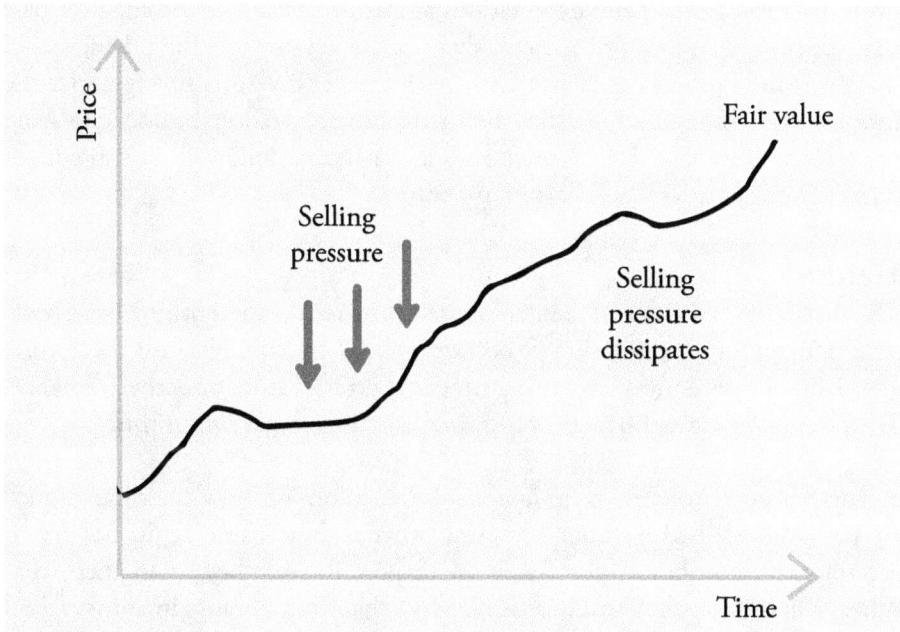

How the disposition effect contributes to short-term positive momentum

Paying attention and updating beliefs

While the disposition effect is arguably the most important contributor to short-term momentum, other decision-making biases can play a role too. Some of these biases relate to how people pay attention and update their beliefs. If investors fail to pay attention or to sufficiently change their views, this could result in them under-reacting to important new information about a company. Like with the disposition effect, when this happens a company's share price might rise in response to good news, but not by as much as it should.

Investors' under-reaction to important new information could occur where they simply don't notice the information; it's hard to react appropriately to something you haven't noticed! Or it could be the result of 'confirmation bias' – people's tendency to disregard or discount new information that conflicts with their existing beliefs. In the case of good news, those existing beliefs are likely to be less favourable. Or it could be as a result of 'anchoring', whereby investors anchor their price expectations and sense of value to a company's past share prices. Those past prices are likely to create low anchors for a rising stock, making it now appear expensive. Only over time, as investors slowly notice the new information and adjust their beliefs to properly reflect it, does the share price reach fair value. Initial price rises are therefore followed by subsequent ones, thereby creating short-term momentum.

Herding

The biases discussed above contribute to short-term momentum. But short-term momentum cannot simply be extrapolated indefinitely into the future. Eventually prices go too far, setting investors up for future underperformance. The power of social influence, or 'herding', is one explanation for this.

Keynes' beauty contest is a famous articulation of how herding works. As Keynes described it, when choosing what to buy investors do not try to ascertain the most beautiful stock in the market. Rather, they try to guess what others will think is the most beautiful. More than this, because investors are all playing the same game, each investor will need to guess what others will guess that others will think is the most beautiful, and so on. Taking this view of the market, a company's fundamental value becomes secondary; primacy goes to understanding investor behaviour.

Unfortunately, problems can occur in playing this investor-behaviour-guessing-game. When people witness other investors buying a stock, they might interpret this as being because those investors are privy to superior information or analysis. But those other investors' decisions might merely indicate that they witnessed yet other investors buying and similarly assumed that they knew what they were doing. Because people tend to under-estimate the role of the social context in others peoples' decisions, this latter interpretation can receive less credence than it deserves.

Investors following others, in the belief that they know something important, is akin to the trailing driver from the previous chapter assuming that the car ahead was changing lanes because they had seen a looming road blockage. However, the reality could be that the leading driver had merely witnessed the car in front of them indicating to change lanes. Just as multiple drivers can vacate a perfectly good lane for no valid reason, when one investor follows another who is then followed by more investors, a stock's momentum can be extended beyond its fair value. And just as the vacant lane doesn't stay vacant when the drivers realise their mistake, neither does a stock's price remain permanently disconnected from its fair value. Eventually long-term reversion results.

QUALITY & LOW VOLATILITY EFFECTS
In addition to value and momentum, stocks with low volatility and those possessing a range of 'quality' characteristics have been found to produce a superior return/risk ratio than the share market generally.[7] Low volatility companies are typically defined as having less volatile share prices, either in absolute terms or relative to the market. There are different definitions of high-quality companies, but they are often defined based on their high profitability, growth, safety and payout ratio. In contrast, companies that are low on these measures are referred to as 'junk'. Low volatility and quality strategies are related, as having low volatility is sometimes used as one of the measures of quality.

As with the value effect and momentum, in a rational world the opportunity to earn superior risk-adjusted returns from investing in low volatility and quality companies should not exist or persist. Arguably, deviations from rational decision-making are occurring here too.

Overconfidence in 'junk' stocks

Part of the explanation for the out-performance of quality stocks relative to junk is that investors have unreasonably rosy expectations for some junk stocks. If investors rightly expect these junk stocks to become less 'junky' in the future, they would be justified in paying more for them. However, the unfortunate reality is that junk in one year tends to remain junk in the next.

Investors shouldn't be surprised by junk stocks' inter-temporal consistency, but apparently they are. Why? Arguably it is because investors are over-confident in their analysis of junk stocks. For some of these stocks investors might forecast reductions in leverage and credit risk, or increases in profitability and payout ratios. If realised, each would move junk stocks towards becoming quality and, presumably, would result in favourable outcomes for shareholders.

However, overconfident investors don't know as much about the future of junk stocks as they think. When decisions are beset with uncertainty and unpredictability, which describes much investing, decision-making research suggests that investors should try not to deviate too far from 'base rates' (ie relevant statistical averages). In this case, the base rate tells investors that junk stocks don't tend to change their spots from one year to the next. Only where investors can reliably predict the future outcomes for individual companies should they justifiably have confidence in deviating from base rates. There will be exceptions to the base rate-rule, of course, but as a rule the exceptions will be fewer than overconfident investors expect. Junk remains junk.

Paying too much attention to high volatility & junk stocks

Investors can only hope to process a small portion of the burgeoning supply of available information. Of the total, the information that best attracts investors' attention will have a disproportionate effect on their decision-making. Do these information-processing effects impact different companies differently? In some ways, yes they do. According to researchers Blitz, Falkenstein and Van Vliet, *'attention-grabbing stocks are typically found in the high-volatility segment of the market. Boring low-volatility stocks are the flip side of the coin, suffering from investor neglect.'* [8]

Stocks with higher volatility tend to attract attention simply as a result of their share price movements. Stocks with large share price movements are often newsworthy. Companies with volatile business fundamentals are too. Each change seeks explanation, and there is no shortage of commentators to provide them.

Which companies capture investors' attention is important because it helps determine what those investors buy.[9] If high volatility and junk stocks are more likely to attract investors' attention then on average they are likely to be systematically overbought and overpriced. When they are, they provide their shareholders lower future risk-adjusted returns.

Corporate management and the quality effect

One important consideration in assessing a potential share investment can be the quality of the management team. Are the CEO, CFO and other senior corporate decision-makers likely to make wise decisions that will benefit shareholders? If there is a systematic bias in the way investors assess companies' management teams then this could also contribute to the quality effect.

Standard finance theory assumes that corporate managers act rationally in their own self-interest. Behavioural finance extends this analysis by contemplating these managers' irrational decisions too. Chief among the biases that can apply in this context is overconfidence. Overconfidence can be a great people-leadership quality; confident leaders tend to inspire confidence in others. However, effective decision-making requires one's confidence to be properly calibrated with reality. Being confident and wrong is a dangerous combination!

Research shows that CEO- and CFO-overconfidence matters for investors. This is demonstrated by the fact that various measures of a senior management team's overconfidence have been correlated with them undertaking value-destroying mergers and acquisitions, as well as with their companies having higher leverage and greater short-term debt.[10] Greater CEO- and CFO-overconfidence therefore equates to greater risk for shareholders.

The connection between management overconfidence and the quality effect comes from the fact that several of the measures of higher quality companies are also proxies for reduced management overconfidence. For example, high quality companies' low stock issuance and high dividend payout ratios suggests that these companies' management teams don't assume they have better uses for shareholders' capital than their shareholders can find elsewhere. This is equivalent to the almost non-existent sentiment: *'I am not an above average driver.'*

Two other characteristics of high-quality companies are low leverage and low accruals. While specific explanations are likely to be relevant in individual cases, overall these measures suggest that the managers of quality companies recognise future uncertainty; they are not sufficiently certain about future cashflows to burden their companies with additional debt or to accrue anticipated future earnings. Recognising uncertainty is the antithesis of overconfidence.

However, while it is a benefit for shareholders to have a CEO who is devoid of overconfidence, it can be natural for investors to take a negative view of these CEOs and their companies. People tend to dislike the uncertainty that these CEOs might express. In addition, because people often conflate someone's confidence with their competence, investors are also likely to perceive these CEOs as being less competent.

In combination, it is understandable that investors might therefore conclude that if the CEO isn't confident about their company's future prospects, how can an investor possibly be? What these investors overlook is that the CEO's expression of uncertainty isn't necessarily a sign of weakness; rather, it could be a sign that they have a good understanding of the uncertain world in which they operate.[11]

If the CEOs and CFOs of quality companies are more likely to avoid common decision-making traps associated with overconfidence then they are more likely to achieve consistent profitable growth, such as by avoiding value-destroying M&A decisions. In turn, if this guide to management decision-making is currently being overlooked by some investors then quality companies could become undervalued relative to junk.

CHALLENGES IN CAPTURING THE BENEFITS

The preceding discussion suggests that people should invest in companies with value, momentum, low volatility and quality characteristics. However, attempting to achieve this can be like trying to take a large piece of cheese from a loaded mousetrap. There are significant decision-making challenges that can thwart investors' attempts to profitably exploit these effects and to make off with the cheese.

Some of the challenges that advisers might need to overcome to help clients capture the benefits of these strategies are discussed below. Educating clients is one approach but, as has been discussed previously, has its limitations. By accounting for decision-making research in both their client engagement and in their own decisions, advisers can help their clients to avoid the mousetrap's wrath. In doing so, their clients can potentially achieve investment outcomes that other investors cannot.

The need for second-order thinking

Appreciating the strategies discussed in this chapter could require some clients to change their mindsets; they need to be able to apply 'second-order thinking'. Whereas first-order thinking focusses on the characteristics of companies, second-order thinking requires investors to also think about how other investors think about those company. It requires investors appreciating the perspectives of the judges in Keynes' beauty contest.

A potentially engaging way that advisers can demonstrate second-order thinking to an interested client is by describing the following game. Advisers can ask clients to imagine that they are in a room full of other investors. Everyone in the room is given the challenge of choosing a number between 0 and 100. The winner of the game will be the person whose choice is closest to the target number. That target number will be determined by averaging all of the numbers that everyone in the room chooses, and then taking two thirds of that average.

A first-order thinker might say to themselves: *'if everyone's choices are random, then the average of those random numbers will be 50'*. Based on this analysis, the investor's choice would then be two thirds of 50, which is 33. In contrast, a second-order thinker would anticipate that other investors would undertake this type of analysis and would instead choose two thirds of 33 (ie 22).[12] The simple conclusion from this exercise is that there can be value in moving from first- to second-order thinking.

Aligning with clients' existing beliefs

Another behavioural concept that can be applied to help with client engagement relates to the consistency effect. Recall that people feel a compulsion to remain consistent with their past actions, statements and beliefs. Applying this idea, if advisers can connect their proposed investment strategies with a client's existing beliefs, then the client is more likely to accept them. For example, investors who enjoy making consumer purchases that are both cheap and of high quality should also appreciate using strategies to capture the value and quality effects. After a client has agreed to these principles, the consistency effect smooths the path for them to accept their application.

Dealing with underperformance

None of the strategies discussed in this chapter is a recipe for consistent outperformance. While having a history of delivering long-term benefits, each strategy can sometimes result in sustained periods of underperformance. The run-up to the dot-com bubble was a good example of when value and quality stocks significantly underperformed. Over this period Berkshire Hathaway, the famed value investor Warren Buffett's investment company, underperformed the index by a staggering 76%.[13] When faced with underperformance, many clients are likely to want to change course, by choosing a different investment strategy, and perhaps a different financial adviser too. What can be done to mitigate this risk?

Importantly, the way that portfolios are constructed can significantly influence the chance and severity of underperformance. Because value and momentum are negatively correlated, for example, combining them can reduce the risk compared with using either strategy separately. By combining them, investors can still capture the benefits of value and momentum, but with lower risk.

Another lever that advisers can pull is the size of the 'tilts' towards each strategy. Bigger tilts mean a client's portfolio has stronger value, momentum or quality characteristics, for example. This can create greater opportunity for long-term returns, but can also come at a greater risk of short-term underperformance. Taken to its extreme, a highly concentrated portfolio might create the highest expected return, but also come with unacceptably high risk. Such a portfolio might incorporate unintended exposures to specific industries, to individual countries or to other risks. As discussed in Chapter 7, diversification is arguably the only free lunch in investing; investors should be cautious when making trade-offs against it.

As advisers would already be aware, to help clients cope with underperformance, clients' expectations need to be set appropriately. They need to understand and acknowledge that the journey to long-term returns will include some periods of short-term and medium-term underperformance. In terms of its likely impact on clients' subsequent behaviour, underperformance that is expected and acknowledged in advance is at least partially defanged.

Avoiding data-mining
Unfortunately, some investment strategies that provide solid historical (back-tested) returns, as do those discussed in this chapter, ultimately fail to deliver the benefits that investors expect. The reasons can be abstract, complex and statistical in nature, so may be difficult for some clients to digest. As a result, they rely on advisers to protect them from strategies that are infected with these problems.

One of the problems is data-mining. If you search through enough data and test enough different approaches, you are going to find what seems like a profitable investment strategy. While they might appear to be meaningful, when viewed in the context of the numerous possibilities that have been tested, most of the patterns that are identified are likely to be just noise.

Despite their apparently successful historical track records, only when these patterns are found in multiple markets, using different but related measures, and have been shown to persist after their discovery, should investors take them seriously. It is important for advisers to distinguish the strategies that meet these criteria from those that do not. Of the strategies discussed in this chapter, arguably value and momentum best meet these criteria.

Further credibility about the on-going efficacy of an investment strategy comes from there being limits to the willingness or ability of other investors to exploit that strategy. This could be due to the presence of powerful decision-making biases, such as those discussed in this chapter. It could also come from investors being unable to stick with the strategy through periods of underperformance. Or it could come from larger investors being unable to take positions of sufficient size, or being unable to develop a commercial business model based on exploiting the strategy. Without these characteristics, advisers would be justified in asking why other investors haven't already arbitraged any opportunities into economic insignificance.

Disciplined implementation

Another challenge is implementation. To effectively exploit the strategies discussed in this chapter, the benefits have to be captured without being outweighed by offsetting costs, such as fees, transaction costs, taxes or additional risks. Some strategies are more impacted by these costs than others. For example, because stocks with positive momentum tend to change significantly from one period to the next, the MSCI World Momentum index has an annual turnover of around 127%. This is considerably higher than the between 20% and 30% turnover for MSCI's indices that track value, low volatility and quality stocks.[14] The additional turnover associated with the momentum strategy could result in investors incurring greater transaction costs and taxes.[15] Advisers who are not focused on these costs and taxes could inadvertently make their clients worse off, despite their best intentions.

Another challenge in implementation is avoiding having good strategies undermined by poorly disciplined decisions. The temptation to override robust investment rules with subjective assessments can be overwhelming, potentially for both the client and the adviser. Without strong controls, doing so opens the door to the very behavioural biases that the investment rules were designed to exploit in others. There is more than one way to exploit these strategies, but there are also plenty of ways to fail.

CONCLUSIONS

Investors' decision-making biases can contribute to the value effect, momentum, the low volatility effect and the quality effect. At least in part, these effects exist because of how investors forecast which companies are going to be successful and which aren't, how investors respond to companies with exciting new technologies, how they react to the actions of other investors, and how they assess the competence of corporate CEOs.

These biases are deeply engrained. They often occur automatically, beyond investors' conscious awareness, where they are safely immunised from introspection. To some extent, they can infect the decisions made by both naïve individual investors as well as by teams of sophisticated professionals.

By incorporating these insights into the investment strategies they recommend, advisers have the opportunity to help their clients exploit other investors' biases. However, there are significant challenges in doing so. To capture the benefits means investing in ways that sometimes go against investors' natural tendencies. It can mean buying value companies with below average growth and waiting for the probable impact of mean reversion. Alternatively, it could mean buying companies with positive momentum that now appear expensive compared with their historically lower share prices. Or it could mean buying companies with CEOs who appear cautious, or buying companies which other investors shun. Exploiting these effects requires thinking differently. The challenge is for advisers to help their clients understand and engage in this 'different' thinking.

To benefit from these effects, advisers can help their clients to develop second-order thinking, and can prepare them to deal with the inevitable periods of underperformance. Advisers can also protect their clients from unsustainable strategies that are the product of data-mining, as well as from ones for which the benefits are more than offset by increased costs, risks and taxes. In chasing out-performance it is easy to make things worse.

Given all of these considerations, the most appropriate courses for advisers to take might be at the margins: only following the most robust strategies that most closely align with investors' decision-making biases; taking relatively small tilts that retain broad portfolio diversification; closely managing costs and taxes; and limiting human intervention to a mostly rules-based approach. Advisers need to ensure that in trying to exploit other investors' overconfident decision-making errors, they don't simply replace them with a different variety of their own.

7

BIASES IN DIVERSIFICATION & ASSET ALLOCATION

Simply choosing an appropriate asset allocation and ensuring sufficient diversification should provide clients many of the benefits from long-term investing. In particular, diversification offers the prospect of a true free lunch – reduced risk without a commensurate reduction in expected returns.

However, to access the lunch investors have to overcome a number of biases. As a result of common decision-making errors, investors can fail to sufficiently diversify, such as by holding only a handful of stocks or a single investment property. Or they could own multiple assets, but unknowingly expose themselves to correlated risks across those assets. And there is also the problem of investors who diversify successfully, but who fail to choose an asset allocation that is suitable for their needs.

By understanding how decision-making biases can lead clients to make poor diversification and asset allocation decisions, advisers can help them to achieve higher returns for the same risk, or lower risk for the same returns. They can also help clients choose a combination of risk and return that better suits their risk profile and objectives.

This chapter discusses the decision-making errors that can impact clients' diversification and asset allocation decisions, as well as potential ways that advisers can help to overcome them.

PREFERRING WHAT IS FAMILIAR

One of the decision-making biases that can impact people's diversification decisions is the *familiarity effect*. This refers to the fact that people tend to prefer things that are familiar to them. The psychological evidence in support of this finding is sometimes startling. Controlled experiments, in which all alternative ('rational') explanations can be excluded, show that merely being exposed to something can lead people to like it more than they would otherwise. Even very short exposures can be sufficient to create the familiarity effect. If some seemingly inconsequential exposures can impact people's decisions, then it is reasonable to expect a much more material impact from the exposures people have to the major companies and brands with which they interact throughout their lives.

The consequences of the familiarity effect

One of the consequences of the familiarity effect is that people typically prefer investing in their own country. Consistent with this, researchers have found a strong home-country bias among investors from multiple countries, including among those from Australia.

When they disproportionately invest in their more familiar domestic markets, investors can overlook the diversification benefits that are available elsewhere. Researchers have found that the foregone benefits from international diversification can be substantial, and that missing these benefits cannot be justified by 'rational' explanations. For example, Associate Professor Hisham Foad comments that *observed domestic equity shares can only be justified by implausible rates of risk aversion or transaction costs higher than any reasonable estimates.*[1]

In an Australian context, when choosing the proportion of an equities portfolio to allocate to Australian shares, theoretically the starting point should be 2%. This is equivalent to the proportion of global equity markets that Australia comprises. Arguably the actual allocation should then be higher because some domestic share investors can access franking credits and other tax benefits, or because investing in local assets can potentially help mitigate currency risk.[2]

However, with larger allocations to Australian shares the marginal benefits are increasingly offset by the costs of reduced diversification. Where to draw the line will differ from client to client; an increased allocation to international markets is likely to most benefit investors with the lowest existing international exposures, as well as those who are least able to access the tax advantages from domestic shares.

In addition to the choice of domestic versus international shares, the familiarity effect can also help explain individual investors' preference for well-known 'blue-chip' shares with familiar brands, as well as for residential property and bank deposits. Each provides the psychological comfort of familiarity. While there is sense in investors avoiding exotic and unfamiliar investment products, some investors too readily believe that the best investments happen to be the ones with which they are most familiar.

Using the familiarity effect in client engagement

How can advisers apply insights about investors' preference for the familiar? Educating clients about the familiarity effect and its potential impacts on their investment outcomes is one possibility. Understanding the hidden drivers of their behaviour might be sufficient to spur some clients to greater diversification.

However, as a general rule it is difficult to overcome biases with education and logic. Advisers should anticipate that many clients will assume that the familiarity effect doesn't apply to them. Some will provide apparently 'rational' explanations for their existing portfolio allocations and preferences. These explanations might be valid, but the psychological evidence shows that there is also a significant possibility that they are merely post-decision rationalisations. These rationalisations fill in the blanks left by a client's preference for the familiar that influences their decisions beyond their awareness.

One risk of advisers attempting to counter the familiarity effect by examining a client's investment rational is that asking a client to explain their past decisions could entrench them. Now that the client has told their adviser why they chose not to invest in international shares, for example, to subsequently change their mind risks them feeling and appearing to be inconsistent. The client could also take offense at the suggestion that they might be biased, undermining the adviser's trust and rapport.

As a general theme, an easier path to helping clients is often to work with their decision-making biases, rather than against them. In this case, advisers can use the familiarity effect by creating analogies between what clients are familiar with and the unfamiliar asset classes in which diversification benefits can be obtained. For example, for a property investor who is unfamiliar with equity investments: *'the dividends you receive on your share investments are just like the rent you receive on your investment property'*. Also, as mentioned in Chapter 2, for investors who can benefit from international diversification, advisers can identify the familiar brand names that are represented in the international equities portfolios that they recommend. If clients prefer what is familiar, it pays for advisers to make good choices seem like familiar ones.

The impact of familiarity on investment professionals

The familiarity effect can impact investment professional too, sometimes in subtle ways that can evade detection. For example, when creating diversified portfolios, a home country bias can be implicit in the questions that investment professionals ask their asset allocation models. In such models, Australian shares are commonly elevated to the status of an asset class and stand alongside the equities of all other countries combined. The lucky country indeed!

This is an example of familiarity combining with a framing effect (the fact that the way a problem is framed can significantly impact the conclusions drawn). Creating a category and calling it 'Australian equities' may seem simple and is certainly convenient, but that it is optimal, and that there are no better alternatives is more contentious. If these asset allocation models were allowed to choose from 200+ countries, each having their own set of return, variance and covariance assumptions, would the recommended allocation to Australian shares be quite so illustrious?[3]

It is largely a matter of historical convention, social norm and convenience of data availability that equity investments should be defined by the geographic location of their listing, and that a relatively small country should stand alone while much larger ones are combined. The fact that asset allocations are derived using sophisticated risk models should not blind advisers to the fact that human decision-making biases can still play a role in dictating outcomes. These models are only as good as their assumptions, the way problems are framed for the model to solve, and the types of scenarios that are considered realistic. These assessments are human, demonstrably fallible and subject to many of the biases discussed in this book.

For advisers who use sophisticated models to determine a strategic asset allocation, there are opportunities to reframe their analyses. Advisers could challenge whether it is optimal to use asset class definitions that are based on geographic boundaries. Alternative measures are available, such as those that attempt to look through traditional categories and create a closer connection to the underlying drivers of risk and return.[4] At the very least, when these models suggest large allocations to domestic shares, advisers need to be on guard to ensure that their recommendations are appropriate for each client, and that their advice has not been adversely impacted by an implicit preference for the familiar.

THE ROLE OF OVERCONFIDENCE

In addition to familiarity, another common decision-making bias that can contribute to under-diversification is overconfidence. One way it can do this is where overconfident investors underestimate the amount of uncertainty in their decisions. Another is where investors believe that they are better than average. Both types of overconfidence can lead investors to choosing a smaller number of investments than they should. This type of under-diversification appears to impact a significant minority of individual investors. For example, according to Investment Trends, 18% of Self Managed Superannuation Funds ('SMSFs') that own shares hold 5 stocks or fewer.[5]

Under-estimating uncertainty

I sometimes demonstrate how people under-estimate the amount of uncertainty in their decisions by asking participants in my workshops to estimate the distance to the moon. I assure those who complain about this difficult task that rather than giving me a point estimate, they should provide a range they are comfortable with. More specifically, I ask them for a range that they feel 90% sure the correct answer falls within. The bottom and top of their ranges should represent the distances they feel there is only a 5% chance the moon is either closer or further than, respectively. If they have no idea then their range might be wide, but that's OK.[6]

If participants are *'properly calibrated'* – that is, they recognise the true extent of uncertainty in their decisions – then 90% of them should find the actual distance to the moon falls within their range. But, consistent with the academic literature, this is the case for only about 50% of my participants. Their confidence ranges are, on average, way too narrow. One in ten people should be surprised by the distance to the moon, but about 5 in every ten people actually are. There is considerably more uncertainty in people's estimates than they imagine.

In an investment context, overconfident investors are likely to underestimate the range of possible outcomes that each of their investments could produce. If they do, they are likely to also underestimate the risk-mitigation benefits that they could receive from diversifying those investments. Why would they diversify risks that they don't perceive they are exposed to? When you don't appreciate the real risks you are taking, diversification can seem like an unnecessary hindrance.

Better than average

Another form of overconfidence that can contribute to under-diversification is over-stating one's own skills. If investors believe they have chosen only stocks that will outperform, diversification may be perceived as leading only to worse outcomes (ie to *'diworsification'*). Consistent with this, Werner De Bondt, one of the founding fathers of behavioural finance, found that while a group of individual investors he studied were not over-optimistic about the returns for the market generally, they were about the returns they expected from the specific companies they held in their portfolios.

The reality is that picking winners is not as easy as it might seem to overconfident investors. While Warren Buffet might have sufficient grounds to proclaim that *'diversification is protection against ignorance'* and that *'it makes little sense if you know what you are doing,'* for mere mortal investors without his long-term track record of success, they should worry less about the possibility of *'diworsification'.* We are not all Warren Buffets.[7]

Faced with the problem of overconfident under-diversification, advisers could try educating their clients. However, lack of knowledge about the benefits of diversification doesn't seem to be the problem. For example, the Household, Income and Labour Dynamics in Australia ('HILDA') Survey found that most people (75%) recognised that buying shares in a number of different companies provides a safer return than buying shares in a single company.[8]

However, when applied to their own investments this knowledge appears to be overwhelmed by the combined influences of overconfidence and familiarity. Yes, these investors might agree it's a bad idea to be under-diversified generally, but not in the case of their own stock selections. When it comes to their own investments, they prefer to own a few companies that they know well, rather than many that they know little about.[9] Overconfident investors are, of course, better than other investors at choosing these stocks – or at least, that's how they perceive themselves. Strategies for working with overconfident investors are discussed in Chapter 8.

THE PROBLEM OF NARROW FRAMING

Psychological research demonstrates that the use of *'narrow frames'* can lead to sub-optimal decisions; it is often better to take a broader perspective on a problem. As is discussed below, this generalisation is true of diversification and asset allocation decisions.

Framing diversification decisions

An investor who uses a narrow frame might focus on the risks associated with their investments individually. In contrast, an investor who uses a broader frame might also think about each investment's contribution to their portfolio's total risk. Only when clients apply this broader frame can they appreciate the benefits of diversification. Without doing so it can be difficult for clients to understand that assuming greater risk on one investment can, as a result of it providing greater diversification, actually reduce their overall portfolio risk. As a result, clients could overlook opportunities to benefit from investing in assets which have low or negative correlations with their existing investments. Unfortunately, as De Bondt comments *'the very idea that risk is defined at the level of the portfolio, rather than at the level of individual assets, and that risk depends on covariation between returns, remains foreign to many investors.'* [10]

But not only do many investors appear to adopt a narrow frame, they also implicitly under-estimate the extent of the covariances between the returns of their individual investments. Individual investors' stocks tend to be more influenced by broad market movements than they expect. For example, De Bondt calculated that individual investors' perceived betas, which he based on a regression of investors' forecasted company returns on their forecasted index returns, were about two-thirds of the level of the companies' actual betas. This means that as much as investors might think that their risks can be mitigated by simply avoiding unwise stock selections, their portfolio returns will probably suffer when markets decline nonetheless. These investors are not as diversified as they think.

The challenge for advisers therefore, is to help clients see the broader (portfolio-level) frame, and to convey the significance of the covariances between a client's investments in a simple and engaging way. This challenge should not be under-estimated. Unless they are carefully communicated, the abstract and statistical concepts that underpin diversification are likely to be less influential in clients' decisions than are the causal narratives that often describe individual stock movements.

A broader frame

Even greater benefits can be gained by broadening the perspective further, to incorporate a client's other assets. Many people own substantial non-financial assets in the form of their primary residence. For investors who are mostly invested in property, the under-diversification of a relatively small portfolio of financial assets might have only limited implications. In these cases, the costs of seeking greater diversification of their financial assets might outweigh the relatively meagre benefits. This could be the case where, say, obtaining greater diversification requires crystallising a capital gains tax liability.

A still broader frame incorporates into the diversification decision what for many investors, particularly younger ones, could be their most significant asset: the value of their human capital. Human capital can be thought of in investment terms as the present value of a client's future employment income. Its value is derived from the profile (ie the quantum and timing) of that income. As with a client's other investments, there are risks associated with receiving those income payments. Those risks can have a component that is idiosyncratic and specific to the individual, as well as one that is correlated with the returns from other assets. Risks related to a client's poor health are likely to be specific to the client, for example, whereas the risk of being made redundant might correlate with weak economic, industry or investment markets. However, overall the correlation between the value of a client's human capital and their investment returns is likely to be low, thereby creating substantial diversification benefits.[11]

In terms of asset allocation decisions, one of the implications of considering an investor's human capital is that younger and more highly educated investors could afford to invest in more risky financial assets. They could do this because they have more substantial human capital with which to offset investment risks. This is because the period over which younger investors will receive income is typically longer and, where they have more education, the profile of the payments they will receive is typically steeper and higher.

Similarly, investors with more stable and flexible future incomes could also invest in more risky financial assets. Investors who have stable jobs, or who have alternative employment opportunities, could have relatively low risk associated with their human capital. In contrast, people who rely more on contingent income payments (such as bonuses or commissions), or who have less stable employment income (such as for the self-employed), or who have fewer alternatives available to them (such as those with non-transferable skills), can afford to take fewer additional risks with their investments. Taking a broader view allows for better diversification and asset allocation decisions, decisions that reflect the ways that a client's human capital and other non-financial assets are able to offset their investment risks.

SIMPLE MENTAL SHORTCUTS

For clients, making appropriate diversification and asset allocation decisions can be complex and difficult. Psychological research shows that when faced with complex and difficult decisions people often use simple mental shortcuts. Some common examples are discussed below, along with how advisers can align their recommendations with the shortcuts that their clients are likely to use.

Choosing by default

It is understandable that many people eschew reading long, complex and legalistic product disclosure statements. Instead, when investing their retirement savings most people choose the default investment option of their employer's default superannuation fund. Choosing the default option is a form of mental shortcut that takes a difficult decision about someone's superannuation and makes it simpler, easier and more manageable. Choosing the default option is particularly understandable for investors with lower investment balances or lower financial literacy. These investors have arguably less to gain and greater barriers to understanding their options. We shouldn't expect people with lower financially literacy to come home from a hard day's work and read a PDS.

Choosing the default option has another psychological benefit too. By being a relatively passive choice it can minimise an investor's future regret in case things go wrong. Despite their logical equivalence, acts of commission tend to be more prominent in people's minds than are acts of omission. Identical financial outcomes will probably result regardless of whether a client chooses a particular superannuation option themselves or is allocated the same one by default, but the psychological outcomes could be quite different.

The result of people using simple mental short-cuts is that many investors receive their diversification and asset allocation by default. In the context of their superannuation the level of diversification received in this way is likely to be good. However, their asset allocation might not align with their individual requirements. Super funds that employ 'smart defaults' (ie default options that are more tailored to their members' characteristics – such as their age) can help close this gap. By having a more intimate knowledge of their clients, advisers should be better able to identify and remedy any remaining misalignment.

Spreading investments evenly

Choosing the default option is not the only mental shortcut that is relevant in the context of diversification and asset allocation decisions. Another is the '1/n heuristic'. Investors who use this heuristic split their investments equally between the available options. Following this strategy means that if the options that are presented comprise mostly conservative funds then an investor will tend to choose a low-risk combination. But, if the list comprises mostly equity funds then they will choose a more aggressive mix. An investor's resulting asset allocation will therefore depend on what is presented in the list, rather than just on their relevant circumstances.

As a demonstration of this, in one experiment investors were able to choose to spread their investments between an equity fund and a balanced fund in any proportions they wished. When they were given this choice they selected a combination that gave them an average allocation to equities of 73%. This compared with an allocation of only 35% that was selected by investors who were provided a similar choice, but this time between a bond fund and a balanced fund. This effect was still huge after accounting for the fact that some allocations were not feasible in each scenario.[12]

Naïve diversification strategies are not just the domain of unsophisticated investors. Even Harry Markowitz, Nobel Prize winner and founder of Modern Portfolio Theory, has succumbed. When asked about how he initially chose his investment strategy, he reportedly remarked: '*I should have computed the historic covariances of the asset classes and drawn an efficient frontier. Instead ... I split my contributions fifty-fifty between bonds and equities.*'[13] Given that even some sophisticated clients are likely to have a proclivity for using mental shortcuts, advisers should take care not only in the options that they recommend, but to present those recommendations in ways that align with those mental shortcuts.

Aligning with decision-making shortcuts

If people predictably use simple mental shortcuts, advisers who are aware of those shortcuts can design '*choice architectures*' that facilitate their clients making appropriate decisions. One example of how they can do this relates to the way that clients use different categories. A case study I have used with groups of financial professionals from across the superannuation and investments industry is shown below.

> *A 50-year old married man (Bob) has been assessed by a financial adviser as having a 'balanced' risk profile. He and his wife are both working, with a combined income of $175,000 pa. They have paid off their mortgage and, in addition to their combined superannuation balance of $185,000, have an investment property with equity of $450,000. Bob wants advice on the appropriate asset allocation for his superannuation. Based on this information, what proportion of Bob's super assets would you recommend he allocates to each of:*
>
> *a. Growth assets (shares, property, etc)?*
> *b. Defensive assets (bonds, cash, etc)?*

By presenting this question I don't intend to suggest a correct answer. Rather, it highlights two things. Firstly, when people's responses to this question are tabulated they demonstrate a wide range of opinions. There is no consensus, even among financial advisers. Responses range from allocating 0% to growth assets, all the way up to 100%.[14] If advisers find this type of question difficult, it should be no surprise that investors do too.

The second point that this example demonstrates is the power of categories to influence decisions. In this example, two options are provided, labelled *'growth assets'* and *'defensive assets'*. To what extent did those categories influence people's choices? To test this, I provide half of the participants a different choice:

> *a. Growth assets (shares, property, etc)?*
> *b. Defensive assets (bonds, etc)?*
> *c. Cash?*

Theoretically, the group who saw the second version of the question should provide the same allocation to growth assets as did the first; they should split the remainder between the other two categories (defensive asset and cash). However, my expectation in setting the question was that by elevating cash to its own separate asset class it would better capture people's attention and seem more important. And if people applied the 1/n heuristic it would also draw a higher allocation.

While the financial advisers who have participated in this experiment appear to be immune to its effects, most of the other groups I have tried it with are not. Whereas advisers are often willing to apply their own asset class definitions to the problem, non-advisers tend to rely more on those that are provided in the question.[15] As a result, non-advisers who are given two options tend to allocate roughly 10% more, on average, to growth assets than do those who are given three options. Needless to say, such a difference in asset allocation could have material long-term consequences for Bob and his wife.

The general conclusion from this demonstration, and from the associated behavioural finance literature, is that the way decisions are framed can facilitate people finding and using different decision-making shortcuts. With these shortcuts in mind, advisers could communicate which choice represents the default option, as well as which is the most popular option and which is the recommended option. And, as the example above demonstrates, it helps if advisers are aware of the influence on their clients' decisions of the categories they use and the labels they assign to those categories.

Clients' decisions can also be influenced by the number, composition and order of the choices that advisers present them. For example, a 'growth' option can feel less risky for a client if it is the middle option (perhaps presented between 'balanced' and 'high growth'), compared with if it is presented at the extreme (after options that are labelled 'conservative' and 'balanced', say). If the growth option is what is most suitable for the client it might be sufficient for the adviser to simply recommend it. But the adviser who also presents it as the middle option greases the wheels for their client to accept their recommendation.

HOW ADVISERS INFLUENCE CLIENTS' CHOICES

Advisers can play a key role in helping clients to overcome some of the problems discussed in this chapter. However, advisers can also inadvertently introduce other problems. The results of a study of almost 6,000 Canadian financial advisers, with approximately 600,000 clients and $20bn of assets, are discussed below.[16] The study shows how advisers assist their clients, but also how advisers' own biases can influence their clients' asset allocation and diversification decisions.

Increased risk and return

The study of Canadian advisers found that they induced their clients to invest in higher risk and return assets. The researchers estimated that advisers increased the marginal households' risky asset share by 30%. They remarked that *'advisers facilitate substantially greater financial market participation and risk-taking, perhaps by reducing households' uncertainty about future returns or by relieving households' anxiety when taking financial risk'*. Assuming an equity risk premium of 6% pa, the authors equated this 30% increase in risky assets to an additional expected return of 1.8% pa, although this additional expected return also comes with additional risks and costs.

The increase in clients' allocation to growth assets that was found in the study was an average, with the results varying based on clients' characteristics, such as their assessed risk tolerance and point in their life cycle. For example, the least risk-tolerant clients held an average of 40% of their portfolios in risky assets, while the most risk tolerant clients allocated 80%. The researchers also found that the allocation to higher growth assets declined with age, peaking at 75% before age 40, and declining by 5 to 10% as retirement approached. These results would not surprise many advisers.

However, what might be surprising was how relatively unimportant clients' measured characteristics were in determining their resultant investment allocations. The 33 client characteristics that were available from the data, including clients' assessed risk tolerance and their age, jointly accounted for only 13% of the variability in clients' asset allocations. Yes, there were expected trends in asset allocation profiles across age and risk tolerance groups, but there were also substantial variations in client outcomes away from those trends. In short, other things were more important in determining how much a client allocated to growth assets. So, what were those other things?

The role of the advisers' preferences and biases

Part of the answer lies in looking at advisers' clients as a group. When the researchers did this they found that the portfolio characteristics of an adviser's other clients were a more reliable predictor of a specific client's portfolio composition than were that client's individual characteristics. This means that if Tom was the adviser and Mary was his client, then Tom's other clients' portfolios provided a pretty good guide to Mary's asset allocation, regardless of Mary's age and risk tolerance.

This relationship was even more significant when it came to predicting whether Mary would display a home country bias (by investing more of her portfolio in her own country's equities). The home country bias inherent in Tom's other clients' portfolios was approximately 7 times more predictive of Mary's home country bias than were any of Mary's measurable characteristics. Client characteristics explained approximately 4% of the variability between clients, whereas the characteristics of advisers' other clients' portfolios explained nearly 28%. It appears that these advisers were recommending portfolios with similar characteristics for all of their clients.[17]

One of the reasons that an adviser's clients' portfolios were similar to each other was because they reflected the adviser's own preferences and biases. The researchers could conclude this because they also had data about the advisers' own personal investment portfolios. Using this data they could investigate the relationships between the decisions advisers made regarding their own investments and those made by their clients. These relationships were found to be important. For example, more risk-tolerant advisers allocated more of their clients' assets to equities. The researchers concluded that advisers' *own risk-taking and home bias are far and away the strongest predictor of risk-taking and home bias in their clients' portfolios.*

From these results the researchers speculated that *advisers may project their own preferences and beliefs onto their clients*. They also noted that *although it might be reassuring [for clients] that advisers are willing to hold the portfolio that they recommend, the portfolio that is suitable for the adviser may deviate substantially from what is best for the investor.* Together these results show that when recommending portfolios it is important for advisers to focus on their clients' preferences, beliefs and biases, but that advisers should not overlook the important role of their own preferences, beliefs and biases.

CONCLUSIONS

This chapter has discussed common problems with diversification and asset allocation decisions. These are important because asset allocation can be a long-term driver of client outcomes, and diversification is arguably the only free lunch in investing. Errors in these decisions can result in higher risks, lower returns, and a misalignment with clients' goals and preferences. Compounded over time, the long-term effects can be substantial.

The psychological causes of these problems include the familiarity effect, narrow framing, overconfidence and the use of decision-making shortcuts. They can impact relatively unsophisticated clients holding undiversified portfolios, advisers who rely on sophisticated asset allocation models, and even Nobel Laureates who won their prize for their insights into portfolio diversification. Advisers need to understand not only their clients' biases, but also their own.

These problems can be difficult to overcome. Understanding diversification requires appreciating the importance of abstract statistical relationships between different investments and asset classes. It can feel unnatural for a client to accept that investing in a less familiar and potentially higher risk asset class can actually reduce their portfolio's overall risk. Even when diversification's importance is understood, overconfidence can mean that investors fail to apply it to their own portfolios.

Advisers can nudge their clients towards better outcomes by aligning their recommendations with clients' decision-making shortcuts. And when engaging with clients they can take a broad frame, to help clients see their investment decisions in the context of their broader investment portfolio, their residential property, their human capital and, ultimately, their goals and objectives. When they do so, better diversification and asset allocation decisions are possible. By helping clients to capture these benefits, advisers can make sure they don't miss out on the free lunch.

8

ADVISING OVERCONFIDENT INVESTORS

Many people have low financial literacy and commensurately low confidence in their own ability to make important investment decisions. This chapter is not about them. It is about the people at the other end of the confidence spectrum, those who know enough to be 'dangerous' and are confident enough to take action. These more confident investors probably follow the financial press, keep up with corporate news and events, and maybe subscribe to an investment publication or two. They are typically male, and probably more financially literate and wealthier than other people.

Unfortunately, many of these retail investors want to manage their own investments, but do not have the skills to do so appropriately. This can create frustration for advisers who can see what these clients should do, advise them accordingly, and yet witness their clients make decisions counter to their advice and to their clients' own best interests.

Overconfidence is at the root of many of these problems. According to Professor Scott Plous, *'no problem in judgment and decision making is more prevalent and more potentially catastrophic than overconfidence'.*[1] In an investment context, overconfidence can predispose people to make a range of ill-advised financial decisions that can lead to increased risks and costs, and to reduced returns. At the same time, it can make people resistant to seeking and accepting the advice that they need. Advisers who can transcend their clients' overconfidence can significantly improve the financial outcomes for this under-advised client segment.

This chapter covers the psychological challenges advisers face in working with overconfident clients or prospective clients. It discusses how the illusion of control, the Ikea effect and overconfidence can create rose-coloured glasses through which people view some of their own investment decisions.

This chapter also provides pause for advisers to reflect on how some of the problems associated with overconfidence might also apply to them, either in the way they make decisions or in the way they present those decisions to clients. How should advisers strike a balance between providing clients with confidence and certainty, and yet also reflecting humility in the face of at least partially uncontrollable and unpredictable markets?

CLIENTS WHO THINK THEY CAN DO IT THEMSELVES
A number of biases can push clients to overvalue and over-rely on their own judgments. This section provides a guide for advisers to navigate the behavioural biases that can distort clients' decisions about when to do things themselves, versus when to rely on expert advice and assistance.

The illusion of control
The *'illusion of control'* refers to the fact that people sometimes feel that they are more in control than they actually are. This is particularly relevant in an investment context, given that many outcomes are unpredictable and uncontrollable; it is more likely that people will overestimate their level of control when their actual level of control is low. The individual investors studied by De Bondt, who were discussed in Chapter 7, provide a good example. In this study the illusion of control was evident from the fact that De Bondt's investors under-estimated the extent to which their returns were driven by factors that were beyond their control. Their returns were less influenced by their specific stock selections, and more by broad market movements, than they expected.

In addition, research shows that people tend to feel more optimistic about the things that they can control.[2] This might contribute to why people feel more comfortable with the risk of driving a car than with flying. Being at the wheel creates a greater sense of control than does sitting at the back of a plane, even though the odds of death are stacked against the car driver. Perhaps more tellingly, people feel more comfortable with the risk of being on the road when they are the one who is behind the wheel, rather than when they are in the passenger seat.[3] This form of optimism was also evident among the individual investors studied by De Bondt; while they weren't too optimistic about the (uncontrollable) market generally, they were when thinking about the future returns from their own stock selections.

Overcoming biases like the illusion of control is often difficult; therefore, advisers might want to pick their battles when trying to get clients to accept that they should share the control of some of their investment decisions. One way to do this is by suggesting clients retain control over some decisions, particularly those for which clients can be justified in believing that their input is beneficial. For example, clients could retain control over decisions related to their portfolio's broad asset allocation, as well as to how their investments are structured for tax and estate planning purposes. In this way, clients could ensure that their investments align with their long-term goals, and suit their tax and family circumstances.

Arguably, by focussing clients on these things, advisers can help their clients to maintain a sense of control. This could make it easier to then persuade clients to outsource other decisions, such as the individual shares they invest in, the asset managers they use, or the market timing decisions they make. As discussed later in this chapter, in relation to each of these choices, investors are likely to have less control over outcomes than they expect, and also risk making predictable errors that can endanger their own financial wellbeing.

Advising clients to place limits on their own decisions is another approach that can potentially help clients, while still allowing them to retain a sense of control. For example, clients could agree to allocate the large majority of their capital to a professionally managed portfolio, but retain a small allocation of 'play-money' with which to make their own investment selections. Or advisers could create a model portfolio that is professionally managed, but that also allows clients to create additional rules, such as to exclude tobacco stocks or to exclude investments in the client's employer. Or clients could continue to manage their own investments, but agree to minimum levels of diversification, or to maximum deviations that they will take from their long-term asset allocation.

More broadly, the more clients feel that the recommendations they receive from their adviser have been dictated by their own preferences and requirements, the greater their sense of control is likely to be. Of course, basing advice on an in-depth analysis of a client's beliefs and preferences, and refining that advice based on a client's feedback, helps to ensure the advice is suitable for the client. But by making this tailoring particularly salient to the client, advisers can also leverage the illusion of control. This means that when working with investors who value their sense of control, advisers should not simply tailor the advice they provide; if they want these investors to accept that advice, they should ensure that it is also seen to be tailored.

None of these solutions necessarily leads to the type of optimal investment strategies envisaged by theoretically 'rational' investment models. Clients' desires for control can mean that these ideals are unrealistic. Nonetheless, these solutions reduce the risk of self-inflicted damage and thereby allow self-directed investors to achieve better outcomes.

The Ikea effect

Related to the illusion of control is the *'Ikea effect'*. This refers to the fact that the more energy people put into something, such as assembling their own table purchased from Ikea, the more they tend to value it. This is the case even if that thing is not objectively any better than an equivalent item assembled by someone else.

The Ikea effect provides another good example of how decision-making biases can operate beyond people's conscious awareness. If people were aware of its effect on them then they would realise that other people would not like their creations as much as they do. However, this is not the case; as Professor of Psychology and Behavioural Economics, Dan Ariely concludes: '... *not only do we overvalue our own creations, but also ... we mistakenly believe that others love our work as much as we do.*'[4]

The psychological evidence provides a number of potential explanations for the Ikea effect. One is that people use a simple decision-making shortcut when they assess the value of things they have created. That shortcut is: *'you get out what you put in'*. While this might be true in many facets of life, in investing it doesn't necessarily follow. When investment professionals take advantage of scale, technology and expertise, they can produce well-diversified portfolios with what might appear to the client to be little effort. When the normal relationship between effort and outcomes breaks down, clients can overvalue their own effortful investment selections.

Another explanation for the Ikea effect relates to *'cognitive dissonance'*, a form of psychological discomfort. It is understandably unpleasant for an investor to spend a lot of time and effort making their investment choices, only to achieve poor outcomes. An objective analysis might confront this investor with the realisation that they have wasted their time and energy; or worse, that they are incompetent. These uncomfortable thoughts can be avoided if the investor simply believes that their investments are indeed good. Of course, as discussed previously in the context of clients achieving difficult goals, people don't necessarily switch their beliefs like this consciously. Rather, these automatic psychological comforting mechanisms operate beyond their awareness, deftly changing their beliefs and soothing their ego without them realising.

The strategies for working with the Ikea effect are similar to those for the illusion of control. The key distinction is that with the Ikea effect it is clients' effort that is key, rather than their level of control, although these two things will be related in many cases. However, while additional client effort means a greater Ikea effect, care must be taken in asking clients for effortful contributions to the advice they receive. If not managed appropriately, these requests can create unhelpful *'frictions'* (ie behavioural barriers) in a client engagement process. Finding the appropriate balance is discussed further in Chapter 11.

Overconfidence

Overconfidence has been referred to by psychologists as *'the mother of all decision-making biases'*.[5] It can contribute to a range of problems, one of which is people being too eager to manage their own investments. The problem occurs when investors with below-average skills overconfidently believe that they are actually above-average. Just as the 80% of people who believe that they are above average drivers can't all be right, there are likely to be far fewer above average self-directed investors than there are self-directed investors who believe that they are above average.[6]

Overconfidence can be fostered when there is wriggle-room for investors to interpret the quality of their own decisions. This wriggle-room allows investors to err towards positive self-evaluations. Given this bias, advisers are right to be sceptical about investors' self-reported investment performance. Despite large-scale academic reviews showing that very few investors are able to consistently beat the market on a risk-adjusted basis, it is rare to meet an individual investor who will tell you they have underperformed. Consistent with this, some advisers report that while their self-directed investor clients might say that their investments are going well, after scratching the surface they find that rigorously measuring and assessing how well their share portfolio has performed is something that individual investors rarely do.[7]

Across a range of contexts, receiving appropriate and timely feedback is often a precondition to effective decision-making.[8] Without the reality check that effective feedback provides, investors can continue to believe that they are in control of randomness, they are above average, and they are doing better than they actually are. In the absence of proper feedback, these investors should heed Daniel Kahneman's advice and not trust their own judgment to tell them how much they should trust their own judgment.[9] One way that advisers can help overcome investors' overconfidence, therefore, is to help them to receive and to appropriately interpret feedback about their investment decisions.

What type of feedback would be helpful for self-directed investors? Rigorous performance comparisons would be a good start. The problem, though, is that there are many ways to get this calculation wrong: poor benchmark fit, inappropriate or no risk adjustments, inappropriate adjustments for the timing of cashflows, etc. With so many things to manipulate, ignore or overlook, if investors make this comparison themselves, it is very easy for them to get the answer they are looking for. Ideally, performance comparisons need to be made by someone without a vested interest in the status quo. Investment performance needs to be assessed with a mindset of *'tell me how I could have done better,'* not the brief investors implicitly give themselves: *'show me how good I was'.*

Some advisers already perform a benchmarking service as part of their initial client engagement. Clients who are genuinely interested in improving their financial performance should welcome this feedback. Those who prefer blissful ignorance might not be ready for advice.

The next sections discuss three specific patterns of investment behaviour that overconfidence can lead to: overconfident overtrading, over-active asset manager selection, and misguided market timing.

OVERCONFIDENT OVERTRADING

Investors who trade most frequently have been shown to achieve lower net returns.[10] This can result from high turnover adversely impacting an investor's gross returns, as well as by resulting in investors incurring unnecessary taxes and costs. Overconfidence is a key behavioural factor underpinning this overtrading.

How overconfidence contributes to overtrading can be seen by imagining two investors: Mary, whose decisions are *'properly calibrated'* (ie reflect the true extent of uncertainty), and Fred (who is overconfident and under-estimates uncertainty). Both are considering adding a stock to their portfolios. For simplicity, both Mary and Fred have arrived at identical valuations for the stock – well above the current share price. What differs is the range around their valuations. Mary and Fred may or may not explicitly construct a valuation range, but if they do not, there will be one implicit in the way they think about possible future outcomes. Those implicit or explicit ranges are shown in the diagram below.

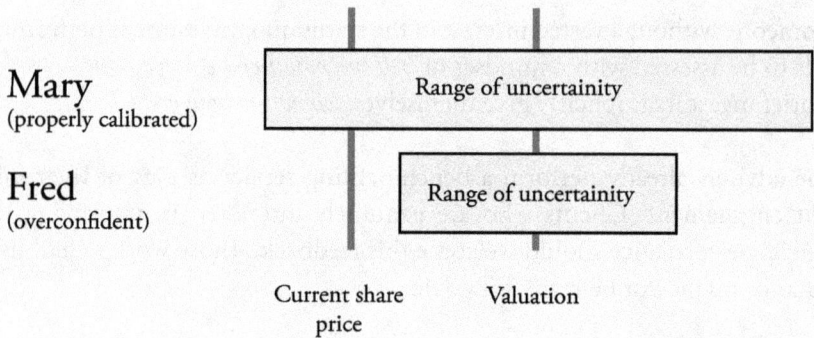

How overconfidence contributes to over-trading.

In Mary's case, because her range is wider, the current share price falls within her valuation range. In Fred's case, with his narrower range, it does not. Other things being equal, Fred is more likely to add the stock to his portfolio. When burdened by his irrationally narrow expectations, it becomes rational for him to bear the potential costs and taxes involved in executing his trade. As researchers Moore, Tenney and Haran comment, investors *'who are too sure they know what an asset is worth will ... be more willing to trade that asset than they should be.'* [11] In contrast, for Mary the choice is less clear-cut. She might buy, or might not. As a result of these dynamics, overconfident Fred will tend to trade more frequently than Mary.

How much difference does trading frequency make to a typical individual share investor? The answer is: it depends, but sometimes quite a lot. In my first book, *'Applying Behavioural Finance in Australia'*, I showed the results of a simple simulation of different trading frequencies on a $1 million share portfolio, over a 10-year period. While the total realised capital gains were the same in all scenarios, as a result of investors sometimes missing the capital gains tax concession, a hypothetical overconfident investor on a 47% marginal tax rate paid approximately $203,000 of extra tax. [12] Of course, a lower total impact would be expected for investors on lower marginal tax rates. There is some complexity in these calculations, but the take-home message is this: for tax-paying individual investors, overcoming overconfident overtrading can have significant long-term financial benefits.

Working with overconfident over-traders

Like with other biases, overcoming overconfident overtrading is likely to be difficult. Stories about stocks rising and falling can make news headlines, and the trading strategies linked to them can form the basis of compelling BBQ conversations. In contrast, the time-value of bringing forward capital gains tax payments, or of missing out on a capital gains tax discount, are likely to captivate only a more select audience. Systematic distortions in investors' estimates of uncertainty are even more arcane.

Given that the tax impacts of a client's investment decisions might not naturally capture their attention, advisers could attempt to make them more explicit. Doing so might open the door to a conversation about the possible ways to improve clients' after-tax outcomes. This is not to say that taxes should always be the most important priority of course. But they should not be hidden in the background of a client's otherwise seemingly profitable trading strategy.

Advisers could also ask their clients about their level of confidence. For example, in relation to a proposed share purchase, an adviser could ask: *'in 12 months-time, what range of share prices would you be 90% sure this company will trade within'*? Given that the range provided by the client is likely to be substantially too narrow, the adviser could continue: *'would you still make this investment if the actual range of outcomes was twice as wide as you expect?'* [13] Discussing this broader range might not change every decision, but it should create pause for at least some overconfident over-traders.

Another question adviser could ask is why their overconfident client has better insight into a stock's prospects than do other investors. By investment transactions being intermediated in an impersonal way, clients are somewhat immunised from the reality that each of their transactions has a counterpart who is making the opposite decision to them. The identity, skills, knowledge and experience of the client's counterpart are unknown and lack salience. Unbeknownst to them, the client might be on the other side of a trade made by a quantitative fund run by a dozen PhD-holding savants, or by an international value manager with a large team of research analysts. The adviser's questions could bring these possibilities better into focus for their client. The client might provide a valid response, but when they don't it becomes more difficult for them to credibly justify that they are above average.

OVER-ACTIVE ASSET MANAGER SELECTION

In addition to over-trading, overconfident investors can also switch between asset managers too frequently. When an active manager underperforms, the temptation for clients can be to cut their losses and switch to another manager. However, switching between active managers is another difficult decision that investors often do poorly. Clients who switch active asset managers after a period of short-term underperformance might feel that they have solved their problems; however, the common reality is that these clients have merely set themselves up for future poor returns. The evidence shows that the returns from the asset managers that investors choose tend to be relatively strong prior to investors investing in their funds, but relatively poor thereafter.[14]

Being able to choose active managers that will outperform in the near future is not necessarily impossible, but requires betting against the odds. Those odds set a high hurdle for choosing an active manager, and a similarly high hurdle for switching between them thereafter. Overconfident investors can overestimate their hurdle-jumping abilities.

The following example shows how relevant 'base rates' (ie statistical averages about choosing asset managers), stack the odds against overconfident investors. Imagine that 20% of asset managers have sufficient skill to beat a benchmark index in the long term, and 80% do not. These proportions might be generous for some market segments and uncharitable for others, but will serve to illustrate the general point. In addition, assume that because of the vagaries of the markets, of those managers who can beat the benchmark index in the long term, only 60% do so in the short term. On the other hand, those same market vagaries allow some of the less capable managers to also beat the market in the short-term. Let's say that half of these managers will get lucky and achieve short-term outperformance.

Given these assumptions, what proportion of the managers who demonstrate short-term out-performance will actually have the skills necessary to deliver out-performance in the long-term? The proportion is lower than most people expect. As shown in the diagram below, the answer is about a quarter (23%). This is the proportion of managers who have outperformed in the short term and that have the skills necessary to outperform in the long term (ie 12%), divided by the total proportion of managers who have outperformed (ie 12% + 40% = 52%). The rest of those with good short-term performance were merely lucky. An investor who bets on a manager's short-term outperformance continuing is, in this example, implicitly taking a bet that they will lose 77% of the time.

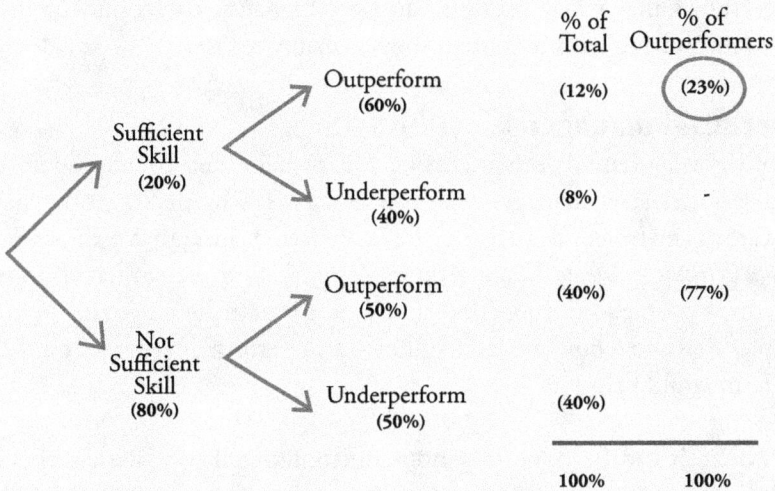

How ignoring base rates can lead to betting against the odds.

Of course, if investors have the expertise to identify which of this pool of managers will be successful, then they can win the bet nonetheless. However, investors are overconfident in their asset manager-selection skills; it is a bet that most investors lose.

What makes choosing an asset manager even more difficult is that the base rate of successful managers is likely to be lower than many investors believe. This is because funds that perform poorly often close their doors to new investors. The list of available funds thereby becomes subject to *'survivorship bias'*. When the typically poorly performing closed funds are naturally removed from the list, what remains is no longer representative. The result is that the base rate appears more favourable than it actually is.

And while the problem of survivorship bias is well known to many advisers, it can be easily overlooked by individual investors. When making a decision, investors' attention is directed to the information they have, less so to what is missing. Kahneman refers to this effect as *'what you see is all there is'*.[15] Unfortunately, the missing pieces of the puzzle can sometimes paint a quite different picture. That picture shows that when choosing an asset manager, overconfident investors need to jump a higher hurdle than they probably realise.

Better fund manager selection

Part of the way that advisers might be able to help their overconfident clients to make better asset manager selection decisions is by making sure that they are aware of the true odds that they face. By itself, stating that *'past performance is not a reliable guide to future returns'* is unlikely to be sufficient, given the strength of people's intuition that the reverse is actually true. Simple tools or examples that show how ineffective short-term performance is as a guide to the long-term could help.

Also, where it can be done in a non-confrontational way, with a client who is open to learning something new, challenging them to guess the chances of a manager outperforming might facilitate them coming to a surprising realisation. Incorrect guesses tend to focus people's attention more acutely, and facilitate learning more effectively, than when people are simply told something they didn't previously know.

Given the difficulty in influencing overconfident investors, here again, advisers might want to pick their battles. The battles that are most worth fighting could include asset manager choices where the base rates are particularly low, where survivorship bias is high, and where returns are most noisy. These decisions could be particularly risky for clients who are contemplating allocating a significant proportion of their portfolio, or who will incur material costs and taxes in the transfer process. In these cases, clients might benefit from choosing an asset manager from a category with more favourable odds of success, or by sticking with their existing asset manager, or by allocating a smaller proportion of their investments to the new manager. While there is much to contemplate when choosing an appropriate asset manager, for the overconfident client, each of these strategies helps tilt the odds of success more in their favour.

MISGUIDED MARKET TIMING

Market timing is another investment strategy that requires betting against the odds. Market timing is understandably tempting, given that broad market movements are demonstrably impacted by psychological-related factors. For example, behavioural finance researchers have identified a number of statistically and economically significant relationships, such as those based on the weather, the seasons, the numbers of hours of daylight, daylight savings changes, the outcomes of major sporting events, social media content and textual markers in financial media. These measures have been linked with market outcomes, such as stock market returns, treasury security returns, mutual fund flows, analyst earnings forecasts, IPO returns, real estate prices, the level of the VIX index, and bid-ask spreads. Markets are clearly impacted by psychological factors.[16]

But investors underestimate the challenge of market timing. Not only do they have to be right about what will happen, but also when it will happen. Many investors have gone broke being right before their time. To profitably trade on expectations of future gains and losses, some investors assume they have to be correct 51% of the time. However, after accounting for factors like the opportunity costs associated with missing the equity risk premium, this threshold is more like 70%. This was the conclusion drawn by Nobel Laureate, William Sharpe.[17]

Like with active manager selection, this creates a high hurdle for successful market timing. In the case of market timing, reliably jumping the hurdle requires a favourable combination of the probability of being correct, the quantum of the expected excess return, the preciseness of the timeframe in which it will be achieved, and limits to the downside risk if the prediction turns out to be wrong.

Overconfidence can lead investors to believe they possess this precision when they don't. For example, the signals that can potentially guide a market timing strategy, while statistically significant and robust, are mostly weak. Or they only become meaningful when at the extreme, or in the long-term. For example, even something as apparently relevant as dividend yields has little predictive ability for stock price movements in the following year. The relationship becomes stronger when assessed over long periods (of say 10 years), but still fails to account for most of the variability of these longer-term future returns.[18]

Relying on qualitative investment forecasts is not much better. In many cases, where they have been measured and assessed, such forecasts have been shown to have no better predictive validity than blind monkeys throwing darts. The broad conclusion from research about forecasting is that people are often overconfident in their abilities to foretell the future.[19] Given what we know about the forecasts that have been assessed to date, it would be overconfident to think that the much broader set of forecasts and predictions that underpin many market timing decisions, and whose validity has not yet been properly tested, are likely to be better.

Unfortunately, even many attempts by professional investors to time markets merely reduce returns and increase risk. For example, a review of the performance of 210 tactical asset allocation portfolios concluded: *'with a few exceptions, they gained less, were more volatile, or were subject to just as much downside risk as a 60 percent/40 percent mix of U.S. stocks and bonds.'*[20] These attempts at market timing can destroy value by being either systematically wrong or, more kindly, being right but without sufficient certainty or magnitude to offset attendant negative consequences. This is not to say timing the market is necessarily impossible, just that many professional investors who believe they can do it actually cannot.

For overconfident clients who insist on timing the market, advisers could inform them of the odds that they are betting against and the preciseness with which they need to be correct. They could ask clients why they can confidently predict market movements, when the presumably vastly better resourced professional teams who manage tactical asset allocation strategies are largely unable to do so. And if they still insist on trying to time the market, advisers could mitigate the risks their clients face by helping them to establish investment policies that limit the extent or duration of their market timing decisions.

OVERCONFIDENT ADVISERS?

The preceding discussion has focused primarily on clients' behaviour. In contrast, this section considers the adviser. It asks how advisers can avoid falling into the same types of traps that can snare their overconfident clients. And how they can do this while still ensuring that their clients have confidence in their advisers' advice and expertise.

Overconfidence applies to advisers too

Daniel Kahneman, Nobel Prize winning psychologist and founder of much of the thinking about decision-making biases, openly acknowledges that he is unable to escape biased decision-making. Advisers therefore must acknowledge that they too can be impacted, although not necessarily in the same ways as individual investors.

To demonstrate one of the ways that financial professionals can be impacted by overconfidence, I asked a team from a major investment and wealth management group to provide ranges that they expected the ASX200 to fall within after 12 months. As with the distance-to-the-moon exercise discussed in Chapter 7, I requested that participants set the limits of their ranges so that they were 90% sure. When I collated the results, I found that the ranges they provided typically allowed for a rise or fall of roughly 11% (ie a 22% total range around their mid-point estimates).

Unlike with the distance to the moon, the problem with this demonstration was that I needed to wait 12 months to find the actual answer. And, even if the

ASX200 was then outside people's expected ranges, I couldn't conclude that participants were overconfident; perhaps they were merely unlucky. However, what I could do was compare the ranges that participants gave with other indicators of market variability. For example, how did their ranges compare with the volatility of the ASX200 that was implied by the VIX, and how did it compare with the ASX200's historical rolling 12-months returns?

What these comparisons showed was that participants' stated ranges should have been at least twice as wide as they were: the VIX suggested that their ranges should have been 44% wide; a cross-check using the historical volatility of the ASX200 index produced an almost identical result; while rolling 12-month historical returns for the ASX200 suggested that even wider ranges were necessary in order to capture 90% of historical outcomes. Put differently, whereas participants were 90% sure the outcome would fall in the ranges they provided, the evidence suggested that it had only a 60% chance of doing so. These results demonstrated that at least one facet of overconfidence was alive and well in the context of a team of sophisticated investment professionals.

Be wary of where overconfidence is most likely
The fact that sophisticated investment professionals can be overconfident doesn't mean that advisers should always second guess their own judgment. But it does suggest that they should be alert to when overconfidence is most likely to infect their advice. When might this be?

Firstly, advisers should be wary of relying on forecasts or opinions, their own or those proffered by other financial professionals, that do not come with a demonstrable track-record of previous forecasting success. A highly credentialed forecaster with a seemingly compelling narrative, perhaps with pages of supporting charts, and with forecasts made to multiple decimal points, is no substitute. These forecasts sometimes come with only the illusion of accuracy. The future is often much less certain than the decimal points suggest.

Secondly, advisers should be alert to forecasts and predictions about uncertain future events that are made with high confidence. Declarations of high confidence made by forecasters often bear little relationship to their accuracy.

As Kahneman argues, they *'mainly tell you that an individual has constructed a coherent story in his mind, not necessarily that the story is true.'*

High confidence forecasts can simply create greater opportunities for surprise. A forecast made with 90% confidence might be right 60% of the time. In contrast, a higher confidence forecast, one that is made with 98% confidence, is likely to be right 80% of the time. In the former case, the forecaster is surprised 4 times as often as they expected (ie 40% of the time compared with 10%), whereas with the higher confidence forecaster, they are surprised 10 times as often as they expect (ie 20% of the time compared with 2%). When greater accuracy is accompanied by even greater confidence, the risks can be enhanced, rather than mitigated.

Thirdly, advisers should be particularly vigilant in contexts in which forecasting errors are most likely. Complex environments like economies and markets tend to be difficult to forecast accurately. This can be particularly the case in the short-term. Over shorter time periods in particular, market timing, individual stock selection and asset manager selection decisions have poor base rates. To bet against them requires possessing either rare skills or a large dose of overconfidence. Unfortunately, the latter is more common than the former.[21]

For some financial advisers, stepping away from the types of decisions described above might mean focusing more on the value they can contribute to clients by providing strategic advice. This value can be substantial. Vanguard estimates that the value of advisers' alpha is about 3% pa. This excludes alpha from investment selection, but includes the benefits of behavioural coaching, rebalancing and cost-effective implementation.[22]

But just as clients are likely to resist some attempts to challenge their overconfidence, investment professionals should also expect to feel naturally defensive about some of their own decisions. For example, in response to the evidence about how poor many forecasts are, some investment professionals deny forecasting applies to them (eg *'I don't forecast, I just buy companies that are going to increase in value'*). Stating that one buys companies that will rise in value is, of course, a prediction about the future. The prediction might have a sound basis, but is a prediction nonetheless.

Some investment professionals conclude that because falsifiable forecasts have been shown to be wrong, the solution is to avoid falsifiable forecasts, such as by only expressing forecasts in vague terms. Others conclude that it is only economic forecasts and outlook statements that are flawed, and that outside these topics they are safe. They are not. Advisers who hear themselves using these types of rationalisations could remind themselves of this apt quote from Carl Richards: 'overconfidence is a very serious problem. If you don't think it affects you, that's probably because you're overconfident'.

The answer to forecasting errors is not for advisers to stop thinking about the future. Helping clients to plan for the future is, of course, a key part of what many advisers do. This can't be done without having some reasonable expectations for what might happen. But what the psychological evidence does suggests is that in forming expectations about things that are inherently uncertain, advisers should ask questions like 'what happens in most cases, for most investors, most of the time?' To reduce the risk of overconfidence, advice that conflicts with these base rates should be given only on the basis of high quality and reliable information. This information should, of course, be sought and relied on where possible; but where it is not possible, advisers' and clients' expectations should be guided by relevant base rates.

Communicating uncertainty

Avoiding overconfidence means appropriately recognising and dealing with uncertainty. But even if advisers appropriately recognise uncertainty in their own decisions, there can be challenges communicating this to clients. At one of my presentations, an adviser commented that he felt uncomfortable providing a seemingly wide range of possibilities to a client who sought his views on the market. There was a disconnect between his client's unrealistic desire for certainty and precision, and the uncertain market reality faced by the adviser. Ultimately, clients have a choice when they ask their advisers for market forecasts; their adviser can be precise, or they can be accurate, but they can't be both at the same time.

Perhaps a compromise for clients who expect both precision and accuracy, is for advisers to give them a precise prognostication, but with high and low scenarios around it. Compared with abstract statistical concepts like confidence intervals and standard deviations, the narratives around which these scenarios are based can make it easier for clients to engage with uncertainty.

More broadly, when communicating uncertainty and avoiding overconfidence, advisers risk their clients jumping to the wrong conclusions, about both them and their advice. Providing wide ranges risks advisers appearing to lack the expertise required to be more definitive. Similarly, advisers who avoid making investment decisions that have low success-rates risk being seen as inferior to those who claim to have the expertise needed to beat the odds. By creating a greater sense of certainty, the use of specific scenarios could help to avoid some of these perceptions.

Where they can't be directly avoided, a client's potentially negative perceptions need to be quickly allayed. For example, advisers could provide evidence that, despite what some financial professionals might say or do, others can't predict with certainty either. There is no shortage of comical mispredictions an adviser can choose from to help communicate this fact. Clients who accept this will hopefully realise that advisers who effectively communicate the uncertainty inherent in their recommendations actually warrant greater trust and admiration.

CONCLUSIONS

This chapter has discussed the challenges and opportunities in working with overconfident clients. Their overconfidence can lead these clients to wanting to do things themselves. It can also predispose them to make a number of low-probability investment decisions. These decisions can expose them to greater risks, and can result in them achieving lower returns. Herein lies the challenge: finding ways to assist people who need advice, but who don't feel that they do. Finding solutions to this challenge can potentially create better outcomes for these clients and, by engaging an under-advised market segment, better outcomes for advisers too.

When working with overconfidence, there is no silver bullet; it would be overconfident to believe that there was! The strategies discussed in this chapter are aimed at making improvements at the margin. They are intended to help advisers to pick the battles that matter, and for which they have at least some chance of winning. The potential approaches to winning these battles include allowing clients to continue to maintain control within agreed limits, constructively challenge overconfident clients with evidence that they might have overlooked, and posing questions with surprising answers. In each case, uncertainty should be communicated in ways that help ensure that clients reach the right conclusions, including about their adviser's expertise.

Overcoming overconfidence requires being vulnerable. It requires recognising that we don't know as much as we think, that the world is less certain that we imagine, and that we are not as superior to others as we like to believe. Being overconfident might feel good, but can also be destructive to one's wealth. The key is to find solutions that allow clients to maintain the positive feeling, but without the negative financial consequences.

9

RESIDENTIAL REAL ESTATE; THE MOST BIASED ASSET CLASS?

Residential real estate often comprises the largest portion of an investor's assets. It can also play an important role in people's lives more generally. But property-related decisions can be difficult. Is it best for a client to buy or to rent? If they choose to buy, which property should they choose? How much should they bid, either at auction or at a private sale? And, for property owners, when is it best to sell? These decisions can be subject to a range of biases that mean that people's property choices don't lead to the financial or life outcomes that they desire.

This chapter outlines the biases that can impact property buyers and sellers. It discusses how advisers can apply decision-making research to help clients find a residential property to live in that will maximise their long-term happiness. This research can also be used to help clients decide whether to buy or to rent, and to ensure they don't inadvertently pay too much. This chapter also covers the decision-making concepts that are relevant in the context of selling a property, as well as how decision-making biases can, in aggregate, lead to property market cycles.

Even if they don't provide specific residential property advice, advisers who are versed in behavioural finance concepts can help their clients make better property decisions.

BUY OR RENT?

The first question a prospective property owner faces is whether to buy residential property at all, or whether it is better to rent. This section discusses how simple mental shortcuts can result in people overlooking important aspects of this decision. It also examines the impact of property ownership on people's subjective wellbeing, and whether owning a property contributes to their long-term happiness.

Simple mental shortcuts

Should a client buy or rent? For many people there is no debate. For them, a simple mental shortcut provides a ready answer: *'rent money is dead money.'* Whereas loan repayments ultimately lead to unencumbered property ownership, rental payments do not. Using this reasoning, who would want to 'throw money away' on rent? In comparison, property investing is neatly conceptualised as being like a ladder, one that leads inexorably upwards towards wealth and prosperity. If the decision to rent or to buy is represented as being the choice between recklessly throwing money away and conscientiously climbing a ladder, it is understandable that people would gravitate to the latter.

These popular mental shortcuts contain an element of truth, but they also obscure important complexities, and they suffer from narrow framing. The narrow frame involves focusing only on whether unencumbered property ownership results from the decision to buy or to rent. In contrast, a broader frame incorporates all of the costs and benefits of owning versus renting.

Some aspects of this calculation are difficult. How does one place a value on the sense of security a family might enjoy from owning their own home, for example? What future increase in property prices should investors assume they will receive? How much will a property owner need to spend on maintenance each year? What is the chance that a change in family circumstances necessitates incurring the costs and hassles of selling and moving earlier than expected? And for renters, what is the chance they are required to move earlier than they hoped due to their landlord wanting to take possession?

Because people tend to focus on what most attracts their attention, among these complexities the low-salience opportunity costs of property ownership can be overlooked. These opportunity costs include the size of the investment portfolio that property owners could accumulate if they chose to rent. This investment portfolio would be seeded with the amount of the deposit, stamp duty and other costs they incurred to purchase their property. It would then be added to with the differences between the payments that they were required to make as a property owner, compared with if they were to rent an equivalent property. Depending on the assumptions made, the financial benefits of property ownership might be positive or negative.[1]

One important assumption when undertaking this calculation is that renters have the financial discipline to invest their surplus cashflows into growth assets and to maintain them in the long term. In contrast, for property owners mortgage payments are a form of 'enforced saving' (in layman's terms), or what psychologists might call a *commitment device*. For people without the discipline to avoid spending their surplus cashflows, the commitment device that property ownership provides can be particularly advantageous.

As with other types of financial decisions, advisers can assist their clients to recognise low-salience opportunity costs, and to correctly factor them into their buy-versus-rent assessments. They can also help clients to make appropriate assumptions that reflect their personalities and their circumstances. And they can improve their clients' options and outcomes by enhancing the financial discipline with which they use any surplus cashflows.

Does property ownership lead to happiness?

Regardless of whether or not there are financial benefits to property ownership, one of the assumptions that is often implicit in a person's decision to purchase a residential property to live in is that it will lead to their greater overall psychological well-being or happiness. But while there is ample anecdotal evidence to support the idea that property provides psychological advantages, researchers have so far been unable to confirm that property ownership leads to happiness. For example, in a review of the extant psychological literature, Professor David Fagundes concluded that '... *the relationship between property and happiness is at best deeply conflicted'*.[2] While the current literature on the topic is relatively thin, Professor Fagundes cites a handful of studies that have found little connection between one's property and one's happiness. This research suggests that while buying a property might increase people's satisfaction with their homes, it might not increase their happiness overall.

There are a number of reasons why this might be the case. One is the tendency for people to habituate to their purchases. A purchaser might be excited when they first move in to their new home, but over time they grow used to it, and it fades into the background of their lives. More generally, people's happiness is the result of all of their lived experiences, meaning that changing one aspect of their lives, such as their property ownership, is only likely to have a large impact if it also has a broad influence on their lives. This might be the case when buying a house corresponds with moving to a different city, for example, but will be less relevant in other circumstances. When people contemplate the psychological benefits of buying a house, it is likely that they don't focus enough on how much of their lives will remain the same.[3]

Another problem is that people's happiness can be impacted by the comparisons that they make. Purchasing a nice house might still make people feel depressed if nearby houses are even nicer. Counter to conventional wisdom, this suggests that to maximise their happiness, clients should buy the best house on the worst street. As with the share investment strategies discussed in Chapter 6, what is economically beneficial (in this case, buying the worst house on the best street), can also be psychologically uncomfortable.

In addition, even if a property makes its purchaser feel good, this can be offset by the adverse effect of any debt the purchaser incurs in the process. Having a nice house is obviously little comfort for people for whom the stress of a large mortgage contributes to their marital or health breakdown.

None of these considerations mean that purchasing a property is necessarily the wrong decision. However, they do provide grounds for advisers to constructively challenge their clients' beliefs and assumptions about property ownership. The answer to whether owning their own home is the best path to a client's financial success, or to their emotional well-being, is 'it depends'.

FINDING THE RIGHT PROPERTY

If a client has decided to buy a residential property to live in, and they want to purchase one that will have the largest impact on their long-term happiness, what characteristics should they look for? Research suggests that they should focus on how the property will impact their on-going experiences and the way they spend their time. For example, does the property have a large living area that is suitable for family gatherings? Or is it in close proximity to a walking track through the woods?

On the negative side, happiness might be diminished by properties that require additional maintenance (assuming people undertake but don't enjoy this maintenance), and by properties that necessitate their owners having longer commutes to work. Long commutes, spending time on chores, and having little free time tend to reduce people's subjective well-being.

Obviously, trade-offs are required, and what suits one person won't be right for another. However, the problem is that in making these trade-offs people can sometimes be poor at predicting which things are likely to lead to their own long-term happiness. There can be a gap between what currently makes people happy, and what makes them happy in the years of property ownership that follow. Advisers can use psychological insights about the drivers of people's happiness to help their clients to narrow this gap.

Shopping around and making comparisons

Buying a property is a big decision that requires much diligence. But these investigations obviously cannot continue indefinitely. How many properties should a prospective purchaser review before being willing to commit? Perhaps surprisingly, there is a theoretical mathematical answer to this question: a prospective purchaser should look at 37% of potentially appropriate properties, and then settle for the next one that is better than any of the others that they have already seen.[4] To view fewer properties than this risks not having established a high-enough benchmark, and then accepting something that is sub-standard. On the other hand, to view more properties before choosing risks passing up a high-quality property and then failing to find anything better thereafter. The 37% threshold has been calculated to strike an optimal balance between these countervailing forces; it is referred to as 'optimal stopping'.

Optimal stopping was based on the 'secretary problem', a theoretical scenario in which an employer seeks to hire the best secretary from a pool of candidates. As the problem is formulated, the applicants are interviewed one-by-one in random order. If all candidates could be interviewed, and the decision deferred until the end, finding the best candidate would be relatively straightforward.[5] But in the problem, a decision about whether to hire or reject each candidate has to be made immediately following each interview. And once rejected, an applicant cannot be recalled. The optimal solution to the secretary problem is to first interview 37% of the candidates and reject them all, no matter how apparently suitable they might appear, and then to accept the next candidate who is better than any of those already interviewed.

Of course, the practical reality of choosing a property is messier than this neat mathematical formulation. Firstly, unless property hunting is a client's favourite pastime, the time they spend viewing properties comes with an opportunity cost. This means that the client should stop sooner than the theoretical optimum. Secondly, a buyer's preferences can evolve and change during their search process. When preferences and search criteria change, past properties might become irrelevant. And thirdly, calculating the pool of properties from which to view 37% can also be difficult. These complexities, among others, mean that while the broad principle holds (ie that there is a balance between waiting too long and striking too early), a simpler approach than optimal stopping might be more practicable.

An alternative to optimal stopping is 'satisficing'. Satisficing involves setting a minimum threshold and purchasing any property that is above that threshold. When several needles are scattered in the property market haystack, satisficing suggests accepting any needle that you find, rather than continuing to search for the perfect one.

Clients using this approach could establish 'must-haves' and assign each property they view an overall score. Despite its defects, a property that rates 7.5 out of 10 and that has all of the necessities might be worth buying. Satisficing seeks to reframe a client's point of comparison from the theoretical ideal that they may never find, to something more realistic. And it is an approach to life that can have broader benefits too. Individuals who satisfice, rather than seek to maximise outcomes, tend to have higher life satisfaction and self-esteem.[6]

Another problem clients face is in how they make comparisons between properties. When making comparisons, research shows that people tend to focus on the things that are easiest to compare, and not necessarily on the things that are most important. In the context of comparing properties, what is easy to compare might include prices, numbers of bedrooms and bathrooms, and land sizes. It takes a little more effort to compare distances to the nearest schools, commute times, and ambient traffic noise. And more difficult still is comparing the pleasure from owning a property that allows its occupants to sit on the balcony and read a book on a sunny Sunday afternoon, say, with an alternative property that offers additional opportunities for socialising, by having a spare room to accommodate interstate visitors. In choosing between properties, the characteristics that are both difficult to compare and good indicators of people's subjective well-being risk being overlooked or under-weighted. Advisers can help to refocus clients' comparisons on what matters most.

BUYING AT AUCTION

Last year I was invited by Chris Bates and Veronica Morgan as a guest on their property podcast, *'The Elephant in the Room'*.[7] The topic was how decision-making biases impacted participants at residential property auctions. In preparation for the podcast I observed a property being auctioned across the road from my house in the eastern suburbs of Melbourne. As it happened, the auctioneer was quite expert in using psychological principles to influence bidders, meaning that I had plenty to talk about with Chris and Veronica. Some of my observations from that auction are discussed below.

The first thing I noticed when I arrived at the auction was a coffee van parked at the front of the house, and that potential bidders had been given free coffees. The caffeine might have stimulated bidders, perhaps, but I was more interested in how being given the coffee might trigger the *'reciprocity effect'*. The reciprocity effect is the fact that when somebody is given something they tend to feel an obligation to reciprocate in some form.[8] Anyone who has received an unexpected Christmas present, but not had a present to give in return, knows how this feels.

The reciprocity effect is particularly important because people don't need to give an identical gift to feel that they have reciprocated. This means that if an auctioneer gives bidders a coffee, the reciprocity effect could predispose those bidders to giving the auctioneer an extra $5,000 bid, say. In this way, the free coffee might actually turn out to be a very expensive one.

The next psychological strategy that I noticed was the auctioneer creating a sense of 'scarcity'. He did this by describing how unique some positive aspects of the house were. What he said was correct to some extent, as no two properties are perfectly identical, but his scarcity narrative belied the relative abundance of opportunities available to purchasers. There was another property for sale a couple of houses further up the street, for example. In addition, the auctioneer mentioned that this was the third time that he had sold the same property, demonstrating that even this particular property would eventually be available again.

The auctioneer's approach complemented how a sense of scarcity is often baked into property auction processes themselves. For example, when bids are taken before a property is 'on the market' (ie the bids are made at a price below what the vendor is willing to accept), this effectively says to would-be purchasers that 'you can bid, but you can't have it!' And, at the other end of the auction, time becomes scarce, as the auctioneer counts down the 1st, 2nd and 3rd calls, before time runs out.

The sense of scarcity that the auctioneer and the auction process created neatly aligns with psychological research. That research shows that when things seem scarce people want them more, and they tend to ascribe more positive qualities to them. Wanting things that are scarce is normally a good rule to follow when buying a property, as well as in life generally. But valuing things that seem scarce is a decision-making shortcut that can lead people astray when things are artificially made to appear scarcer than they actually are.

The next psychological issue that I noticed was *'anchoring'*. As the auction progressed, the auctioneer mentioned that houses in the area commonly sold for (the relatively high amount of) $2 million. In doing so, he created a high anchor. Psychological evidence suggests that, unless they were armed with countervailing anchors which they called to mind at the right time, the $2 million anchor was likely to drag buyers' value perceptions upwards, towards this amount. Any bidders who had not fixed their valuations and maximum bid amounts prior to the auction thereby risked having them inflated during the auction process.[9]

The anchor was likely to be effective despite the fact that it was presented without much evidence of its relevance. Research shows that even obviously irrelevant anchors, including those derived from rolling dice or reading the last digits from a phone number, can significantly impact judgments, for both experienced professionals and amateurs alike. In one experiment, the supposedly independent valuations provided by property professionals were influenced by being shown the vendor's asking price. This was despite the professionals saying that the vendor's expectations were irrelevant for their valuations.[10]

Another reason people might have been influenced to raise their bids at the auction I attended, and at auctions more generally, is the *'consistency effect'*. For prospective purchasers who have made an initial bid, that bid signals their intention to purchase the property. For them to subsequently decline to make further bids risks being seen as an inconsistent act, by the bidder themselves, as well as by the auctioneer and the crowd of on-lookers. In this way, seemingly irrelevant and innocuous bids that are made below the reserve price can impact subsequent bids that have real economic consequences. Arguably this is why bidding is allowed to start below the reserve price at all.

The same principle applies to any pre-bid statements that prospective purchasers make about their bidding intentions. Even if they are not legally binding, the evidence about the power of the consistency effect suggests that those statements can carry psychological force. Influencing strategies begin well before the auction – clients need to be on guard from the outset.

As bidding slowed and the auction looked set to stall below the reserve price, the auctioneer deftly employed another psychological strategy to influence bidders: *'loss aversion'*. At this point the auctioneer could have highlighted the benefits of making a further bid; purchasers could gain the opportunity to negotiate exclusively with the vendor after the property was passed in. Instead, he warned how failing to bid would result in losing the opportunity to negotiate. Unsuccessful bidders risked waking up in the morning to find that somebody else had bought their house, he said. By choosing to frame his comments in the form of losses rather than gains, he aligned his communications with research about the power of loss aversion, as well as with the popular conception of 'FOMO' (fear of missing out).

During this lull in bidding, the auctioneer was also faced with a psychological effect that worked against him. Bidders stood in a crowd of perhaps 50 or 60 people, none of whom were bidding. As has been highlighted throughout this book, the messages received from others can powerfully impact people's actions and beliefs. Unfortunately for the auctioneer, the message this crowd was sending to its members was that the property was not worth buying. The auctioneer had to find a way to overcome the negative social feedback loop that his auction risked being sucked into.

The auctioneer found a clever way to do this. He used his colleagues who were assisting at the auction to create a countervailing social norm. Referring to his assistants, he said something like: *"I know this property is a great buy; Mary knows it, Bill knows it, and Frank knows it."* The proclaimed knowledge of these property insiders thereby suggested that the lack of bidding didn't really mean that the property wasn't worth buying. The implicit negative social norm generated by the crowd of non-bidders was cleverly countered with an explicit positive one.[11]

The broad conclusion from my observations at the auction is that prospective purchasers could confront a number of psychological strategies that are either used explicitly by auctioneers, or are implicit in the auction process itself. Without needing to make any specific property recommendations, advisers can potentially assist their clients by helping to mitigate the effects of these strategies. For example, to limit the impact of high anchors, advisers can help their clients to establish more objective property valuations that they can call to mind as they bid. And, just as having a pre-committed strategy can help share investors, advisers can also recommend that clients who plan to bid at auction predetermine their maximum bid amount and have a strategy to stick to it. Like Ulysses tying himself to the mast, having somebody bid on their behalf could help clients achieve this. And, as is discussed in the next section, advisers could suggest their clients also consider other ways to purchase residential property, such as via a private sale.

BUYING VIA A PRIVATE SALE

An alternative to an auction is buying a property through a private sale process. This avoids some of the psychological issues that can impact bidders at auctions. However, buying via a private sale can introduce other decision-making problems. As is discussed below, one of these is the problem of the 'winner's curse'.[12]

The winner's curse refers to purchasers failing to properly account for the impact of uncertainty and conditional probabilities and, as a result, paying too much. To demonstrate how this can happen, imagine 2 families, the Smiths and the Joneses, both of whom are considering buying the same property. For ease of comparison, each family will receive the same benefits from owning the property, and each has an identical capacity to pay for it.

Assume that the property's theoretical 'true value' is $1m, based on all of the costs and benefits that the families would derive from it. However, as neither family is able to precisely determine this value, each makes their own best-guess estimate. On average, these estimates are correct, but one family happens to be a little too high and the other a little too low; say $1.1m for the Smiths and $0.9m for the Joneses.

The two families now each have the opportunity to place one confidential bid, on the basis that the highest bid will be accepted without further negotiation. Given these assumptions, how much should each family offer for the property?

One strategy is for each family to simply place a bid equivalent to their estimated valuation. If those estimates are, on average, correct then there is roughly an equal chance that the true value is either higher or lower that each family's estimate. Therefore, the risk of paying too much appears to be offset by an equivalent possibility of getting a bargain.

However, the situation is actually less favourable for the two families than it appears. If the Joneses offer $0.9m, it will be rejected; only the Smith's offer of $1.1m will be accepted. Unfortunately, the Smith's estimate was too high, meaning that they have paid too much for the property and have suffered the winner's curse. The somewhat counterintuitive conclusion is that, even if prospective purchasers are correct about their valuations on average, they can still systematically pay too much.

There are a number of strategies that purchasers can use to help mitigate the risk of suffering from the winner's curse. Perhaps the most obvious one is to simply make lower offers. However, while this reduces the risk of overpaying, it also reduces the chances of people successfully acquiring a property at all.

A second strategy is for people to avoid making offers on properties for which there are many other interested parties. Other things being equal, the more offers that a vendor receives, the more extreme a purchaser's offer needs to be in order to be accepted. This means that where possible, purchasers should try to find out the number of other parties that they are competing with. Where that number is large, they should be more cautious about the size of their offer, or whether they should make an offer at all.

A third strategy is to only make offers where there is a relatively low amount of uncertainty in the property's value. A property for which there has been a number of recent comparable sales would have less uncertainty about its value than would a relatively unique property, for example. Prospective purchasers' valuations might be unbiased and, on average, correct in both cases, but their distribution of valuations would be different. The wider range of values for the unique property means that the purchaser who suffers the winner's curse is likely to suffer it more acutely.

And a fourth strategy is for prospective purchasers to only bid on properties for which they receive some special benefits from ownership that others don't. For example, having a home that is near a nuclear power plant might be seen as a disadvantage for many, but not necessarily for those who work at the plant. Compared with other buyers, the nuclear power plant employee might value the short commute and also be less concerned with the risk of a meltdown. For this purchaser, buying a property above market value might not be a curse at all.

Each of these strategies requires purchasers taking a broader frame, one that steps back from the specific property and looks at the context in which it is being sold. That broader frame also considers the behaviours of other bidders and of the vendor. In each case, advisers can potentially assist by helping clients to focus their attention on the types of information that they can easily overlook.

SELLING A PROPERTY
While auctions and private sale processes seem to favour vendors, sellers can also face psychological challenges. Selling can be difficult when the owner doesn't feel like buyers appreciate their property's true value. And it can be doubly difficult when the owner faces the prospect of selling at a loss.

The value disconnect
One of the challenges faced by sellers is the 'endowment effect', which refers to the fact that people tend to value things that they own more than equivalent things that they don't. A famous demonstration of this involved giving students coffee mugs. These students required more to sell their newly acquired mugs than the price their non-mug-receiving peers said they were willing pay for the same mugs. In one experiment, the average selling price was more than double the average buying price ($7.12 versus $2.87). Theoretically, these values should have been roughly equivalent. And while other studies of the endowment effect have found a smaller gap, the effect is likely to be stronger in the context of someone's family home than for a mere mug that they have only recently received.[13]

The *'Ikea effect'* is another bias that could contribute to sellers having unreasonably high expectations. As discussed previously, the Ikea effect is the tendency for people to over-value things into which they have invested effort. In the context of property, this could include the vendor's investments of their time and energy into property maintenance, renovations and gardening, among other things. Even if a purchaser would have made the same renovation choices as the vendor, by not having made those choices themselves, they are unlikely to value them as much.

Of course, if the purchaser's tastes differ from the vendor's then they might have made different renovation choices altogether. Vendors who suffer from *'egocentric bias'* can underestimate this risk. Egocentric bias is the tendency for people to think that others share their own preferences and views more than they actually do. Not everyone appreciates the artistically designed water feature in the front yard.

Sellers can also be impacted by emotional associations. Because *feelings do not say where they came from'*, a seller's joy at watching their child's first steps across the kitchen floor can become associated, not just with the child, but with the kitchen too.[14] In contrast, when the purchaser looks at the kitchen, they might see only a cramped bench-top and an outdated stove. And because memories can be more easily recalled in the same context in which they were formed, losing access to the kitchen risks losing access to its associated memories too.

To help overcome some of these biases the psychological research suggests that advisers should help their clients to think more like traders. Clients should try to think of the property they are selling less as a family home and more as tradeable commodity. There is some evidence that people who are experienced traders are less susceptible to the endowment effect.[15] And for those clients whose personal experiences prevent them from thinking in this way, there is at least the potential that awareness of the psychological challenges associated with selling a property makes them more amenable to obtaining and relying on a fair, objective and impartial assessment of their property's value.

Selling for a loss

A particular challenge for vendors is the potential of selling for a loss. Of course, nobody likes making losses, so vendors should try to avoid them where they can. However, attempts to avoid losses can sometimes backfire, leaving vendors worse off than if they were to accept their loss and move on. Waiting might result in a better outcome, but there is also a risk that it leads to not much improvement, or worse, to further losses and opportunity costs.

One strategy that advisers can use to help clients to sell at a loss, when it is in their best interest to do so, of course, is to find ways to replace the purchase price as the client's primary reference point. Advisers could introduce alternative reference points, such as the amount the client requires to make their next property purchase, for example, or the amount they require to discharge their outstanding debts. By choosing alternative reference points, losses can sometimes be reframed into gains.

Another strategy advisers could use is to help clients attribute different meaning to their experiences. Selling at a loss confronts the client with the possibility of making a negative self-assessment, perhaps that they are financially incompetent, or at least imprudent. If selling at a loss comes with this emotional baggage, then it's understandable that some clients would prefer not to sell.

To counter this, advisers can potentially help their clients to attribute meaning to their experience in more constructive and less confronting ways. Did they happen to buy their property during a period of particularly high prices, for example? Changing the way clients think about the past can potentially open the door for them to make more constructive decisions in the future.

And finally, advisers could assist their clients to sell by framing their property as being part of their overall investment portfolio. People have been shown to be more willing to sell real estate when they consider it as part of a portfolio, rather than in isolation. When it is just one of many things in a portfolio, some of which have probably done well and some less well, there is more countervailing evidence with which to quieten the loss-averse voices that clients hear in their heads.

IMPACT ON RESIDENTIAL PROPERTY MARKETS

The discussion to this point has focussed on the biases that can influence the sale or purchase of an individual property. More broadly, biases can create self-reinforcing feedback loops that result in property price cycles. This can occur, for example, when property owners' recent experiences of price rises or falls feed their expectations for more of the same. These experiences can then become supercharged via the stories people relate around water coolers, or on social media. When they do, recency bias and the power of social influence combine.

In contrast, long-term property price histories are more abstract and statistical in nature, and so don't tend to have as much influence on people's decisions as they should. These histories are the statistical base rates that should typically form the foundation of people's long-term property price appreciation expectations, and are what advisers can help clients to focus more on.

Just like with equities, decision-making biases can result in property markets experiencing momentum: price rises followed by more price rises. A similar dynamic can apply in falling property markets too. However, rather than there being a stampede for the exits, in falling markets transaction volumes tend to diminish, as property owners try to avoid selling at a loss. Overall, property market cycles tend to be slower than for equity markets, perhaps reflecting the lower liquidity and lower frequency of price information.[16]

In aggregate, the impact of decision-making biases is arguably more pronounced for property than for equity markets. One reason this might be the case is the way that residential property is commonly valued. Because property values have a large non-financial component, valuing residential property can be difficult. Rather than trying to determine a property's absolute value, people tend to focus on its relative value, by observing how much other properties have sold for. Social norms are thereby baked straight into the price.

Another reason is that most participants in residential property markets are relatively inexperienced, unsophisticated investors, who are driven by a range of different financial and non-financial motives. There are few institutional investors to apply a more objective financial discipline. Even if there were, the illiquid nature of property markets, the relatively high transaction costs, the unique and indivisible nature of individual properties, and the absence of an ability to take short positions, all make arbitraging differences between price and value difficult or impossible. The result is that behavioural biases in property markets can remain unchecked.

Even if most people's expectations and decision-making were realistic, this might not be enough to avoid property cycles. Because most property doesn't trade from year to year, a relatively small proportion of particularly active investors can have a disproportionate impact on the market. For example, one study found that a small number of extremely optimistic people were largely responsible for the US property bubble.[17]

Given that a relatively small proportion of people are buying and selling properties each year, does that mean that advisers should only think about the impact of property markets on those particular clients? Not necessarily. One reason is that rising and falling property values can also impact people's spending. In what's referred to as the 'wealth effect', when people feel wealthier, such as from a rise in their property value, they tend to be more willing to spend.

The wealth effect associated with rising property prices tends to be stronger than from rising share markets, potentially because property wealth is perceived as being more permanent. But it could also be, at least in part, because spending is facilitated by lending products, such as lines of credit, that allow property owners to consume capital that would have otherwise been difficult to access. In this way, financial advisers need to be aware of the impact of property cycles on their clients, regardless of whether they happen to be buying or selling.

CONCLUSIONS
This chapter has demonstrated how clients' decisions relating to residential property can be subject to a range of biases. Those biases can lead people to misjudge whether they should buy a property at all, and can infect their choice

of property. And, when they come to buy or sell, different decision-making biases can result in buyers paying too much, and in sellers failing to accept fair offers. Given the important role that residential property plays in many people's lives, the consequences of these decisions can be significant.

In making these difficult decisions, advisers can help their clients to take a broad view about residential property, one that incorporates the impacts of property-related decisions on the rest of their lives, recognises non-salient opportunity costs, and considers clients' properties in the context of their broader investment portfolios. Advisers can also help better align their clients' property purchase decisions with the psychological drivers of their long-term happiness, they can help mitigate the risks associated with buyers paying too much, and they can help sellers to rely on objective valuations.

The fact that property decisions include an important non-financial component does not exclude them from the disciplines of sound decision-making. Similarly, the fact that many advisers do not provide specific advice on residential property does not mean that they cannot contribute in meaningful ways to their clients' residential property decisions. Psychological insights can add to an adviser's toolkit to help them have the most effective conversations with their clients about residential property.

10

THE PSYCHOLOGY OF SAVING & RETIREMENT PLANNING

Complex and difficult long-term decisions are often required in order for clients to meet their retirement needs and objectives. Clients must contemplate how much they will need in retirement and for how long, how much investment return they can expect to achieve, and therefore what savings will be required. Standard economic theory assumes that people are able to make these calculations and determine the actions that are necessary.

However, a number of psychological barriers stand in the way of people making the appropriate assessments and taking the necessary actions. Despite wanting to save more, many people are seduced into procrastination and inertia, or lack the self-control required to sacrifice current pleasures for future security. As a result, they can fail to experience the retirement outcomes they desire.

'Rational' approaches that seek to implore or incentivise people to save for retirement can sometimes help, but other times can have limited success.[1] The good news is that there are many psychological strategies that advisers can use to complement these approaches. Psychological strategies can help clients to manage their spending and saving, and to choose appropriate financial products and services. With the benefits of long-term compounding, advisers who use these strategies can make big differences to their clients' financial well-being.

SPENDING AND SAVING

Not everyone has the capacity to save for their retirement, of course. But for those who do, the challenge is less about their financial capacity and more about the psychological barriers that can prevent them from doing so. Part of the challenge for clients is making trade-offs between the happiness they derive from spending in different periods. Failure to save appropriately for retirement can occur when people place too much priority on the present. But because people don't always make these trade-offs explicitly, clients might not have strong convictions about their preferred savings behaviour. This can make them open to being influenced by various psychological strategies that can help them save for retirement, a number of which are discussed below.

Finding easy savings from psychological blind-spots

Cutting expenditure can be hard, but not all spending cuts are equally difficult. In some cases, relatively easy opportunities to save exist but, because they inhabit people's psychological blind-spots, are overlooked. For example, while people might be willing to shop around to save $100 on a $1,500 TV, they would typically be less inclined to seek out an equivalent saving on a $40,000 car. This is not 'rational'; if someone is prepared to drive to a different shop to save $100 on a TV, then they should be prepared to invest just as much effort to save $100 on a car, other things being equal. When $100 is saved for retirement, it matters not whether it was saved off the price of a TV or off the price of a car. But because people naturally compare a potential saving with the price of the item, the saving on the car seems less important.

If people tend to overlook savings that appear small in the context of big-ticket items, then relatively easy savings might be found by negotiating a better rate with a real estate agent, finding a cheaper mortgage, or selecting a managed fund with a lower fee. Because they appear small compared with the price of a property, the amount of a mortgage, or the size of an investment portfolio, each is an area in which clients might overlook meaningful savings opportunities.

Another psychological blind-spot where savings can potentially be found relates to expenses that clients hardly notice they incur. The less people notice that they incur a cost, the less sensitive to it they become. While paying via credit card makes payment less noticeable and less memorable than when paying with cash, the problems of low salience and inertia combine in an even more powerful way when a payment is automatically deducted from a bank account, or automatically added to a loan. In these cases, the barriers to clients noticing and taking action are particularly high. Savings opportunities from this psychological blind-spot might include cancelling subscriptions to little-used services, or finding more competitive deals on utilities and mobile phones.

Advisers could also help to create greater salience for the expenses that clients barely notice. For example, costs that seem small because they are 'only a dollar a day' or 'just the price of a coffee' can seem more important when they are expressed as annual equivalent amounts. Similarly, amounts expressed as percentages can carry more psychological weight when they are converted to dollars, particularly where the percentage is of a large amount. So, a harmless $3.50 daily coffee might become a more apparently meaningful $1,000 annual expense, and a seemingly inconsequential 0.25% reduction in a mortgage interest rate could turn into an annual saving of $1,250.

Having taken the first step towards greater salience, advisers could then convert dollar amounts into even more tangible terms. *'Did you know that the amount of interest you could save on your mortgage each year is equivalent to 10 nice restaurant dinners?'* for example. In doing so, these expenses become more accessible to clients' conscious decision-making and are less likely to be incurred simply as a result of their inattention.

Avoiding making acquisitions in 'hot states'
Another psychological strategy that can help clients save for retirement is to avoid making acquisitions while they are in *'hot states'*. Just as grocery shopping when hungry is a bad idea, arguably so too is shopping while excited by one's potential purchase.

Whereas hunger can be cured by eating, excitement can often be cured with the passage of time. There is psychological sense in sleeping on major purchase decisions. To leverage this effect, advisers could ask clients *'how long have you been thinking about buying x?'* and *'do you have to have it now, or could you wait until next month to make a decision?'* If the client delays the decision but doesn't change their mind, at least they can have comfort that their choice wasn't adversely impacted by short-term emotional influences. Better still, like the joy of unwrapping a Christmas present, research suggests that the increased anticipation associated with the delay could actually enhance the pleasure they obtain from their acquisition.[2]

In addition to changing the timing of a decision, another strategy is to change the location. Changing the location can reduce the salience of the object being purchased. For example, a shiny new car is salient for a prospective purchaser who is standing in the car yard. However, when the same decision is made elsewhere, such as back home at the kitchen table, the purchaser's decision-making can become more abstract.

A famous example of how salience can impact decision-making involved children and marshmallows. In a series of experiments, children were offered a choice: eat a single marshmallow now, or resist the temptation and be rewarded with a second marshmallow later. What is particularly relevant for advisers and their clients is that when the marshmallow was either absent or represented by a drawing, the children were able to wait twice as long as when the temptation was in full view.[3] The less tangible and more abstract the marshmallow was, the more easily resisted it became. Advisers could therefore encourage their clients to make major purchases away from the object of their desire.

Reducing temptations

In a rational world, all money is the same; it is entirely fungible. But the reality is that people find some 'types' of money more tempting to spend than others. This is because people create separate mental accounts, notional psychological buckets of money into which they allocate different components of their income, expenditure and wealth. Each bucket can have a different meaning, and can therefore have a different associated propensity to be spent versus saved. This *'mental accounting'* can create both problems and opportunities.

For clients who are trying to save more, one of the problems occurs when they allocate money to a bucket for which expenditure has a low threshold, such as money kept in cash or in a transaction account. The benefit of this approach is that people tend to feel better if they have more money that is readily available to spend; but the problem is that having excess cash in a transaction account can burn a hole in one's electronic pocket, in a way that money kept in a savings account does not.

Automatically transferring some money out of transaction accounts and into savings or loan accounts can help mitigate this effect, making it less likely that the money will be wasted on frivolous purchases. Inheritances, gifts, lottery winnings, tax returns and bonuses are particularly in danger of being spent unwisely. As Professor of Behavioural Science and Economics, and now Nobel Laureate, Richard Thaler puts it, *'people match the seriousness of the source of a windfall with the seriousness of its use.'*[4] Easy come, easy go!

Advisers could also use their clients' predilection for mental accounting to help them to make trade-offs among competing uses of funds. For example, bringing to mind a concrete representation of the opportunity costs of a $150 concert ticket might be difficult, given the multitudinous ways $150 could otherwise be spent. But if the expense comes from an 'entertainment budget', then the set of alternative uses for the $150 is narrowed. A client can then compare a night at the concert with, say, the pleasure that they would derive from purchasing 10 movie tickets.[5] The movie tickets are not necessarily the true opportunity cost of attending the concert, but if the alternative is that clients fail to consider opportunity costs at all, they can be a useful proxy nonetheless.

Creating a connection with the future

Making comparisons between two spending options can be particularly difficult when the benefits are experienced now for one option and in retirement for the other. It's literally as if different people are having each of the two experiences. That is the conclusion from fMRI scans that show the parts of the brain that people use when they think about their future selves. When they do, the pattern of brain activation is quite different from when they think about their current selves; it more closely resembles their brain activity when they think about a stranger.[6]

These findings become even more compelling when individual differences are considered. The people whose future-self brain activity is most similar to that when thinking about a stranger are the most likely to prioritise the present over the future. Viewed through this lens, saving for retirement is akin to giving money to a stranger and, understandably, the more like a stranger their future self seems, the less people want to save.

People's future selves are at a number of psychological disadvantages when it comes to prioritising their happiness. Whereas people's current selves live in a tangible, high-salience world of sights, sounds, smells and emotions; their future selves are abstract, and are split between multiple possible future worlds. High-salience environments that are rich in detail, like the current world, tend to attract attention and direct decision-making, whereas abstract and uncertain ones, like the future, do not. Together, these neurological and psychological barriers can prevent clients from translating their acceptance of the need to save into the motivation to do something about it.

Advisers can help their clients to overcome these barriers by fostering a greater sense that they share their identity with their future selves. There is some evidence that relatively simple behavioural strategies can help achieve this. For example, showing people a computer-generated aged version of themselves has been shown to increase people's savings intentions.[7] The technology that enables this is now readily available.

Research also shows that clients' connections with their future selves can be strengthened by simply suggesting to them that even though some aspects of their lives will change over time, their core identity will remain the same. And people who feel at least some connection with their future self can be influenced to save by appealing to their sense of moral responsibility. For example, in one study saving was successfully encouraged by saying *we urge you to consider the responsibility you have to your future self. After all, your future self is completely dependent on you.*[8]

Advisers can also assist clients to create a greater connection with their future experiences and emotions. With all of the potential ways the future can play out, it can be difficult to bring to mind a single scenario around which detail can be elaborated. One exercise that aims to help overcome this problem is known as *'mental time travel'*. Using this approach, advisers could ask clients to envisage a specific desired version of their retirement future, and to elaborate on it in tangible terms. For example, if they envisage spending time at their beach house, they could try to think about the feeling of the sand between their toes, the smell of the salty air, the sound of the waves crashing in the background and of seagulls flying overhead. They could imagine sitting on the beach reading a book by their favourite author and glancing up to see their spouse returning to dry off from a swim. And they could think about the associated feeling they hope to feel, perhaps of contentment, of relaxation, or satisfaction.

Mental time travel has been found to increase people's willingness to save because the details elaborated on help create the vividness that the future lacks. This approach also allows clients to experience at least a small taste of their future emotions. And while the idealised scenario that is envisaged might be replaced countless times as a client's priorities and life circumstances evolve, the point is not to predict the future; rather, it is to help prioritise it.

Using pre-commitments

Saving for retirement can sometimes be deprioritised simply because the emotional burdens of saving are felt in the present; people are hyper-sensitive to these emotions. In comparison, not only do future emotions tend to lack salience, but people tend to believe that their emotional responses to the same event will be less intense in the future.[9] As a result, asking a client to save today triggers negative emotions in a way that asking them to give up something in the future does not. If clients are going to save more, now is not the time to do it!

To avoid this problem, advisers could ask their clients about their future savings intentions. Decisions made about the future are more likely to be based on abstract ideals, such as what a client thinks is the best or right thing to do, rather than on short-term emotional considerations. This is why people who are asked to choose food to eat in the future select something healthy, why those who are asked what movies they might enjoy in the future select something high-brow, and why people buy gym memberships. In comparison, people making similar choices in the present are more likely to be found on the couch with a box of chocolates and a trashy movie. Saving is like eating an apple, watching a documentary and heading to the gym, something that people often agree that they should do, but fail to do as much as they would like.

Advisers can leverage this effect by asking clients who have difficulty saving to pre-commit to save more in the future. Because they avoid immediate negative emotions and employ more abstract thinking, these pre-commitments should be easier for clients to agree to. Thereafter, clients who have made a commitment to themselves and to their adviser are likely to feel some obligation to remain true to that commitment. Savings measures that are specific in their timing and amount are likely to be hardest for clients to psychologically wriggle out of. Advice relationships should be well suited to setting savings objectives and timeframes that are meaningful and achievable, and for holding clients accountable for their achievement.

The efficacy of pre-commitment strategies could be enhanced using the power of inertia. This could be achieved by making future savings occur automatically, such as by setting up an automatic transfer into a savings account or superannuation fund. Insights about loss aversion can also be used, by arranging additional savings to correspond to a time a client expects a pay rise. In this way, the additional savings don't seem like a (psychologically unpalatable) loss, they are merely the client giving up a (less psychologically impactful) future gain. Each of these strategies recruits biases that favour saving, to counterbalance those that oppose it.

Compared with attempts to save more in the present, the discussions advisers have with their clients about their future actions and intentions should be less difficult for both clients and advisers. And when the future turns into the present, rather than there being a sense of paternalism, the adviser can position their advice as merely helping their client to stay true to their own intentions.

Framing & communication

As has been alluded to earlier, people can be impacted by the way dollar amounts are shown. When a client sees their investment balance, because it is likely to be large compared with amounts they typically deal with day-to-day, it can create the 'illusion of wealth'. But whereas a $300k balance might seem large, an equivalent income of, say, $300 per week, seems much more modest. As a result, displaying retirement incomes has the potential to better influence clients to save for retirement. Research has confirmed this. For example, in one study, participants who were shown the increase in income that would result from boosting their savings increased their rate of savings by 8% more than did those who just saw the impact of their additional savings on their projected balance.[10]

But when they discuss incomes, should advisers refer to annual amounts, or to their monthly or weekly equivalents? Because people tend to insufficiently adjust for the frequency of payment, annual salaries seem larger. Following the advice of Ariely and Kreisler, therefore, to persuade clients to save money out of their salaries, advisers should express those salaries as an annual amount (to make them seem big). To make saving seem even more compelling, Ariely and Kreisler recommend that, in contrast, clients' projected incomes in retirement should be expressed as a monthly or weekly equivalent (to make them seem small).[11]

Making it simple and easy

An important finding of behavioural research is that small 'frictions' can sometimes influence people's behaviour. A friction is a point in a process where a person is required to exert some effort. Research shows that even tiny frictions can sometimes make a difference, such as when someone is required to turn a page or to click a link. If people are sufficiently motivated then they will, of course, turn the page or click the link. But for people whose motivation borders on apathy, a small friction can be the difference between their action and inaction.

One way advisers can use the concept of frictions to facilitate their clients' savings is by ensuring that the strategies they recommend are simple and easy. Setting up automatic transfers, deductions and alerts makes saving easy, whereas relying on willpower and vigilance does not. Similarly, to reduce frictions, simple budgets and account structures that require little effort to monitor and maintain should be preferred. Arguably, there is a risk that well-intentioned savings measures that are too complex or difficult merely influence a client's spending expectations, rather than their actual spending behaviour.

In addition to removing frictions to clear the way for savings-related behaviours, for clients who have difficulty saving as much as they would like, advisers could add frictions to help reduce spending-related behaviours. Having clients' savings kept in accounts that cannot be easily accessed with credit or debit cards is one example of how this could be achieved. The incremental effort required to manually transfer money from these accounts might be enough to avoid some expenditures. If it's not worth the trouble of transferring money to effect a purchase then the item probably wasn't worth buying in the first place.

Targeting those most in need

The savings strategies discussed above will not be equally relevant and applicable for all clients. Given their longer periods to retirement, younger clients potentially have the most to gain from increased savings. But younger clients are also likely to have the weakest connections with their future selves, making saving for retirement seem less relevant. This has been evident on the occasions I have asked groups of financial advisers attending my workshops to close their eyes and envision their own retirements. Younger advisers understandably find this exercise more difficult. When working with younger clients, advisers might need to provide them more assistance to envisage their ideal retirement.

More broadly, people have different preferences for spending in the present versus saving for the future. They display different abilities to delay gratification, control their impulses, and stick to a plan. They have different habits, beliefs and peer groups that can support saving or encourage profligacy. Advisers who understand these differences can target their savings strategies to the clients who are likely to benefit from them most, and can tailor those strategies in ways that make them most effective for each client.

RETIREMENT PLANNING & INCOMES

In addition to saving for retirement, clients must make choices about the types of investments and other financial products that will help them to achieve their retirement goals. In doing so, there are many risks to consider and much complexity. How long will they want to, and be able to, work before retiring? How long will they and their partner live? How much will they want and need to spend during their retirement? And what sequence of investment returns can they expect?

As advisers would appreciate, there are no simple answers to these questions, and nor are there simple solutions to the risks that these questions present. There are merely alternatives that can manage different risks and provide different financial rewards. This section discusses some of the decision-making biases that can impact clients as they choose between these alternatives, as well as the psychological strategies advisers can use to help their clients make the most appropriate choices for their circumstances.

Insurance

In terms of the risks and uncertainties faced by people across their working lives, arguably for many the uncertainty of their labour income is most important. However, empirical studies have shown that under-insurance is prevalent. This means that individuals and their families are exposed to sometimes ruinous financial outcomes, such as in the event of their death or incapacity, where their labour income is no longer available.

A number of decision-making biases are relevant in explaining this under-insurance gap. One is a lack of salience. Unless a client has experienced a similar life-changing event with a friend or family member, it can be hard for them to envisage their own potential untimely death or incapacity. In contrast, annual insurance premiums can be a much more tangible reminder of their costs.[12]

In addition, because people's automatic psychological machinery is designed to protect them from unpleasant thoughts, this can lead them to downplay or neglect the possibility that highly adverse scenarios could apply to them. While this 'optimism bias' can be a useful tool to bolster one's mood, it can also leave people exposed to the risk of negative outcomes. Why bother with exercise, sunscreen or insurance if the risks these things are designed to mitigate only apply to others?

Even if clients believe that the benefits of insurance outweigh the costs, there are further barriers to them acquiring adequate cover. Insurance products can be complex, the options numerous, comparisons between them difficult, and the underwriting processes lengthy and sometimes burdensome. There is no shortage of potential frictions. Every time the client has to go hunting for an old policy number, or has to complete a medical form, there is a chance that they will fail to proceed. In many cases, acquiring adequate and appropriate insurance is neither simple nor easy.[13] As a result, clients can easily become overwhelmed, disengaged and overcome by inertia.

There are a number of potential solutions to counter these behavioural barriers. For example, as many already do, advisers can create greater salience of the benefits of insurance by using relevant stories and case studies. By demonstrating the choices made by other people, these case studies can employ the power of social influence. Advisers can also remove some of the frictions in their client experience, and they can try to ensure that it is easy for clients to make comparisons, ideally between a small number of relevant insurance options.

A major super fund recently employed me to advise them on the design of their insurance application form and associated process. One of the areas of opportunity that I highlighted was helping members to see the specific steps they would need to take, and then to be able to track their progress through those steps. This can help because people tend to be initially motivated by seeing that they have made some progress through a process, and subsequently by seeing the gap close as they approach their objective. A digital form can achieve this by having a progress bar. When the conversation is face-to-face, advisers can achieve the same outcome by giving clients regular feedback about their progress through a process.

If their adviser doesn't simplify insurance-related decisions and make them easy, then clients are likely to employ their own strategies to do so. For example, they could choose their insurance cover only on the basis of price, or simply choose to do nothing. Cheaper insurance or no insurance will suit some clients, but other clients are likely to need nudging towards the insurance solutions that better suit their needs.

Bucket and yield strategies

A broad behavioural principle is that, to encourage clients to make appropriate choices, advisers could try to align those choices with how clients naturally think. So, if people tend to think in terms of separate mental accounts, for example, then why not create investments that follow a similar structure? This approach is referred to as a *'bucket strategy'*, where different investment 'buckets' are earmarked to satisfy separate client goals.

Compared with using a single pool of money that is intended to satisfy multiple objectives, the one-to-one correspondence between a client's investments and their goals makes the purpose of each investment more salient. This type of earmarking has been shown to be effective at influencing people's behaviour in some contexts.

But bucket strategies also have drawbacks. Matching investments to multiple specific goals can create complexity and inefficiency, relative to investing in a single portfolio. Also, as discussed in Chapter 3, investors' goals can sometimes be fuzzy and imprecise, and prone to changing over time. Bucket strategies that attempt to match specific investments to fuzzy and changeable goals could create inflexibility. This inflexibility could relate to transaction costs or taxes, or simply to clients feeling wedded to past decisions, despite their changing preferences. When clients' goals change, their buckets need to change too.

Buckets might be most suitable where clients have a relatively small number of high-level goals, or their goals cover short time-frames. In these cases, the risk of complexity, and of failing to adapt to change, are lower. Having a bucket of cash to cover short-term expenditures and emergencies, and another bucket of investments to cover longer-term objectives, might be an example. But, as Brooks, Davies and Smith comment, *'when the goal system becomes more complex and dynamic ... the accompanying costs of jam-jar mental accounting too often are missed, ignored, or glossed over.'*[14]

Regardless of whether buckets are used, sometimes investments naturally align with people's mental accounts. The income investors earn on their portfolio, for example, allows them to mentally account for it separately from their capital. This mental accounting facilitates people's self-imposed discipline of spending their income and leaving their capital untouched. While spending income or capital might be logically equivalent (ignoring transaction costs and taxes), these alternatives can be psychologically distinct.

Given this, retirees who enjoy spending will understandably prefer higher yielding investments. This means that advisers who wish to recommend investments that provide mostly capital growth might need to also recommend ways to help retired clients to mentally account for their expenditure.

Guaranteed incomes

Guaranteed income products like annuities can also provide a source of income in retirement. As advisers would be aware, guaranteed income products can take away the risks that clients outlive their savings. Research has found that retirees holding annuities tend to be more satisfied with their retirement, other things being equal.[15] This suggests that at least partial annuitisation may provide peace of mind for some clients.

However, clients face another set of decision-making challenges when considering whether to purchase an annuity. For example, purchasing an annuity involves translating an apparently large sum (the amount of capital required to purchase the annuity), into a relatively small one (an on-going monthly income). It is not surprising that asking clients to irreversibly turn a big dollar amount into a small one can trigger anxiety.

As was discussed previously, the problem is that people can fail to sufficiently account for the periods over which payments are made. To allow for more balanced decision-making, advisers could potentially sum the future income a client would derive from owning an annuity over multiple years, and then compare this amount with the annuity's purchase price. Alternatively, the monthly annuity income could be compared with the income that would be derived if the client's capital was invested in other ways. However, while each approach is intended to foster more effective decision-making, depending on the circumstances, various complexities could make these calculations and comparisons difficult.

Another problem for the purchase of annuities is that while they take away the risk of a client outliving their savings, they can actually seem like a gamble. The gamble is one in which the client hopes not to die early, and thereby suffer the apparently unfair loss of their capital. Counter to rational expectations, because they are sometimes seen as a gamble, rather than as a way to gain control over their income and expenditure, people who are risk-averse have actually been found to be less inclined to purchase annuities.[16]

Clients who focus on the risks of dying early, or on only reaching their average life expectancy, can be justified in considering annuities unattractive. To counter this, advisers can make more salient the real possibility of clients enjoying an extended old age. As a demonstration of how people's longevity expectation can be influenced, I sometimes ask half of my workshop participants to estimate the proportion of their clients they think will die before their 85th birthday. At the same time, I ask the other half the proportion they think will die on or after their 85th birthday. Theoretically, these two proportions should sum to around 100%. However, because people tend to overestimate the probability of the particular scenario that they have been asked to think about, the total is typically greater than this. The implication is that advisers who ask their clients to envisage living well beyond their average life expectancy, or who provide relevant examples and case studies of people doing so, could increase the importance their clients place on this scenario. Hopefully, these clients will then be better prepared if and when it eventuates.

COGNITIVE DECLINE
One of the challenges in advising clients as they approach and then enter retirement is dealing with the potential for their cognitive decline. After age 60, the prevalence of dementia roughly doubles every five years. By the time

people reach their 80s, more than half will suffer from either dementia or other significant cognitive deficits.[17]

Cognitive decline tends to be most pronounced in people's *fluid intelligence*. This refers to their capacity to think logically and solve problems in novel situations. It is less pronounced in people's *crystallised intelligence*, being their ability to use their acquired skills, knowledge and experience.[18] These differences are perhaps best reflected in some older people's difficulty in adopting new technologies. Doing so sometimes requires solving novel problems about things for which their previously acquired skills, knowledge and experience has little relevance.

In a review of some of the relevant research on age-related cognitive decline, Schlomo Benartzi highlights that older adults have marked declines in numeracy (ie the mathematical skills needed to cope with everyday life, and to understand information in graphs, charts or tables), and that they have been found to have difficulty understanding simple measures of risk. For example, in one study, when asked which numbers represented the biggest risk of getting a disease, '1 in 10', '1 in 100' or '1 in 1,000', 29% of older adults (ages 65-94) could not answer the question correctly.[19] Unfortunately, problem solving, numeracy and risk assessments are central to much financial decision-making.

One of the challenges in dealing with cognitive decline is its unpredictability. The path can be slow or rapid, and onset can be early or late; individual experiences can stray far from the average. Another challenge is recognising cognitive decline when it happens. Obtaining good feedback on financial decision-making is difficult at the best of times, let alone determining whether a judgment was impaired by cognitive decline.

And even if it is clear to an adviser that a client's judgment was impacted by their cognitive decline, for the client to recognise this requires them coming to potentially very unpleasant conclusions about their competence and independence. As has been discussed previously, people don't reach unpleasant conclusions about themselves lightly, particularly ones with such potentially profound implications.

Reflecting some older people's unwillingness and inability to accept signs of their reduced cognitive function, in a survey conducted by State Street, advisers reported that *'it is the investors' refusal to recognise the onset of cognitive decline that is preventing conversations about diminished capacity'*. State Street also found that clients' refusal was underpinned by an understandable fear, with investors indicating that *'their fear of losing independence is blocking them from action'*. But it is not just actions that are blocked, certain conclusions are also blocked; while financial literacy scores decline with age, self-assessments often remain in-tact.[20]

In a way, making decisions when a client is impaired by cognitive decline is similar to making decisions when they are in a hot state. In both cases predictable decision-making errors can be expected, and in both cases making choices prior to those adverse situations arising can help. This suggests that advisers should try to start planning early for the possibility of cognitive decline.

Early conversations about cognitive decline still require clients to face an uncomfortable future scenario, and could still be resisted. For example, the State Street researchers found that while 85% of advisers say they encourage their clients to have a plan in case of cognitive decline, only 41% of investors think they need a plan. But while these conversations are not entirely effective, at least they have the advantage of being framed as being about merely the theoretical possibility of a client's future cognitive decline, rather than the much scarier thought of its actual occurrence.

To further de-escalate the psychological stakes, these conversations could also be couched in broader terms, including anticipating changes in a client's future motivations, preferences, available time and energy. It is not just their cognitive capacity that is likely to change as they enter old age. In what has been referred to as the *'end of history illusion'*, people often under-estimate the extent of these changes. History seemingly 'ends' because while people recognise the significant personal changes they have experienced in the past, they don't sufficiently anticipate the changes that will probably occur in the future.[21]

Of course, an elderly client's family can also play an important role. In this case, the family members have the far easier task of recognising someone else's decision-making problems, rather than their own. Despite this, the task is not without its challenges. For example, people tend to project their own preferences onto the elderly people they seek to assist.[22] Nonetheless, overcoming the significant psychological challenges advisers face in helping clients during their cognitive decline could require a team effort.

CONCLUSIONS

Planning for retirement is complex, uncertain and difficult. As Professor Olivia Mitchell and Stephen Utkus from Wharton put it, *'it is because retirement savings decisions are at least an order of magnitude more complex than other economic decisions that people need help.'* [23] These decisions can be beset with a range of biases that leave clients and their families exposed to various adverse scenarios. Chief among them are the death or incapacity of a family's main income earner, as well as the risk that retirees have inadequate savings to last what might be an unexpectedly long retirement. By applying psychological insights, advisers can better influence their clients to save for retirement, to manage their risks and, ultimately, to enjoy adequate retirement incomes.

Behaviour change and the formation of new habits can be difficult, particularly if it requires people making sacrifices. But decision-making research suggests a number of strategies that advisers can use to help clients save for retirement. These include saving money that seems unimportant, and paying attention to expenditures that go unnoticed. Advisers can help prevent clients making rash decisions, such as by avoiding 'hot states' and by limiting temptations. They can also help clients to form stronger connections with their future selves. To have the greatest impact, the strategies advisers employ should make saving simple and easy. As a result of long-term compounding, small things can make a big difference.

In terms of choosing appropriate investment and other financial products, advisers can make things more salient that are easily overlooked. This could include the risk of dying early and leaving a dependent family, or the risk of living well into old age and running short of money. It is not the average life that people risk overlooking, it is the potential variability around it.

When it comes to helping clients to prioritise their futures, advisers' personal client relationships give them an advantage. When retirement is represented in mass communications as a couple of old men on a golf course, no room is left for the client to envisage their own personalised retirement outcomes. It's hard to feel an emotional connection with someone else's retirement. Envisioning one's own retirement should be a personal exercise, not a pre-cooked meal. Not everyone likes golf.

11

CLIENT ENGAGEMENT & INFLUENCE

This chapter examines how advisers can apply behavioural insights to improve their client engagement across a range of contexts. For example, how can advisers help their clients to deal with information overload and complexity? The strategies covered in this chapter can be used to better attract clients' attention, to focus them on what is important, and to reduce the risk of them becoming overwhelmed.

This chapter also covers the ways that advisers can build trust and commitment in their client relationships, and ensure that clients appreciate the value of their advice. It is not sufficient for advisers just to be trustworthy and to provide valuable advice; they must also appear to be trustworthy and their advice must also appear to be valuable. Applying psychological insights about how clients judge both trustworthiness and value, can help.

Also covered in this chapter are a number of approaches advisers can use to better understand and communicate with their clients. Because clients can have poor visibility of the real drivers of their own decisions, this can make their subjective assessments and introspections an unreliable guide for advisers to follow. But communication is a two-way street; it helps if advisers are also aware of the ways that their own psychological blind-spots can contribute to miscommunications and misunderstandings.

INFORMATION OVERLOAD & COMPLEXITY

Some financial decisions are inherently complex and require the synthesis of large amounts of information. Simplification can be beneficial, but this sometimes risks obscuring important details, thereby potentially failing to satisfy advisers' legal requirements, and undermining clients' trust. This section outlines a number of strategies that advisers can use to provide clients necessary information, while limiting the risk of them becoming overwhelmed.

Reducing and tailoring

Perhaps the simplest way for advisers to reduce the risk of their clients becoming overwhelmed, is to convey their messages using fewer words, simpler language and more images. Wordy and unnecessary text is not harmless; it reduces people's willingness and ability to pay attention to what really matters. A pertinent diagram or video can often replace much text.

If text needs to be included, say for legal reasons, advisers could ask whether the legal requirements could be satisfied using fewer words. While working with lawyers can sometimes be frustrating, I have found at least some of them amenable to reviewing legal disclosures with an eye to conveying the same message using less ink. As Ulrich Boser argues, *fewer words – and more breaks between ideas – make it easier for people to grapple with new information*.[1]

Another way to potentially remove unnecessary text from client communications is through increased tailoring. Because people tend to pay more attention to information that they perceive to be personally relevant, I typically implore my clients to be ruthless in removing material that is not. Sometimes this means creating different versions of a document for different client segments, so that each client segment sees only what is most relevant for them. The personal relevance of a piece of client communication could also be enhanced by populating it with clients' actual data, or by ensuring that it is only sent at the time it is most relevant for each client. The take-home message about personal relevance is this: if an intended piece of client communication cannot clearly articulate *what this means for you right now is …* 'then advisers should question whether it should be sent at all.

Layering and chunking

Where text can't be removed altogether, another strategy is to provide information only in small doses. *'Layering'* can help achieve this. Layering means providing clients with all of the relevant information, but only progressively, as they digest each piece and are ready to move onto the next. The first layers should provide the information that is most important and most easily understood, before proceeding into the detail thereafter. Google search results provide a ready example of the use of this principle; they show a heading and a pertinent sentence from each site, before users click through to access more content.

Layering allows advisers to focus their clients on the main messages and recommendations, but also gives clients the opportunity to understand the detailed reasoning and underlying information, if they wish. As many advisers do already, a simple example of layering is providing a short executive summary and a detailed set of appendices as part of a Statement of Advice. The same principle can be applied to structure face-to-face communications. In both contexts, by revealing additional detail only when the client is ready to process and/or act on it, they are shielded from the sense of cognitive overload they might otherwise experience.

A similar concept to layering is 'chunking', whereby discrete pieces of information are combined together into 'chunks'. The reason this can be effective is that people's short-term memories can only hold about 5 to 7 pieces of information. However, if that information is grouped into meaningful chunks, then people can remember much more. For example, remembering the 6 letters E, S, R, O, H and A in sequence, is more difficult than remembering the single chunk of information 'A HORSE, spelt backwards'.

As an example of how these concepts can be applied, for one client I reviewed a Powerpoint slide that contained 15 bullet points. My concern was that, because of the limits of clients' short-term memory, by the time they were halfway through reading the list, they would probably have forgotten the first point. As it happens, this problem seemed to have applied to the slide's author too, as one of the bullet points had been unintentionally repeated. To counter the problem, I suggested that the bullet points be grouped into a smaller number of subheadings, under which the more detailed bullet points were then arranged. Not only did the subheadings represented a more manageable number of chunks of information for clients to remember, they helped to layer the information too.

Offering fewer, easier choices

Related to having too many bullet points is the problem of having too many choices. This is referred to as the *paradox of choice*. The paradox is that while having many choices should facilitate people finding more suitable alternatives, when presented with many options, they can sometimes make no choices at all. As a result, they can stick with the default option or with their existing arrangements.

These are often regret-minimising choices. If things turn out poorly, the less active the choice people make, the less regret they tend to feel. The effect is somewhat ironic; the fear of not choosing the best option and regretting it later can actually leave clients with a less suitable alternative. This is compounded by the fact that the more options there are to choose from, the more chance there is for error. When there are 10 options, there are 9 ways to be wrong.[2]

The challenge, therefore, is for advisers to reduce the number of choices that they present to clients, while still giving them options that suit their needs. To do this, they could use a series of simple choices that allow the universe of options to be filtered into a manageable shortlist. When options are presented as a single long menu, the choices that clients are required to make are compounded. As was discussed in Chapter 4 in the context of choosing an asset manager, separating these decisions simplifies the choices, makes comparisons easier, and shortens the list of suitable alternatives.

Appropriate mental shortcuts

Psychological research shows that to reduce the burden of information overload and complexity, people often use simple mental shortcuts. For example, in the survey discussed in Chapter 1, in which most people failed to read the 'important information', it appears that investors used a simple mental shortcut. That shortcut was that information labelled as 'important' is actually unimportant and can be ignored. Given that wordy legal disclaimers are commonly provided under the heading of 'important information', it is understandable why investors could have drawn this conclusion.

If clients are going to use mental shortcuts, then one way advisers can help is by providing clients with shortcuts (or rules-of-thumb) that are aligned with their advice. In terms of advisers' communications, the appropriate shortcut is often the main message from a page, a slide, a table or a chart. When I review documents for my clients, I typically look for the main message to be immediately apparent. One way to do this is to put that message in the heading. So, in the example of the investors who ignored the 'important information', changing the heading from 'Important information' to 'Skip the first question' might have been effective.

Another approach to better draw readers' attention to the main message could be to highlight the pertinent points in bold, in coloured text, or with an arrow or a circle. The same principle applies whether advisers are providing text, tables of numbers, or charts. An adviser at one of my sessions jokingly suggested that for the instructions about skipping to the next question, a skull and cross-bones warning sign might have been appropriate!

These simple approaches are easy to do but, when you are very familiar with your own documents, also easy to forget. If they are not used and if, as a result, the main message the adviser intends to convey is not obvious, the client is likely to apply their own mental shortcuts. As the example of the 'important information' demonstrates, sometimes these shortcuts can be quite different from what the author intends.

Even if the main message is clear, the later it appears in a document the less effect on clients it is likely to have. Research shows that 90% of the impact of some investment statements comes from what's on the first page.[3] Not only are messages that are positioned up-front more likely to be seen at all, they can also influence how subsequent information is interpreted.

A popular example of this is the question *according to the biblical story, how many of each type of animal went on the ark with Moses?'* The fact that many people answer '2' to this question shows that they have probably overlooked the last part of the sentence. In fact, no animals went on the ark with Moses, because it wasn't Moses at all; it was Noah. Because they have probably already reached their conclusion part-way through the question, the mildly incongruous final word slips under many people's radars. What this means for advisers is that by stating their main point clearly and succinctly up-front, clients are more likely to interpret subsequent information in ways that align with their adviser's intended message.

Using social norms

As has been discussed previously, social norms can impact important financial decisions. For example, people's savings decisions can be strongly influenced by their peers, such that people with virtually identical demographic characteristics can have dramatically different savings rates, depending on whether their peers save for retirement or not.[4] This creates an opportunity for advisers to use social norms to help their clients to cut through complexity and to avoid information overload.

For example, an adviser could inform a client who is contemplating how much they should save and how much insurance cover to purchase, that *'most of my clients your age save about 15% of their income, and have enough life insurance to at least pay off their mortgage'* (assuming these things are true). In doing so, advisers can choose the social comparison groups and case studies that best align with their clients' characteristics, circumstances and goals.

Even if advisers don't proactively use social norms to positively influence their clients, they should be careful not to inadvertently use them the wrong way. This can be easily done. For example, in response to a recent bout of market volatility, I observed a major super fund tell its members that an increasing number of people had switched their investments to the cash option. They then urged their members to take no action. As a result, members were provided mixed messages; the social norm and the fund's advice were in conflict.

To align the social norm with their advice, the fund could have said: *'despite the volatility, most members have decided to maintain their current investment mix'.* While it was no doubt true that an above-average number of people had switched to cash, it is also true that the vast majority of people in major super funds rarely switch their investment options at all. When two social comparisons are available, the one that promotes people making the right choice should be used.

Another common example is when a piece of communication states *'did you know that many people hold multiple superannuation accounts? If you are one of these people, you could be paying unnecessary fees. You should therefore consolidate your unwanted accounts'.* As with the previous example, the social norm embedded in this message should align with the intent of the communication, not push against it. As an alternative, this communication could be rewritten as *'did you know that an increasing number of people are consolidating their unwanted superannuation accounts',* which at the time of writing was also true.

Where social comparison groups that display the appropriate behaviour are hard to identify, *'injunctive norms'* can sometimes be used as an alternative. Injunctive norms reflect what people say or think is the right thing to do. So, for example, *'our clients have told us that they dislike paying unnecessary fees. One way to avoid them is to consolidate your unwanted superannuation accounts'.* Some lateral thinking might be required to find the right social or injunctive norm, or the right comparison group.

These types of social comparisons will influence some people more than others. Some clients, perhaps including those who are low in the Big 5 personality trait of *'agreeableness'*, might argue that they don't care what other people say or do. While psychological research shows that the use of social and injunctive norms tends to have a positive impact on people's decisions overall, advisers could improve upon the averages by targeting their use to clients who rely more heavily on social comparisons.

TRUST & COMMITMENT

Another way advisers can positively influence their clients is by fostering feelings of trust and commitment. Trust is critical for client-professional relationship quality, given the level of personal disclosure that is often required and the extent that some clients rely on their advisers. Higher levels of trust and commitment are associated with higher client satisfaction and retention; they are also associated with clients having a greater propensity to reveal personal and financial information, to implement planning recommendation, and to resolve conflicts effectively.[5]

Unfortunately, advisers tend to overestimate their clients' levels of trust and commitment, meaning that as a group, advisers need to establish trust more than they think.[6] As is discussed in this section, to be judged as trustworthy, advisers need to display the proxies that clients use to judge their trustworthiness.

Demonstrating expertise

One proxy for trustworthiness that clients use is expertise; if clients view their adviser as an expert, they are more likely to trust their advice. Consistent with this, when reporting on the findings of a mystery shopping exercise into retirement advice, ASIC commented that people *'may simply view the adviser as the expert in what is generally a complex subject matter, and assume, as a result, that the advice and service is high quality'.*[7]

But judging an adviser's expertise can be difficult. How can advisers help clients make this assessment? A direct way for advisers to demonstrate their expertise is, as many already do, to have their qualifications and accreditations on display for their clients to see when they visit. This could be particularly helpful for younger advisers, whose age might count against them when clients judge their experience, and therefore their expertise. ASIC's mystery shopping revealed this, with one client commenting that his adviser *'didn't seem very old, so I was wondering how much experience he had'.*

Beyond an adviser's age, other aspects of their appearance can matter too. Research shows that judgments of competence can be made on the basis of people's appearance within a fraction of a second.[8] And while advisers can't easily change some aspects of their appearance, others can be changed. For example, as most advisers would already appreciate, professional clothing can make a difference. One study showed that more than 3 times as many people were willing to follow a J-walker across the street when they were wearing a suit, compared with another J-walker in casual clothes.[9] When it comes to risking death or serious injury, people are more willing to trust someone who simply looks professional!

And professionally presented documents can also help, as was demonstrated by ASIC's shadow shopping research. Clients in that study revealed being impressed by advice documents that were nicely bound. When it comes to financial advice, some clients literally judge the book by its cover.

Advisers could also ensure that they appear confident. ASIC noted that *for some participants, comfort was derived from the adviser having confidence and good communication skills.'* This is consistent with psychological research that shows that people often use confidence as a proxy for competence. Being well prepared, and potentially rehearsing difficult conversations, could help achieve this.

Finally, because people understand things through the prism of what they already know, clients are likely to judge their adviser's expertise, at least in part, by whether the advice they receive accords with their initial beliefs and expectations.[10] When advisers presents advice that runs counter to a client's beliefs, there are two possibilities: the client changes those beliefs, or they keep their beliefs and instead reject the advice. Of these two options, because changing beliefs can consume considerable mental effort, as well as challenge a client's ego and sense of competence, rejecting the advice can be more psychologically palatable. The risk for advisers is that clients interpret their own rejection of the advice as being indicative of the poor quality of that advice, rather than as the outcome of their own subconscious psychological self-defence mechanisms.

To counter this effect, advisers could try to find ways to agree with their clients first. Seemingly contentious concepts could be introduced slowly thereafter, once trust and credibility has been established. As with layering, this suggests that advisers should try to pay close attention to the order in which they present their advice. Easy to understand, big-ticket concepts that accord with a client's existing beliefs, should come first.

Creating ownership and commitment
Related to trust is a client's sense that they are committed to their advice relationship, to achieving their goals, and to following the advice they receive. One strategy advisers can use to help build commitment is to ensure that clients actively participate in the advice process. An Australian survey of financial advisers and their clients found that *'the more active a client is in the relationship*

the more ownership they will have over relationship outcomes.'[11]

Getting active client contributions to the advice they receive leverages three related psychological effects that have been discussed previously: the Ikea effect, cognitive dissonance and the consistency effect. Subconsciously increasing their assessment of the advice they receive is one way for clients to avoid the uncomfortable thought that they might have invested energy into advice which is of little value. The more effort they contribute, the greater the psychological imperative to appreciate the advice they receive.

Advisers can potentially accentuate the benefits of these psychological forces by simply asking for feedback. In one study, asking customers about their satisfaction with their current firm led to an increased likelihood of them opening an additional account, and a decreased likelihood of them ending their relationship with the firm.[12] For clients to do otherwise would have created dissonance, in light of the presumably favourable survey responses that these clients provided. This result relies on the survey responses being favourable, of course, but by providing an opportunity to identify unhappy clients and to resolve their problems, unfavourable survey responses are obviously also valuable.

Client contributions to the advice process can also create a greater sense of control. There is less need for a client to worry about how much they trust their adviser if they feel in control of the advice they receive. An advice process that follows a 'rules-based' or 'policy-based' approach, where those rules or policies are based on a client's stated beliefs or goals, is one way that advisers can help clients to feel in control of the advice they receive.

Another way is through education. Clients have been found to be more likely to renew business with advisers who take the time to educate and empower their clients, compared with those who place themselves in a position of power over them.[13] This demonstrates an indirect benefit of advisers providing financial literacy education to their clients, even if the direct benefits of financial literacy education are often weak.

With each of these strategies there is what Dan Ariely refers to as a *'delicate trade-off'* between the benefits of making the advice process easy for clients, and the benefits of asking them to invest their time and effort into it.[14] Asking clients for too much effort risks driving them away; but asking for too little risks missing the opportunity to build their sense of ownership and commitment. In striking the right balance, the amount of effort sought from clients can be escalated throughout an advice process – small amounts of effort initially, with larger efforts later, after an initial level of commitment has been established. Ensuring that clients' efforts have a clear net benefit for them should also help. Client effort is a resource to be used wisely.

Is my adviser on my side?

Part of trusting someone is believing that they have your interests at heart. How can advisers demonstrate this? Asking questions and displaying empathy is a good start. One of the questions in my survey of individual investors that I referred to previously demonstrated this. Simply inserting the words *'he asked you a little about what you were trying to achieve with your investments'* into a hypothetical investment scenario, led to an 11% increase in the likelihood that investors would use a particular asset manager. This was despite the hypothetical investment manager presumably being in no position to give advice.

Clients might also judge whether their adviser is on their side by whether they feel that they are being sold something. People who sense that others are attempting to persuade them can become resistant.[15] In contrast, advisers admitting their own failings, admitting their own luck, or admitting to not knowing something, can each counter this sense.

To be effective, these statements should be made in ways that don't compromise a client's faith in their adviser's competence. For example, in response to a client's poor investment choices, an adviser could say: *'I too cursed myself for making seemingly foolish investments when I started out … but what I've learnt is that investing is very easy in hindsight, and that as long as you are sufficiently diversified, making the occasional loss is not problematic.'* An adviser's historical failings have thereby been transformed into current-day wisdom.

Clients could also be helped to appreciate that their adviser is on their side by perceiving their adviser to be like them. People tend to treat members of their own groups more favourably than they treat members of 'out-groups'. This makes sense from a historical perspective, when there were clear benefits to favouring members of one's own tribe, but it also works in the modern day. Psychological research shows that it even works when the categorisation rules that divide in-groups from out-groups are based on superficial or logically irrelevant factors.

Advisers can use people's tendency to favour those whom they perceive to be similar to them by finding things that they share in common with their clients. An adviser and client discovering that their children went to the same school, or that they holidayed at the same resort last year, or that they support the same football team, isn't just idle chatter; it could be a pathway to greater trust.

Do I like my adviser?
Advisers can also build trust simply by being liked. When people don't like the messenger, they tend to ignore the message.[16] The social psychological research suggests a number of strategies that advisers can use to help foster a warm relationship with their clients. One is engaging in *mutual self-disclosure*. This approach has been tested in a laboratory setting by having pairs of people disclose increasingly personal information about themselves to each other. Commenting on the power of mutual-self disclosure, Professor Robert Cialdini notes that these pairs *generated feelings of emotional closeness and interpersonal unity that are unparalleled within a forty-five minute span, especially among complete strangers in an emotionally sterile laboratory setting*. He continues: *hundreds of studies using the method have since confirmed the effect, and some participants have even married as a result!*[17]

While advisers are probably best not to marry too many of their clients, two findings from the research about mutual self-disclosure are particularly relevant. Firstly, people who disclose personal information tend to be more liked. And secondly, people tend to disclose more to those they like.[18] The normal social rules apply to these dynamics; disclosure of negative information, or of inappropriate highly personal information, will probably backfire. And, of course, not all clients are likely to respond the same way. But, within these limits, advisers who are willing to reveal some of their own personal details to their clients stand to benefit, by being more liked and being more trusted with clients' sensitive personal information.

Finding genuine ways to enhance a client's ego could also help. People who provide positive feedback tend to be viewed favourably.[19] But again, there are limits. Blatant flattery could backfire; subtlety is required. Depending on the circumstances, to enhance clients' self-perceptions, advisers could position their recommendations using phrases such as *'I think that the smart thing to do is...'* or *'I think that the responsible thing to do is...'* or *'for people who like a bargain...'*. Accepting the associated recommendations comes with the embedded compliment that the adviser thinks that the client is smart, responsible, or has an eye for a bargain.

More generally, there is a benefit to humanising client interactions. As most advisers would probably be aware, face-to-face meetings allow for more trust and co-operation than do discussions conducted by email or phone. Among others, studies of negotiations tend to bear this out. People negotiating face-to-face are both more trustworthy and more trusting, compared with when negotiations are conducted over email or phone. Negotiators are also more likely to engage in the mutual revelation of their interests when communicating face-to-face, less likely to do so when communicating by telephone, and least likely when communicating in writing.[20]

As negotiations researchers Don Moore and his colleagues argue, *face-to-face communications offer a more immediate two-way flow of information and access to nonverbal cues, making misunderstandings easier to correct than in textual communications.'*[21] This suggests a substantial benefit for advisers who meet their clients face-to-face, at least initially, or when discussing particularly sensitive matters, or when opportunities for misunderstandings and miscommunications are high. Telephone and email might be an expedient alternative in other circumstances.

VALUING & PRICING ADVICE

According to the ASIC mystery shopping survey discussed previously, *'people have difficulty assessing the value of advice, even after it has been provided'*.[22] Strikingly, ASIC found no difference in clients' satisfaction, between those who received what ASIC determined to be good versus poor quality advice. This demonstrates that it is not enough that advisers provide high value, high quality advice; they must also ensure that clients believe that it is of high value and quality. Strategies to help clients see the value of valuable advice are the topic for this section.

What is the value of advice?

One of the decision-making shortcuts clients could use to assess the value of the advice they receive is to equate its value with the apparent effort required to produce the advice. While in life generally, effort and value might often be correlated, in some cases this shortcut can lead clients astray. To demonstrate how this can happen, Ariely provides the example of a locksmith. As a novice, the locksmith was ineffective, taking some time to open locks, and destroying many of them in the process. Over time his skills improved, so that he could open locks more quickly and without damaging them. As he became more experienced, his value-proposition should have been stronger; a faster service with less damage. Despite this, as a result of his clients witnessing the ease with which he now completed his task, their willingness to pay diminished.[23]

Advisers face the same challenge as the locksmith. To the client, the years of education and experience on which their adviser's expertise might have been built risk fading into the background. Directly observable measures of effort are likely to be more salient. These could include the time their adviser spends meeting with them, as well as the length of the advice document that they receive. Of course, one obvious solution is for advisers to spend more time with their clients and to provide longer advice documents. However, each comes with a cost, to the adviser's time, and to their clients' ability to cope with information overload, respectively.

As many advisers already do, another solution is for them to ensure that they clearly articulate the value that they provide, including both the financial and non-financial benefits. One problem many advisers face is that at least some of the value they provide is intangible. What value can be ascribed to a client feeling that their financial situation is now under control, and that their financial future is secure? Articulating these things at least brings to clients' attention some of the benefits they might not have focussed on otherwise.

In addition to these approaches, advisers could increase the salience of the work that is required to formulate their advice. This is sometimes referred to as 'operational transparency'.[24] For example, an adviser could mention that 'the shortlist that I have provided has been derived from a detailed review of over 150 funds'. This could help to make clients aware that much more work was undertaken on their behalf than what the shortlist might suggest; the shortlist was just the tip of the iceberg.

This approach can be complemented by advisers making sure that they avoid inadvertently providing signals to clients that suggest that little work has been done. Any generic documents that ask clients questions or that provide information that the adviser should already know is irrelevant, tell clients that either the adviser hasn't been listening, or that they haven't been working. Given the limited window clients have through which to view the value of the advice they receive, it is important for advisers to pay attention to what is visible through that window. A small amount of additional effort to better tailor these documents could create a disproportionate increase in a client's value perceptions.

Pricing

The next challenge for advisers is to determine how to charge, and how much to charge, for their advice. Behavioural research suggests that payments that seem small, that clients often don't notice, and that are easy for them to make, will be easier for advisers to charge and to receive. On-going fees that are based on a percentage of a client's assets, and that are deducted directly and automatically from their investments, are an example. However, these fees have the potential disadvantage of clients paying them without having proper regard to the value of the advice that they receive. Of course, advisers who have their clients' best interests at heart will want to ensure that their fees do not exceed the value that they provide.

As Australian advisers will be aware, regulatory changes stemming from the Royal Commission mean that in the future, advice fees are likely to be more difficult for advisers to charge and receive than they were in the past. This could occur as a result of increasing the frequency with which advisers need to gain their clients' consent to fees, or by restricting the fees that can be automatically deducted from a client's superannuation balance, for example. Some advisers risk losing clients and revenue as a result.

Whether or not they are transitioning to a new fee model, advisers could use a number of psychological strategies to nudge clients towards being willing to pay a fee that is commensurate with the value of the advice they receive. One is the use of social norms, such as by informing clients that *'most of my clients prefer to pay a flat fee of $2,500 per year'*. Another is the use of anchors, such as by commenting that *'in the event of your inability to work, the income you'll receive is $75,000 per annum. My fee for advising you on your insurance requirements is $3,500.'* More directly relevant anchors should be preferred where they are available, but the psychological research suggests that less directly relevant ones could influence clients' willingness to pay, nonetheless.

A few years ago, I tested the impact of anchoring on financial advice fee estimates with a group of around 400 financial advisers. The advisers completed a short survey in which half of them were asked *'how much do you think the average investor spends on financial advice (including financial planning, stock broking and tax advice) each year? Is it above or below $500?'* and then *'what is your estimate?'* The other half of the group received the same questions, but with '$500' replaced with '$2,000'.

My expectation was that the advisers' estimates would be heavily influenced by the $500 and $2,000 anchors. This is what happened; the estimates provided by those who had seen the high anchor were, on average, 65% higher than the group who saw the low anchor ($2,077 versus $1,257). If financial advisers' estimates were heavily influenced by anchors then less-informed clients, who face more uncertainty about the value of financial advice and who are probably less able to bring to mind alternative anchors, are likely to be even more influenced.

How fee options are structured could also influence clients. At the very least, by giving clients a number of options, the more expensive ones create high anchors that make the less expensive ones seem more reasonable. The highest priced wine on the menu sells the second most expensive one. Having multiple options also potentially allows client conversations to be transitioned from whether to pay for advice at all, to being about which advice option to choose.

Other structuring techniques could influence clients too. A well-known example is Ariely's demonstration of how, by introducing a redundant option, *The Economist* magazine nudged people to purchase a more expensive subscription package.[25] While making a comparison between the cheap and expensive packages was difficult, as the redundant option was clearly inferior to the expensive package, it made that part of the comparison easier. As a result, the presence of the redundant option facilitated people choosing the more expensive one.

I confirmed a similar result with the advisers mentioned earlier. Their willingness to pay was 14% higher, on average, when I introduced a redundant option into a survey question. However, offered pricing packages that advisers don't believe are genuinely beneficial for their clients risks not only undermining the confidence clients have in their adviser, but also the confidence that the adviser has in discussing their pricing options with their clients. Pricing structures can be tailored to incorporate psychological insights, but still need to be reasonable.

When it comes to using psychological strategies, doing nothing is not necessarily a safe option. If advisers do not employ the types of strategies discussed in this section, then they risk their clients using their own set of social norms, anchors and points of comparison, be they appropriate or otherwise. Arguably, so long as the value clients receive is greater than the price they pay, and the price they pay is greater than the cost to deliver the advice, employing the strategies discussed in this section can help everyone. And if clients then use the price they pay as a proxy for the value of the advice that they receive (which people tend to do), paying a fair price (rather than a low price) for high quality advice could make them more likely to rely on it too.

UNDERSTANDING CLIENTS BETTER

Arguably the most important part of client engagement is being able to understand clients. To provide appropriate advice, advisers need to understand their clients' needs, preferences, decisions and behaviours. But clients are not necessarily open books. Even if they try to be transparent, psychological barriers can make them opaque. This section discusses the psychological issues associated with several different approaches that advisers could use to better understand their clients.

Rationale and process

Perhaps the most obvious approach advisers can use to understand their clients' decisions and actions, is to ask them to explain their rationale. However, as has been discussed throughout this book, the problem with this approach is that people can often be blind to the real reasons for their decisions and actions.

But even if they are often flawed, the reasons clients give can sometimes provide important clues to their decision-making. As clients articulate their thinking, advisers might be able to identify the decision-making biases that could apply. For example, in contemplating a specific investment, a client who reveals a desire to recoup past losses is evidencing the 'sunk cost fallacy' (past losses should be irrelevant to future decisions). This client has also framed their investment decision narrowly, and has used the purchase price as their reference point. Advisers could use each of these observations to guide them to the influencing strategies that are likely to be most effective; in this case, potentially by using a broader, forward-looking frame of reference.

As with the reasons for their decisions, the processes that clients say they follow might not be entirely accurate, but could still reveal some important information. For example, the sources of information clients use for their decisions could suggest the influence of the 'availability bias' (ie focusing on what most attracts their attention, rather than on what is most important).

They could also suggest various social dynamics, such as where information and advice are received from friends or family members. These insights could allow advisers to redirect their clients' attention, and to challenge unhelpful social influences. And, if the client is unable to articulate the decision-making process they use, this could provide the opportunity for the adviser to recommend one that they should.

Behaviours and habits

Advisers could also ask clients about their behaviours and habits, and assess the implications for their financial decisions and outcomes. For example, by exposing themselves to short-term returns, clients who have a habit of checking the markets daily might accentuate the effect of loss aversion. They could also create an increased risk of over-reacting to patterns in the short-term noise. These clients might benefit from having frictions added to their investment decision-making processes, to reduce the risk of relatively harmless thoughts crystallising into much more dangerous actions. In contrast, clients who don't pay attention to markets at all might benefit from strategies that help to manage the risks associated with inertia.

However, advisers should be careful not to read too much into clients' reported behaviours. Because the context can heavily influence what people do, the past is typically only a reliable guide to the future decisions a client will make in a similar context. In what is referred to as the *fundamental attribution error*, people's behaviours reveal less about their enduring personal characteristics than we tend to believe. If a client's life circumstances change substantially, their behaviours and habits could change too.

In addition to asking clients about their behaviours, advisers can sometimes observe them directly. For example, an adviser could notice that a client appeared tired and stressed on the day they came to see the adviser and to complete a risk tolerance questionnaire. In this case, the adviser could suggest that the client completes it again, on a different day. Doing so could help ensure that the short-term impact of the client's negative mood didn't overly influence their assessed risk profile, and therefore their long-term investment strategy.

The danger with the direct observation of clients and their behaviours is that, like with other methods of understanding clients, they can sometimes be unreliable. The often difficult and error-prone task of reading body language and faces risks distracting advisers from more reliable information about their clients' advice requirements. A client with crossed arms might be unhappy, or they might simply feel comfortable sitting that way. Reading someone else's body language can sometimes be useful, but it is a less reliable window on their soul than many people expect. Insights drawn from body language are clues to clients' thoughts and feelings, but ones that should be treated with scepticism until corroborated.

Experiences and beliefs

Another approach advisers could take is to ask clients about their experiences and beliefs. A client's experiences and beliefs can heavily influence how they interpret the information and advice they receive. As discussed previously, clients are more likely to accept advice that accords with their beliefs, and to reject advice that doesn't. And because they have high salience, a client's own experiences can weigh heavily against any countervailing statistical evidence that their adviser might present. Past experiences can also introduce various reference points, frames and anchors, such as the purchase price of an investment property, or a client's past annual salary. Uncovering each of these allows advisers to anticipate when their advice is most likely to be accepted, and when and why it might be challenged.

However, asking clients about their experiences and beliefs also has its limitations. What clients remember is likely to be subject to 'recall bias' (ie that some experiences happen to be more easily recalled than others), and 'hindsight bias' (ie the way people reinterpret history, sometimes in self-serving ways, often beyond their awareness). And, on top of this, what clients tell their advisers is likely to be subject to 'social desirability' (ie how people favour reporting things they think others will approve of). But regardless of whether they are entirely true, clients' stories might still help advisers understand the lens through which they view the world.

Hypothetical scenarios

Another alternative is for advisers to ask their clients about hypothetical scenarios. Planning for future scenarios is ultimately what is most relevant for many clients. Constructing scenarios and asking clients how they would respond holds the promise of allowing a client's preferences and behaviours to be measured, not just in the past and the present, but in the multiple hypothetical future worlds that they might visit.

However, the problem with this approach is that people are often poor at predicting their own decisions. This is particularly the case in contexts that are different from those that clients have experienced in the past, and particularly when their future decisions are likely to be made in 'hot' emotional states. As discussed previously, while clients might proclaim that they are a long-term investor who is unfazed by market volatility, when the market falls by 25% and they experience the associated fear and anxiety, they might want to switch to cash nonetheless.[26]

Talking about biases

And finally, advisers can potentially talk to their clients about decision-making biases directly. In my experience, many people are interested in psychological research and the hidden influences on their behaviour. As I wrote in my previous book: *'behavioural finance offers a potential double benefit for client engagement. It can help guide how financial professionals should communicate with and influence clients, as well as potentially being the content of the communication itself.'* [27]

But the challenge with this approach is that while people often enjoy hearing about others' biases, they don't easily recognise that biases apply to them. This is referred to as the *'blind-spot bias'*, and it is one of the reasons why awareness of decision-making errors does not directly translate into actions and outcomes. As Greg Davies and Peter Brooks note, *'a central theme of decision science is the consistent finding that merely informing people of their adverse behavioural proclivities is very seldom effective in combating them.'* [28]

Client behaviour is complex and, despite advisers' best efforts and the use of various psychological strategies, is likely to remain only partly understood. Each of the approaches discussed in this section has strengths and weaknesses. There is no silver bullet, or single right way for advisers to understand their clients. Rather, they can pick and choose from a range of options as each is relevant and as the circumstances allow.

Advisers can also use different approaches in combination. For example, if a client suggests that they will confidently focus on the long term when confronted with a future market correction, the adviser can cross-check their client's self-prediction against their actions during the last downturn. Similarly, a client's belief that saving for retirement is a good idea can be cross-checked with their reported shopping habits. Each gap between their intentions and expectations (on the one hand) and their behaviours and outcomes (on the other), creates an opportunity for the client to benefit from advice.

EFFECTIVE COMMUNICATION

Most of the client engagement problems discussed in the preceding sections relate to clients, including their ability to deal with information overload, to properly assess their adviser's trustworthiness, and to accurately predict and recall their decisions. But effective communication is a collaborative exercise, one that requires advisers to acknowledge that they are human too, and so bring their own set of biases to their client engagement.

One bias that could be relevant for advisers is the tendency for people to think that they know more about other people's thoughts and actions than they actually do. To paraphrase psychologist Nicholas Epley, *'people's confidence in their mind-reading abilities outstrips their accuracy.'*[29] If advisers become overconfident that they understand their clients' minds, then they risk being surprised when their clients fail to conform to the mental images of them that their advisers have constructed.

Psychological research highlights several common ways in which disconnects can occur between the beliefs people have about others, and reality. As discussed above, reading too much meaning into a client's face and body language is one example. Under-estimating the role in people's decisions of contextual factors is another. As is attempting to take a client's perspective without genuinely understanding their circumstances. To metaphorically walk a mile in a client's shoes requires first understanding what type of shoes they wear.

Clients can also contribute to this problem. People tend to suffer from the *'illusion of transparency'*, which refers to the sense people have that others can read our thoughts more accurately than they actually can. Whether someone is nervous about giving a speech, or is trying to conceal a lie, their audience is probably less aware of this fact than they think. If they feel that their adviser can read their mind, clients might not feel the need to clarify their ambiguous words and actions.

One study showed that these dynamics are particularly problematic when communicating via email. Study participants who sent emails predicted that their recipients would be roughly 80% accurate in understanding the (somewhat ambiguous) messages they sent. The recipients were even more confident, thinking that they had interpreted the messages with around 90% accuracy. But when assessed, both were mistaken: the actual accuracy was only 56%. After reviewing this research, Epley concludes, *'people who communicate in ambiguous mediums think they are communicating clearly because they know what they mean to say, receivers are unable to get this meaning accurately but are certain that they have interpreted the message accurately, and both are amazed that the other side can be so stupid.'* [30]

These types of communication problems reinforce the need for advisers to be extra sensitive to situations in which their clients provide potentially ambiguous messages, be they verbal or non-verbal. In these cases, asking clarifying questions could help resolve the ambiguity. But in doing so, advisers should be careful to not simply ask questions that seek to confirm their expectations. Confirming questions are likely to solicit confirming answers.

Another risk of miscommunications occurring is if advisers implicitly assume that their clients are similar to the them. Chapter 7 discussed one way this could occur, by advisers projecting their own risk tolerance onto their clients. More broadly, the *false consensus effect* refers to the fact that people tend to be biased towards believing that others share their opinions, beliefs, preferences and values. Similarly, advisers need to be careful about the *curse of knowledge*, which refers to the difficulty people can have in understanding the perspective of others who don't share their knowledge.

These biases mean that clients are likely to be more different from their advisers than their advisers might think. They suggest that, while exploring similarities between advisers and their clients can help to build trust, advisers need to be careful that they sufficiently explore the differences too. They need to challenge the assumption that their clients understand them, and that they understand their clients. And they need to accept their potential role in contributing to, as well as in overcoming, any misunderstandings.

CONCLUSIONS

People's trust in financial advisers has been understandably shaken as a result of various well-publicised scandals, such as have been highlighted in Australia by the Royal Commission. Obvious harm has been done to clients who received poor advice, or who paid fees but received no advice at all. However, less obvious is the harm caused to people who, as a result of their diminished trust in the advice profession, failed to seek advice from trustworthy advisers. Less headline-grabbing harm was also done to people who received sound advice, but who failed to act on it. By helping advisers to build trust and commitment, as well as to better understand and communicate with their clients, this chapter aims to reduce these hidden harms. Both clients and advisers stand to benefit.

When clients trust advisers and recognise their expertise, their influence can be substantial. As a demonstration of the influence of experts, in a study in which an expert's opinion was presented to experimental subjects who were asked to make unfamiliar financial choices, the areas of their brains linked to critical thinking and counter-arguments were found to be almost silent.[31] A similar lack of critical thinking in the face of expertise was demonstrated by nurses who administered eardrops to patients rectally, in supposed compliance with doctors' instructions. Those instructions were to put the eardrops in each patient's right ear (written as 'r ear').[32]

Like the patients in this example, in the context of a trusted advice relationship, clients are vulnerable to misunderstandings. To quote Spider Man's Uncle Ben, *'with great power comes great responsibility'*. This responsibility includes advisers being vigilant, not just about their clients' decision-making biases, but also about the adviser's own role in contributing to miscommunications. Even superheroes have weaknesses.

12

TOPICAL ISSUES: ETHICS, TECHNOLOGY & COGNITIVE DIVERSITY

This chapter covers the psychological challenges related to three topical issues: ethics, technology and the role of cognitive diversity. The ethical issues are relevant for advisers who, for example, wish to avoid the sometimes-hidden influences of conflicts of interest on their advice. Conflicts can impact advisers beyond their conscious awareness and intentionality, making their influence surprisingly hard to recognise and overcome. Because well-intentioned advisers can still act counter to their clients' best interests, advisers need to understand the psychology of ethical decision-making.

Also covered in this chapter are the psychological issues related to group decision-making. Governance structures such as boards, investment committees and leadership teams can play an important role in ensuring that appropriate advice is provided to clients. However, teams can be subject to their own psychological problems, resulting in important information being overlooked, differing views being silenced, and people with expertise being ignored. Cognitively diverse teams that use effective team decision-making processes can potentially overcome these problems.

This chapter also discusses the psychological issues related to the use of technology, data and automated decision-making tools as part of an advice process. Technology can identify and sometimes overcome human biases and errors, and it can present information in ways that facilitate clients' choices and actions, but it can also create new opportunities for misunderstandings and errors. Arguably, the thoughtful combination of human advisers with advice tools and data is superior to either human advisers or technology alone.

CONFLICTS OF INTEREST

Conflicts of interest matter. A research paper prepared by Professor Sunita Sah for the Australian Royal Commission outlined what it described as *'a large body of evidence that documents how conflicts of interest play a substantial role in influencing advisers' attitudes and decision-making.'*[1] Consistent with this, the Royal Commission's final report focussed heavily on the role of conflicted remuneration as a contributor to various forms of misconduct.

These findings are unlikely to be new or surprising to most financial advisers. But advisers might be surprised by how conflicts can influence people's decisions beyond their awareness, how they can sometimes have the strongest impact on those who believe they are immune, and how their effects can persist in spite of seemingly logical strategies aimed at addressing them. A key conclusion from psychological research is that conflicts are more relevant for more advisers than they might expect. This section discusses these issues, along with the strategies that advisers can employ to mitigate or avoid the adverse impacts of conflicts of interest on their advice.

Why conflicts matter more than we think

Conflicts are likely to matter more than many people think because the psychological mechanisms that are involved can sometimes operate beyond people's conscious awareness. As Professor Sah puts it, *'many people have the wrong mental model of conflicts of interest and believe that succumbing to such conflicts is a matter of corruption: deliberate favouring of self-interest over professionalism. In reality, many conflicts of interest that influence advisers occur on a subconscious and unintentional level.'* Of course, some cases of misconduct do involve the deliberate favouring of one's self-interest. However, the risk is that by focussing on only these cases, both clients and advisers can be blindsided by the broader impacts of conflicts that lurk beneath consciousness.

As has been highlighted already, subconscious processes are both difficult for people to detect through introspection and to overcome through conscious mental effort. As a result, people who are motivated to avoid bias and who are educated about their impacts can still succumb to their effects. This means that advisers who are subject to conflicted remuneration but who sincerely attest that they act only in their clients' best interests, can potentially be both right about the benevolence of their intentions and yet wrong about the integrity and objectivity of their advice. According to Professor Sah, *even advisers who are ethically engaged can give biased advice.*

One of the psychological mechanisms that makes it difficult to overcome the impact of conflicts of interest is *motivated reasoning*; people are more likely to believe things which they have an incentive to believe. The more they want something to be true, the more they search for supporting evidence and the more credible they tend to find that evidence.

At a neurological level, brain scans show that people who are asked to reach conclusions in the presence of a motivation to do so more heavily use parts of the brain associated with processing emotional activity, compared with those parts that are more associated with logical analysis. When a conflict between logical and emotional reasoning is resolved there is a burst of activity in the brain's pleasure centres.[2] The result is that while they might not do so consciously, people find a way to align their reasoning and the evidence with the conclusions that they are motivated to reach.

When considering whether an asset manager will outperform, advisers will probably support their conclusions with relevant information and justifications. But when advisers are required to make difficult assessments like these in the presence of a conflict of interest the door is opened for motivated reasoning. This could be manifest in an adviser disproportionately searching for and recalling information that reflects well on their preferred manager. When a manager has outperformed over 3 years, but underperformed over 5, motivated reasoning tells us which time period to focus on.

Not only are more advisers likely to be impacted by conflicts than they think, they are also likely to be impacted to a greater extent. Based on a review of the relevant research, Professor Sah concluded that *individuals that did concede they may be biased ... tended to drastically underestimate the extent of their bias.* This is consistent with broader evidence that demonstrates that people often underestimate the impacts of a variety of different decision-making biases on their judgments.

And advisers could also be impacted by a broader array of conflicts than they expect. As I said in my first book *'we need to think more broadly than just incentives. Material interests are not the only factor that can introduce conflicts of interest. Personal affiliations, in the absence of any monetary incentive, have also been shown to be sufficient to produce bias in judgments, for example.'*[3]

Some approaches to managing conflicts don't work

What can be done to overcome the adverse effects of conflicts of interest? Some strategies that focus on the conscious and intentional aspects of decision-making could have limited impact. For example, removing 'bad apples' from the advice industry might prevent intentionally corrupt individuals from providing advice. While this would be welcomed, this approach ignores the problem of how conflicts can impact the much larger group of well-meaning advisers. Psychological experiments demonstrate that ordinary people who are put in certain contexts will do all manner of things that they would ordinarily find abhorrent. The psychological evidence suggests that the problem is less about removing bad apples, and more about fixing the bad barrels that they populate.

What if advisers who are subject to a conflict of interest disclose that conflict to their clients, so that clients could choose whether to accept the conflicted advice? While this approach has some intuitive appeal, unfortunately, as was demonstrated with the example of the 'important information' in Chapter 1, many retail investors are unlikely to read such disclosures. As Professor Sah puts it, *'even the clearest and boldest disclosure may fail to protect consumers.'*

Even if these disclosures were read, given the difficulty people have in predicting how conflicts impact decisions, and given the interpersonal dynamics between the client and the adviser, it is unlikely that many clients would know how to respond. Rejecting the advice could be awkward if it is seen as the client insinuating that their adviser's advice is corrupt.[4] According to Professor Sah, *'given the mixed response of advisees to conflict of interest disclosures, it is apparent that we cannot rely on consumers to respond as anticipated by policy-makers.'*

Advisers becoming more aware of the impacts of conflicts is also likely to have limited benefits, at least by itself. Awareness tends to lead people to believe that others are impacted by conflicts and biases, but not to accepting that conflicts and biases could impact them personally. Even if they accept that the problem applies to them, overcoming subconscious decision-making biases with effortful conscious processes is at best difficult, and in many cases appears to be entirely futile.

Unfortunately, futility might not be the worst-case scenario. Making advisers aware of the impacts of conflicts could actually make things worse. This could happen if, for example, advisers become complacent and self-assured about their ability to manage conflicts. However, while awareness is not the whole answer, it might be part of the answer. It could help if it lays the groundwork for advisers to accept approaches that actually do improve advice. Some of these are discussed below.

Should conflicts simply be avoided?
Given the difficulties in overcoming the effects of conflicts, avoiding them appears to be a simple solution. But this is not as straightforward as it might seem. For example, avoiding conflicted remuneration alone is unlikely to be sufficient; conflicted sponsorships would also have to be avoided. Advisers might not feel that their advice is impacted by sponsorship arrangements, but neither did the participants of studies whose responses were monitored and whose brains were scanned as they made decisions in the presence of a sponsor's logo. Their judgments revealed a bias in favour of the sponsor and their brain scans revealed that the presence of the sponsor's logo increased the activity in the parts of their brains that are related to pleasure.[5]

In the context of financial advice, the good news for product providers is that this evidence supports the efficacy of them sponsoring advisers' conferences. The bad news is that it also calls into question the integrity of the advice provided by some conference attendees. However, a real-world context might be expected to at least partially mitigate the effects that have been found in an experimental setting; conferences often have multiple sponsors, and there could be a material gap between the time an adviser attends a conference and the time at which they provide advice to a client.

Advisers avoiding conflicted remuneration might also be insufficient if conflicts remain elsewhere in their organisations. Conflicts have been shown to impact people where they feel that they are accountable to someone, particularly someone to whom they need to justify their decisions, and where they are aware of that person's conflicted preferences.[6] This suggests an adviser whose remuneration is free of conflicts might still be impacted if their boss' remuneration is conflicted. Unlike explicitly conflicted remuneration, biases that are implicitly conveyed in social relationships are arguably less likely to attract the attention and concern that they warrant.

Even if advisers receive only remuneration agreed to and paid by their client, there is still the possibility of a conflict. This conflict can arise as a result of a divergence between the actual value of advice and the value that clients perceive. If clients judge the value of advice by its complexity, by the apparent effort involved in providing it and by the confidence with which it is delivered, then advisers have an incentive to deliver complex advice, to make frequent changes to portfolios and to make bold predictions. This can sometimes conflict with the benefits of providing relatively simple advice, of following relatively passive investment strategies and of sticking with long-term base rates. No conflicted third-party remuneration is involved, but through no fault of their own, advisers could be conflicted nonetheless.

And even if all forms of conflict of interest were somehow avoided, there is the question of whether all clients would necessarily be better off. Where a conflict of interest offsets another decision-making bias, retaining the conflict might actually advantage the client. For example, people with financial dependents who do not proactively purchase insurance and who have a low willingness to pay for advice, could benefit from being provided insurance via an adviser who receives a commission from an insurer. When a broader view of both clients' and advisers' circumstances and decision-making is considered, two 'wrongs' can sometimes make a 'right'.[7]

Assuming that some forms of conflicts of interest are likely to persist into the future, what does the psychological research tell us about how advisers can most effectively manage these conflicts? None of the following strategies is a panacea, but each can help to create a context in which appropriate advice is more likely to be provided.

Avoiding small moral liberties

One of my favourite exponents of psychological strategies is Derren Brown. In one of his entertaining TV programs, 'The Push', he led a number of volunteers to push a man off a tall building to what they believed was the man's likely death. Derren got them to perform this extreme act by taking the volunteers through a series of well-choreographed and increasingly compliant morally questionable acts. What started with them mislabelling a vegetarian dish, led to them concealing what they believed to be a dead body, to them falsely impersonating an after-dinner speaker, and ultimately to murder. The program echoes Milgram's famous study in the 1960s in which people progressively increased the electric shocks that they believed they were administering to an apparently distressed person who they could hear in a nearby room, even when those electric shocks reached life-threatening levels.

What these demonstrations show is that moral disengagement is not instantaneous; rather, it is a slippery slope down which well-intentioned people don't necessarily recognise they are sliding. Each additional slip seems small given one's past transgressions. This can be further buttressed with the observed transgressions or implied consent of others across a team or organisation, particularly where those others are in positions of leadership or authority. Advisers need to be aware that if their circumstances conspire against them in this way, they might find themselves doing things that they previously considered unthinkable. To avoid sliding down the slope it is best not to step on it at all.

Making the desired behaviour easy

Because people tend to avoid effort, as far as possible, advice processes should ensure that compliance with moral standards is easy. Onerous processes are less likely to be followed consistently. For example, the greater the burden that is placed on clients to complete documents, the less likely they are to do so. This can create more risk of well-meaning advisers cutting corners in order to expedite the process. People who are responsible for designing advice processes, fact-find documents and application forms can assist by removing, reducing and simplifying the requirements where possible. Adding requirements can sometimes be prudent, but so can eliminating unnecessary ones.

Client engagement training is another way that could help make it easier for advisers to provide appropriate advice. Being better able to influence clients, to challenge their beliefs and to educate those with poor financial literacy, could make it easier for advisers to give clients what they really need, rather than just what they think they want.

A targeted approach

Not all conflicts of interest present the same risk. Where there is more room for interpretation there is also more room for bias. For example, arguably there is more subjectivity and uncertainty in choosing an asset manager than there is in deciding whether a client should make an additional contribution to their superannuation. Conflicts related to the former are therefore likely to be more problematic than are those related to the latter.

Red flags should also be raised where base rates suggest that financial professionals have a poor track record of success. Successfully selecting a high-fee investment product is an example; it's not that it can't be done, just that because the base rate is low there is a high risk that attempting to do so will result in a poor client outcome. If advisers have an incentive to provide types of advice that are rarely successful, they should be particularly on guard to ensure that any such advice is in their clients' best interests.

In addition to identifying the types of advice that are most at risk from conflicts, psychological research can be used to identify the advisers who are most at risk. High-risk advisers include those who have not accepted the ways that conflicts can impact their decisions beyond their awareness, or who are overconfident in their ability to overcome them. People who incorrectly assume that they can overcome conflicts expose themselves to greater risk of bias.[8]

The risks are compounded where high-risk advisers work within high-risk organisations. These organisations might have cultures that provide inappropriate social norms, or which have advice processes that make it difficult for advisers to do the right thing. They could also have greater 'psychological distance' between advisers and their clients. This could occur where advisers have large numbers of clients, where clients are shared between advisers, or where advisers otherwise have low engagement with their clients. The less personal the adviser-client relationship, the easier it is to dehumanise clients, to blame them for poor outcomes and to downplay the impact of conflicted advice on them. When one client receives poor advice it is a tragedy; when a million do it is merely a statistic.

The psychological research discussed in this section does not suggests a single best approach for dealing with conflicts of interest for all types of advice, for all advisers, for all organisations, or for all clients. A targeted approach that combines removing some conflicts and introducing different behavioural solutions could be best. That combination could vary depending on the circumstances. However, what is consistent is that an approach is likely to fail if it ignores the fact that well-intentioned advisers can be impacted by conflicts beyond their awareness.

BOARDS, COMMITTEES & LEADERSHIP TEAMS
As has been alluded to already, advisers don't operate in a vacuum – they are often part of broader organisations. Those organisations bring a cultural context, as well as decision-making structures like boards, investment committees and leadership teams. By influencing the processes advisers must follow and the products and services they can provide, these bodies can have a significant impact on the advice that clients ultimately receive.

Because they often sit at the apex of organisational hierarchies, the implicit presumption is that these bodies make decisions more effectively than do individuals. However, the evidence for this is mixed. It is true that super-additive synergistic teams can outperform individuals, but it is also true that teams can be just as biased as their individual members. And various manifestations of of 'group-think' can result in teams actually making worse decisions. When it comes to team decision-making, often conventional wisdom, common practice and what feels comfortable are poor guides to what is most effective.

Common problems with team decision-making

One of the problems teams face is how best to combine the judgments of their individual team members. Whose opinion should be relied on most? In the workshop exercises I run with teams, the teams rarely do as well as their best individual member. If they could identify who had the best answer to the problem I gave them, they would do well by simply relying on that person. But sometimes it is difficult to judge who that person is. The apparent plausibility of their approach, the confidence with which they articulate it and the person's relative seniority can each be a poor guide to their accuracy.

In contrast, decision-making research suggests a better guide to finding genuine expertise is whether someone has had the opportunity to practice and to learn from feedback. Unfortunately, the teams that participate in my workshops don't tend to explore the expertise of their members in a rigorous way. They implicitly fall back on less accurate proxies instead, meaning that the true expert among them remains unrecognised, often to that person's chagrin.

Another problem can occur with team deliberations where important information that would change a team's decision remains hidden. This is referred to by psychologists as a 'hidden profile'. Theoretically, a collaborative team could do better than individuals acting alone by pooling the information that is spread across their team members. However, research shows that the information that tends to be discussed and repeated at meetings is that which is most commonly known and that which confirms people's existing beliefs and expectations. This is, at least in part, because those who share information that confirms the group view are typically seen as more competent and more credible, by both themselves and their peers.[9] When teams ignore important information and overlook the contributions of people with genuine expertise, poor decisions can result.

Strategies for better team decision-making

The types of problems that can beset teams suggest a number of potential solutions. For example, the problem of information remaining hidden from team deliberations can be at least partially mitigated by requiring team members to disclose the factual basis for their statements and opinions. This is a discipline with which advisers will be well-acquainted in the context of providing advice, and is arguably equally relevant for teams. The use of secret ballots, turn-taking rules, pre-mortems, devil's advocates and checklists could also help bring to light information, perspectives and alternatives that might otherwise be overlooked or underweighted in team deliberations.

Because of the psychological barriers involved, people should not expect constructive challenge, uncomfortable feedback and disconfirming evidence to naturally emerge in team conversations. Asking a colleague to disclose the facts from which they have derived a conclusion could be confronting; the quest for robust team decision-making could be interpreted as a slight on a colleague's judgment. Pre-agreed team processes and decision-making rules can standardise and depersonalise the process, leading team members to the conclusion that frank feedback, requests for supporting information and the identification of conflicting views are simply 'the way we do things around here'.

Perhaps not surprisingly, leaders can play an important role in fostering effective team decision-making. Because of their potential disproportionate influence on team deliberations, leaders should try to avoid expressing their view early. Leaders can also assist by establishing team cultures and mindsets that make it OK to challenge and to be challenged, OK to be wrong and OK to be different. Making these things psychologically safe for team members helps remove barriers to disconfirming information and views being disclosed.

Leaders can also help by ensuring a level of openness and a willingness to hear uniquely held information. They can ask questions like 'are there any alternatives not yet examined?' or 'have we missed any information?' or 'does anyone have doubts they have not yet expressed?' Asking these types of questions may seem like simple good governance. However, within both small advice firms and large integrated financial services groups, sometimes the reality is far from this ideal. For example, a recent review by APRA revealed a host of problems at CBA that related to ineffective team decision-making, including there not being enough constructive challenge and there being too much collaboration in pursuit of consensus. It is unlikely that CBA is unique.[10]

The role of cognitive diversity

A team's composition can also be important. Research shows that where they work well, cognitively diverse teams (ie teams of people who think in different ways) can overcome some of the problems discussed above and can outperform individuals.[11] Having a cognitively diverse team can help if it creates even a single non-conforming voice. An individual dissenter, even one voicing only a moderately different view, can substantially reduce the probability that other group members will conform or will silence their dissent.[12]

Cognitively diverse teams can benefit from their members bringing different perspectives to a problem. To be useful, these perspectives need to organise the world in distinct and meaningful ways.[13] A number of examples that are relevant for financial advice have been provided throughout this book. For example, when thinking about investment decisions, 'value' is one perspective, while 'quality' is another. Other alternative perspectives include 'first-order' versus 'second-order thinking', or focusing on a specific decision versus broader base rates, or on what a theoretically rational person should do versus what real people actually do in the real world. No one perspective is necessarily superior to its counterpart; the magic comes from combining different perspectives in ways that leverage their respective strengths.

This type of cognitive diversity can be found in teams regardless of team members' ages, genders or ethnicities. But a team's 'identity diversity' can also matter, particularly for teams with diverse clients. An adviser's gender or age could make it easier for them to understand and empathise with clients of the same gender or of a similar age, for example. The policies and processes agreed to by any teams comprising only older men risk being disconnected from the needs and preferences of their younger female clients.

Unfortunately, capturing the benefits of cognitive diversity is sometimes difficult; there are considerable barriers to overcome. Larger and more diverse teams bring with them both the benefits of different perspectives, expertise and sources of information, but also greater problems with communication, co-ordination and trust. The value that each team member contributes must be assessed and a determination made of the circumstances and ways in which their contributions are likely to be most valuable. Understanding someone else's perspective takes time, energy and motivation.

Given these constraints, when I have asked teams who attend my workshops what they consider to be the optimal team size, a common response is not really a team at all; it is a 'team' of one. It is often easy for participants to bring to mind examples of poor decisions made by their teams, circumstances in which their views were ignored or when it was clear to them that sub-optimal decisions were made.

In light of the empirical psychological research, as well as the experiences of my workshop participants, to suggest that many teams' current approaches are optimal seems optimistic. When team decision-making is less than optimal the important governance function that boards, investment committees and leadership teams provide can be ineffective, or worse. By helping to overcome the problems of ineffective teams and to unlock the benefits of cognitively diverse ones, the strategies discussed above are intended to benefit both advisers and their clients.

THE ROLE OF TECHNOLOGY

This chapter has so far discussed aspects of individual and team decision-making. This section broadens the discussion to incorporate the use of data and technology-driven decision-making tools, models, structures and interfaces. In the context of advice, technology can improve decisions by being used to identity and overcome human biases and errors, or to present information in ways that facilitate client choices and actions. It can also lead to better outcomes by creating more effective investment structures, or by reducing the cost and increase the efficiency of providing advice. But with these opportunities comes a number of potential ethical and psychological issues. These are discussed below.

Technology and ethics

Automated decision-making tools can provide a potential solution to the problem of conflicts impacting well-intentioned advisers beyond their awareness. With the benefits of data and technology, advisers could establish explicit and transparent rules and policies that align with their good intentions. They could then rely on technology to automatically and consistently apply those rules and policies. By removing the element of subjectivity and discretion, the opportunity for conflicts to influence advice is thereby diminished. So long as the decision-making rules and data are unbiased and objective, the advice clients receive should be too.

But offsetting the potential benefits are the ways that technology can sometimes introduce other ethical issues. This is not because technology is naturally wicked; rather, because it lacks a value system of its own it can sometimes learn unethical values from data. It can simply reflect and perpetuate the biases it finds in the world. So, for example, if data shows that women are more likely to default on some loans (perhaps due to the greater chance they have of their careers being interrupted by family responsibilities), blindly following the data might result in women being charged a higher interest rate than men. Human judgment is required to determine if this is the right thing to do.

In the context of advice, the patterns found in past data can potentially be perpetuated by advice that naively reflects a clients' past spending or investment decisions. While they can sometimes be a good starting point to work from, these decisions reflect what has happened in the past, not necessarily what ought to happen in the future. Automated decision-making tools might not be able to see the potential for change and improvement, but human advisers could.

Data insights

So long as the ethical issues can be overcome, data offers the promise of better understanding and predicting client behaviour. In an often-repeated demonstration of this, the retail store, Target, reportedly used data analytics to predict a young customer's pregnancy before her angry father was aware of his pending grand-parenthood. And from an investment perspective, new and alternative datasets might also create investment opportunities by predicting commercial, economic and financial market outcomes.

But these types of data-driven insights are not without their problems. It is easy to simply find patterns in the noise. Technology doesn't intuitively know which of the relationships it finds in the data are meaningful and which are reasonable. Statistical models can sometimes create only the appearance of accuracy and insight. Where these models attempt to predict human behaviour, because of the inherent uncertainty and complexity, they are unlikely to be as accurate as their users might hope; often there is much to client behaviour that is left unexplained. Very precise predictions in noisy environments can simply be very precisely wrong.

As I discussed in my second book, *Cyborg*, while the story of the Target customer appears compelling, having read mixed accounts of it, I'm still not sure if it is true and, if it is true, the reliability of the prediction. For example, did Target 'predict' that 10,000 of their female teenage customers were pregnant, each with a 10% probability of being correct? Was the success story plucked from a much larger pool of failures, all shrouded in a murky cloud of uncertainty? If so, how should an adviser respond if given a similarly uncertain data-driven insight about their clients? Given that decision-making tends to be most effective when people focus on only a handful of the most important pieces of information, in many contexts simply ignoring the insights might be the best approach. There are enough things to distract advisers already; data insights shouldn't add to the noise.

Care must also be taken if advisers rely on insights from client surveys and questionnaires. It is easy to conclude that what clients say about themselves is accurate. But as has been discussed already, psychological research shows they are often mistaken. If clients underestimate the chance they'll be forced to retire early, or underestimate their future medical expenses in retirement, or underestimate their future longevity, then they may need a higher return to meet their future needs than they perceive. Arguably, a portfolio 'optimised' by an algorithmic process to meet a client's perceived needs, but that then leaves a predictable shortfall when one of these types of risks materialises, is not really optimised at all.

Another challenge with capturing the benefits of data analytics is dealing with data errors. Unless they are obvious, it can require humans to spot errors and to assess their consequences. For example, if two databases both include a 'John Smith', but these client accounts have not been linked, is it safe to merge them? Doing so when there are, in reality, two different John Smiths might result in a breach of their privacy, if personal information is then disclosed to their namesake. On the other hand, not combining the accounts when there is only a single John Smith might miss the opportunity to offer him a more streamlined and tailored service. While the real number of John Smiths might be obvious to their adviser, due to multiple incompatible legacy systems, this scenario reflects the current reality for some financial institutions. For at least the near term, advisers will need to be expert at applying their judgment to identify and deal with data errors.

Data offers the promise of advisers better understanding their clients. However, if the weaknesses and uncertainties in using data insights are overlooked, the sense that an adviser gets that they know their client will not be matched with reality. To offset the problems in understanding clients, advisers need to be armed with both psychological insights and with open-ended clarifying questions. Until there are substantial improvements in artificial intelligence, technology is unlikely to ask these types of questions or to understand the responses to them that clients provide.

Technology interfaces

One of the problems discussed previously is how information overload can impact clients. Technology interfaces can help mitigate this problem in ways that hard copy documents cannot. Menus, filters and hyperlinks can be used to layer and chunk information. And technology interfaces can remove clutter by showing only what is personally relevant for each client and only showing it at a time when each client is likely to be most receptive. They can also help motivate action, by presenting clients with one step at a time, by removing small frictions from processes and by showing clients their progress as they move towards their goals. A technology-enabled behavioural toolkit provides advisers with a broad range of options to influence and engage with their clients.

But technology interfaces can also create problems. For example, making it easy for clients to check their investment returns and to switch between investment options, could increase the risk of clients suffering from loss aversion and of over-reacting to short-term volatility. This might be mitigated to some extent if people habituate to seeing short-term losses, but it's probably safer not to have to rely on habituation occurring.

Similarly, the more cashless and effortless payment options become, the less likely clients are to save. For example, as discussed in Chapter 11, there is more 'pain of paying' when making a purchase with cash than with a credit card. While clients might not be aware of how these conveniences can adversely impact them, many would benefit from there being more frictions in these technological tools, rather than fewer.

Rather than becoming unpopular with clients by making information less available and making things more difficult, advisers could at least ensure that the information clients see when they log-in to check their investments is framed in ways that minimise any adverse impacts. The incentive for a client to check their investments daily is likely to be diminished if most days they see a slowly increasing projected income in retirement, say, or a relatively consistent long-term return. When clients risk jeopardising their financial well-being, boring investment returns are better. There are plenty of other ways for clients to get their excitement on-line than from checking their investment returns, just as there are plenty of other ways that advisers can motivate and engage with their clients than by showing them.

Working with automation

In 1995 the Royal Majesty, a cruise ship with 1,200 passengers and fitted with a GPS plotting aid and other sophisticated navigational equipment, grounded off the East coast of the US. The reason for the mishap? The ship's GPS receiver aerial cable had frayed and failed. As a result, the ship's navigational systems had reverted to 'dead reckoning' mode (which doesn't correct for the prevailing tides or winds). Consequently, the ship gradually drifted off course and steered toward a sand bank in shallow water. The crew failed to notice – either that the GPS signal was no longer working, or that the ship was off course. The National Transport Safety Board report on the incident cited crew over-reliance on the navigational system, as well as complacency associated with insufficient monitoring of other sources of navigational information.

The broader conclusion from this type of real-world failure, and from the academic literature on the psychological processes involved, is that while well-designed automated systems and decision-making tools can deliver a raft of benefits, they can sometimes lead to unintended consequences. When advisers work with automated advice tools they need to be careful not to be lulled into complacency.

Several strategies can help to ensure that advisers remain vigilant. One is ensuring accountability; it should be clear who is accountable for any problems. In one experiment involving the use of automated tools in a flight simulator, people who were told that they would have to justify their performance in a debriefing interview after the experiment were more attentive and committed significantly fewer errors.[14] In the case of advice, if the data on which an adviser has relied is incorrect, is it the adviser who is accountable, the adviser's licensee, a technology provider, or perhaps the client?

Providing transparency can also help. The ability to access an advice tool's underlying information and reasoning has the potential to help both advisers and clients to assess how much to rely on a tool's outputs. Related to this is ensuring that advisers receive specific information about a tool's reliability. Research suggests that the more specific the information about the circumstances and ways in which the tool might fail, the better. This can then be a cue for advisers to critically examine relevant assumptions and sensitivities.

From a psychological perspective, the use of technology and data-centric tools as part of a financial advice process is a balancing act. Having too much trust in data and technology risks advisers being blindsided by the types of errors that these tools can be prone to. It also creates the risk of the data providing advisers an overconfident sense that they understand their clients, and of automation lulling them into complacency.

But on the other hand, advisers who are too suspicious of technology risk missing out on many important benefits. Finding the right balance requires calibrating an adviser's use of data and technology, not just with the reliability of the tools, but also with the reliability of the adviser's own un-aided judgments. Both have their strengths, but also their weaknesses.

The risks and benefits of technology and data-driven advice tools vary in different circumstances. Their reliability and scalability are likely to suit less complex client circumstances and advice requirements. In contrast, advisers' own judgments could be superior where client circumstances and requirements are more complex, uncertain and subjective. For the vast range in between, a *'cyborg'* combination of human advisers supported with various advice tools and data could be best.

CONCLUSIONS

This chapter covered three topical issues for advisers: ethics, technology and the role of cognitive diversity. The psychological issues in relation to each provide a mixed bag of risks and benefits. For example, conflicts of interest can create more pervasive problems than many advisers might anticipate, and yet can sometimes help clients achieve their goals. Also, advisers can be supported by teams with diverse perspectives and insights, but if not managed well, these teams can overlook important information and can create frustration and discontent among people whose expertise is ignored. And technology and data can sometimes help advisers to provide appropriate advice, but can also introduce their own set of biases and blind-spots.

The way that conflicts of interest can influence advice shares a lot in common with other decision-making biases. Just as with other biases, conflicts canoperate beyond conscious awareness to prevent an adviser's good intentions from translating into good advice. Is there much difference between two well-

-intentioned advisers, one whose advice is adversely influenced by a conflict and the other by an anchor? The former has a stigma attached that is absent for the latter, but only because we have the wrong mental model about conflicts as necessarily resulting from a corruption. Arguably, any failure to overcome decision-making biases that results in harm to clients should be an ethical concern.

The psychological issues associated with technology and teams also share some commonalities. In some ways, the use of technology and data as part of an advice process is similar to the role played by different individuals in a cognitively diverse team. By 'thinking' quite differently from its human counterparts, technology creates substantial cognitive diversity. It is vastly superior at crunching large datasets, and yet is naïve to human values and motivations. It is like having a teammate with deep numerical and technical expertise, but no real-world experience. This hypothetical person's teammates would be justified in reserving their judgments if he or she failed to support his or her opinions with evidence. Similarly, for technology to be trusted it needs to be at least somewhat transparent. To be a valuable part of an advice team, neither technology nor advisers can afford to hide their strengths and weaknesses within a black box. This chapter attempted to lift the lid on both.

13

CONCLUSIONS & PRACTICAL CHALLENGES

The intention of this book has been to serve as a guide for advisers in how to best apply insights from behavioural finance. The first half of the book showed that doing so can help advisers to better align their advice with clients' risk profiles, to assist clients to set goals and to spend their money in ways that lead to their future happiness, to provide financial literacy education that clients respond to, to coach clients through market cycles, and to invest in portfolios that exploit other investors' decision-making biases. The second half discussed how advisers can help clients to avoid asset allocation and diversification errors, how they can more effectively communicate with and influence clients, how they can assist them to buy residential property and to save for retirement, and how they can mitigate the impacts of conflicts of interest.

Behavioural finance can be used to improve face-to-face conversations, risk questionnaires, fact-finders, advice documents, application forms, websites and investment reports. It can be used to better understand and influence clients, to manage an adviser's own decision-making biases, and to improve organisational cultures and practices. And it can be used with clients ranging from those who are financially illiterate and overwhelmed, to those who think they are too sophisticated to be biased. In these ways, the strategies discussed throughout this book have the potential to improve outcomes for advisers, their clients, and the organisations that advisers represent.

However, there are many ways that seemingly good behavioural strategies can fail. Just as joining a gym can make things worse if the gym-goer then feels justified in eating a chocolate cake, sometimes well-intentioned approaches to applying behavioural insights can backfire. What works in a laboratory won't necessarily work in practice. Whereas labs can control the environment, additional variables apply in the real world. Those additional variables can sometimes be important. This means that what works for one client in one context, won't necessarily work for another client or context. This chapter discusses some of the principles that can help ensure that behavioural finance doesn't fail in implementation.

OVERCOMING BARRIERS TO SUCCESS

Successfully applying behavioural insights requires asking *'what behaviours do which particular clients display, in which contexts, and that lead to what outcomes?'* It requires analysing the psychological and financial problems different people face and the circumstances in which they face them. That analysis is likely to find a web of different decision-making biases that apply to different types of clients, in different ways and with different consequences. Successfully applying behavioural finance needs to balance simplicity with the need to account for these complexities.

Simple but not simplistic

One way overly simplistic approaches can fail is by trying to overcome a particular bias without due regard for its multiple effects. For example, overconfidence can lead investors to being under-diversified, but potentially also to them achieving greater expected returns from choosing higher risk/return asset classes. In this case, it might be only in the context of diversification that a client's overconfidence is a problem. An adviser's approach to this client could therefore focus on helping to overcome their overconfident under-diversification, rather than their overconfidence per se.

Tackling a decision-making bias could also backfire where a bias' effects offset those of another bias. This was discussed in the context of insurance commissions in Chapter 12, where an adviser's incentive to recommend insurance products could offset a client's inability to recognise the risks resulting from their own underinsurance. While this scenario deviates from theoretical ideals in which neither the client nor the adviser is biased, retaining biases can sometimes be a pragmatic way to achieve good outcomes for both.

Another complexity that needs to be addressed is differences between clients. For example, providing detailed investment reports to overconfident clients might lead them to over-react to short-term noise. In contrast, the same reports might lead other clients to feel overwhelmed and to ignore the report entirely. The solution in the first case might involve framing the reports in a way that focuses clients' attention on longer-term and more meaningful comparisons, while in the latter case it might be reducing, layering and chunking the information to reduce clients' cognitive load.

Individual differences don't stop there. The consequences for two different clients who both feel overwhelmed by their respective investment reports could be quite different. There might be little risk for a client who ignores an investment report if their investments are already appropriate for their circumstances and are being automatically rebalanced. However, the risks of doing nothing might be material for other clients. It is for this second group of clients that advisers might need to also apply behavioural strategies that are aimed at motivating action, such as by highlighting a small, easy next step for them to take.

But while there are some complexities to consider, behavioural solutions don't need to be complex. For example, approaches to finely partition clients into discrete risk buckets, or that match investment portfolios to a complex set of future goals, are likely to be spuriously precise. A client's measured risk tolerance can be sensitive to the way questions are framed, investment strategies can be similarly sensitive to assumptions about risk, returns and correlations, and future goals can change over time. Providing advice that combines risk tolerances, future goals and investment forecasts is replete with uncertainty and unpredictability.

In response to uncertainty and unpredictability, decision-making research shows that it is often best to focus on what is most important and on what can be measured and predicted most reliably. For example, advisers could seek to avoid the noise of clients' unstable and context-dependent short-term preferences by designing portfolios to satisfy clients' fuzzy long-term goals. Or they could focus more heavily on the more objectively measurable aspects of a client's risk profile, such as their risk capacity. When dealing with uncertainty, simple strategies are both more easily understood by clients and more likely to meet their needs. There is obviously no point advisers being sophisticated, misunderstood and wrong.

What prevents change?

While advisers are increasing incorporating behavioural insights into their advice processes, the way that some advisers and organisations provide advice is still not well aligned with the psychological evidence about how people think and behave. Unfortunately, each deviation from best practice is an opportunity for a client to make a poor choice that impacts their own financial future. Or it is an opportunity for a client to discontinue an advice relationship that they would otherwise benefit from, or an opportunity for an adviser to inadvertently provide sub-optimal advice.

A number of barriers can prevent advisers from moving to best practice. One of these is where teams have inconsistent knowledge and understanding of behavioural finance. It can be difficult for one person who is well versed in behavioural finance to change their organisation when other advisers in their team, or their legal and compliance colleagues, are still at square one.

When viewed from square one, changing the order in which returns are shown or reducing the amount of information on a page could seem like unnecessary deviations from convention, rather than simple ways to positively influence clients' behaviour. As Davies and Brooks argue, among these people there can be a *'great reluctance to genuinely believe that shielding ourselves, employees, or clients from too much information and reducing the detail and frequency of data is something that should be pursued.'*[1]

By helping teams to become more conversant with the psychological evidence, behavioural finance education and training can help gain broader acceptance for these types of changes. In my experience, as they move from square one and understand more about how clients think and behave, even the much-maligned legal and compliance teams can sometimes be amenable to change. Client engagement should comply with both the law and with how clients think. Hopefully this book is a step in that direction.

But while knowledge of behavioural finance is a good start, often it is not sufficient. Because they are human, advisers who are knowledgeable about behavioural finance will not necessarily see all of its applications. Being human, they could forget to apply it, or could apply it inconsistently, or could fail to apply it to themselves.

Where memories fail, checklists can help. Even better is if behavioural strategies happen automatically and consistently, as a result of having been integrated into templates, business processes or IT systems.

Preparation and practice could also assist. In the context of a difficult client conversation, an adviser being prepared to seamlessly weave behavioural strategies into their conversations could leave more cognitive resources for them to listen to and understand their clients. Ideally, advisers shouldn't be distracted during client conversations by having to mentally rehearse what they are going to say next. A prepared adviser is likely to be a more effective adviser.

Part of the solution could also involve a third party. As I am acutely aware in writing this book, it can be hard to identify ways to improve your own work once you've already looked at it a dozen or more times. For advisers, having another adviser to challenge your thinking, to share their experiences, to introduce alternative ways to frame conversations and to keep you accountable could help. As could having a fresh set of eyes to review client-facing documents through a behavioural lens. In my experience, these reviews often find opportunities that are hiding in plain sight.

Whatever is applied will need to be easy for advisers and their teams to implement. In a busy schedule with multiple competing demands, advisers can have little spare time or surplus cognitive capacity. The more frictions in the process and the more time and effort that are required, the less likely a behavioural strategy will be effectively applied. As Davies and Brooks put it, *'a clever behavioural intervention is of no value if not used.'*[2]

Start, learn and improve
Arguably, advisers shouldn't worry too much about getting it perfect the first

time. As Confucius apparently said, *'better a diamond with a flaw than a pebble without'*. In the parlance of loss aversion, this could be rephrased as *'don't let a disproportionate fear of errors paralyse you into inaction'*. Perfection is an unrealistic expectation; more realistic is expecting a series of small incremental improvements.

Within the bounds of appropriate advice, I advocate advisers being creative in the way they employ behavioural insights, to explore what works for them as much as what works for their clients. When undertaking this type of exploration, one of my super fund clients found that using social norms was more effective for their younger members, whereas using concepts linked to loss aversion worked better for older people. Over time it is this type of learning from feedback that will allow advisers to home in on the specific set of strategies that work with specific types of clients, with specific problems, in specific contexts. The advisers who capture the most benefit will be those who have both the willingness to experiment and the discipline to respond to the associated feedback.

Behavioural finance is not a silver bullet. It should not be anticipated to influence all of the decisions, made by all clients, in all circumstances, all of the time. Depending on the circumstances, I think it's reasonable to expect a well-designed, targeted and implemented strategy to create at least a 10% change in behaviour. The question then becomes, what is the benefit of a 10% change? For example, what would be the long-term benefit for clients of them being comfortable choosing a 10% greater allocation to growth assets? Or the benefit of clients saving 10% more of their income for retirement? In these examples, the benefits could be substantial, particularly for clients with longer investment horizons.

Similarly, what would be the benefit for the adviser's business of clients providing 10% more referrals, or of 10% more prospective clients progressing from their first appointment to their second? And what would be the benefit on the adviser's job satisfaction if 10% more clients accepted their advice? A back-of-the-envelope calculation could be used to estimate the financial and commercial benefits in some cases, whereas in other cases the benefits might be less tangible.

Against these benefits, the costs need to be assessed. What is the cost of changing the way investment options are presented as part of template advice documents, or in application forms? What is the cost of changing how returns are shown in investment reports and on technology platforms? What is the cost of changing how questions are framed in fact-find or risk questionnaires? And what is the cost of a day of team training? For the simplest and easiest behavioural strategies, these up-front costs are likely to be small relative to the long-term benefits. There is often plenty of low-hanging fruit within easy reach.

At the time of writing, Australian financial advisers face a number of challenges. In order to continue to provide advice they need to pass the FASEA exam. Many will also need to complete additional tertiary education. Some will have to restructure, and possibly eliminate, remuneration arrangements on which they have historically relied. And, as an industry generally, advisers need to rebuild the trust that has been called into question. Behavioural finance is relevant for each of these issues. It is part of the FASEA exam and broader education requirements, and it can help advisers to build trust and to deliver valuable advice. Therefore, for advisers looking to understand and apply behavioural finance, there is no better time than now.

NOTES, REFERENCES & FURTHER RESOURCES

'*Applying Behavioural Finance in Australia*' is Simon Russell's first book. As well as advisers, this book is intended for asset managers, asset consultants, super funds and other sophisticated investors.

Readers will notice some areas of overlap with the current book, but will enjoy a more in-depth discussion of some behavioural finance topics, and the introduction of others that were not covered herein.

In particular, 'Applying Behavioural Finance in Australia' will be useful for advisers who build portfolios that seek to capture value, momentum, quality and low-volatility effects; who undertake company, industry or economic forecasts and analyses; or who are responsible for assessing and selecting asset managers.

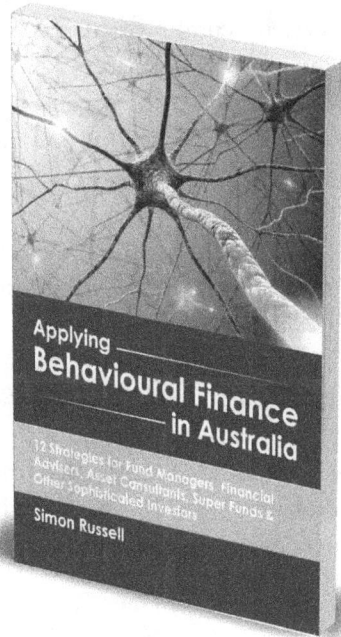

'*Cyborg*' is Simon Russell's second book, written with contributions from Dr Alistair Rew. It applies psychological evidence to the question of how humans, data and technology can best be combined in the context of investment decision-making. It provides far greater depth and breadth to the related discussions included in the current book.

'Cyborg' is a quick read (perhaps 4 hours) and is relevant for professionals who make various strategic and tactical decisions across the investment landscape, including forecasting corporate earnings, deciding which new product to launch, determining what skills to recruit for, or seeking to influence prospective clients.

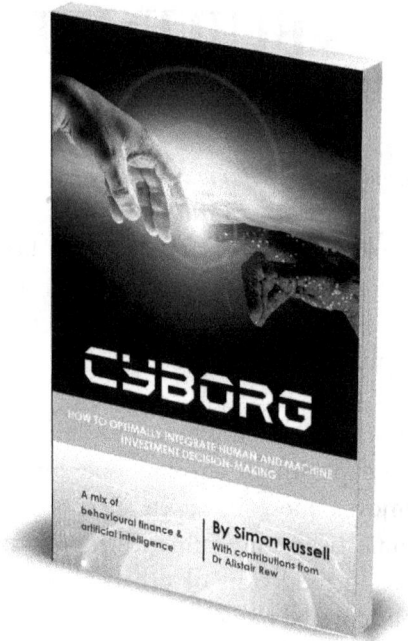

WHAT THIS BOOK IS ABOUT

Notes

1. Russell (2016).

2. For example, see Sah (2018).

References and further reading

Productivity Commission, 2018. "Superannuation: assessing efficiency and competitiveness". No. 91.

Russell, S, 2016. "Why the super industry is like the Titanic". LinkedIn.

Sah, S, 2018. "Conflicts of interest and disclosure". Research Paper. Royal commission into misconduct in the banking, superannuation and financial services industry.

CHAPTER 1: BEHAVIOURAL FINANCE AND THE SUBCONSCIOUS MIND

Notes

1.   For almost every 'irrational' decision-making bias or decision-making shortcut there exists a counterargument for why it might actually be rational or optimal when viewed in a different way, or in a different context. Given this, plus the pejorative nature of the term 'irrational', I tend to be reticent about labelling decisions and behaviours in this way. Certainly, I don't anticipate that many clients would appreciate being told that they were irrational.

2.   Apparently, he has subsequently changed this strategy.

3.   See Moore & Healy (2008) for a review of the components of overconfidence.

4.   Clark et al (2013)

5.   This conclusion excludes investment decisions made for the purpose of rebalancing, creating liquidity, harvesting tax losses, passive investing, etc.

6.   Although the purchase price might still be relevant from a tax perspective.

7.   Soll & Larrick (2009).

References and further reading

Ariely, D, 2008. "Predictably irrational." HarperCollins. New York.

Ariely, D, 2010. "The upside of irrationality." HarperCollins. New York.

Baker, H & Ricciardi, V. (eds), 2014. "Investor Behavior." Wiley. New Jersey. (Chapters 2 & 3)

Clark, G, Duong, H, Gerrans, P, Lajbcygier, P, Moulang, C, Strydom, M, Vaz, J & Wickramanayake, J, 2013. "A Review of Retirement Savings Investment Behaviours: Theory and Evidence". CSIRO-Monash Superannuation Research Cluster Project 3: Better Superannuation Outcomes, Working Paper.

Kahneman, D, 2011. "Thinking fast and slow." Penguin Books. London.

Lewis, M, 2017. "The undoing project." WW Norton & Co. New York.

Moore, D, Tenney, E & Haran, U, 2016. "Overprecision in judgment" in "The Wiley Blackwell Handbook of Judgment and Decision Making", Keren, G & Wu, G (eds). Wiley-Blackwell. New Jersey.

Moore, D & Healy, P, 2008. "The trouble with overconfidence". Psychological Review, 115 (2), 502-517

Montier, J, 2007. "Behavioural investing." Wiley Finance. West Sussex. England.

Ratey, J, 2003. "A user's guide to the brain." Time Warner Books UK. London.

Russell, S, 2015. "The financial advice industry needs more Jedis, but fewer mind tricks." Professional Planner.

Russell, S, 2016. "Applying Behavioural Finance in Australia." Publicious. Melbourne. (Preface)

Soll, J & Larrick, R, 2009. "Strategies for revising judgment: how (and how well) people use others' opinions." Journal of Experimental Psychology, 35 (3), 780-805

Thaler, R, 2016. "Misbehaving". WW Norton & Co. New York.

Thaler, R & Sunstein, C, 2009. "Nudge." Penguin. New York.

CHAPTER 2: RISK TOLERANCE, PERCEPTIONS & PROFILING

Notes

1.   ASIC (2017) states that *'we expect that processes for complying with the best interests duty will ensure that, within the subject matter of the advice sought by the client: (a) the scope of the advice includes all the issues that must be considered for the advice to meet the client's objectives, financial situation and needs (including the client's tolerance for risk)'.*

2.   Ignoring tax consequences.

3.   Consistent with this, in a report on risk profiling, the UK's Financial Services Authority argued that communicating risks with clear language as well as through graphical representations could aid clients' understanding (Financial Services Authority, 2011).

4.   See discussion in Benartzi (2012).

5.   This is quite different from the 'revealed preferences' that some risk profiling tools try to measure by assessing people's decisions in various hypothetical scenarios.

6.   Baker & Ricciardi (2014).

7.   Barber & Odean (2001).

8.   Clark et al (2013).

9.   Baker & Ricciardi (2014).

10.   Adams & Funk (2011), Sheedy (2017).

11.   Baker & Ricciardi (2014).

12.   Benartzi (2010).

13.   Baker & Ricciardi (2014).

14.   Clark et al (2013).

15.   Financial Services Authority (2011).

16.   Davies (2017)

References and further reading

Adams, R & Funk, P, 2011. "Beyond the glass ceiling: does gender matter?" Management Science, 58 (2)

ASIC, 2017. "Licensing: Financial product advisers – conduct and disclosure." Regulatory Guide 175.

Baker, H & Ricciardi, V. (eds), 2014. "Investor Behavior." Wiley. New Jersey. (Chapters 6, 7 & 18)

Barber, B & Odean, T, 2001. "Boys will be boys: gender, overconfidence, and common stock investment." Quarterly Journal of Economics, 116 (1), 261-292.

Barnea, A, Cronqvist, H & Siegel, S, 2010. "Nature or nurture: what determines investor behavior?" Fourth Singapore International Conference on Finance 2010 Paper.

Benartzi, S, 2010. "Behavioral finance and the post-retirement crisis". A Response to the Department of the Treasury/Department of Labor request for information regarding lifetime income options for participants and beneficiaries in retirement plans.

Benartzi, S, 2012. "Save more tomorrow." Penguin. New York.

Clark, G, Duong, H, Gerrans, P, Lajbcygier, P, Moulang, C, Strydom, M, Vaz, J & Wickramanayake, J, 2013. "A Review of Retirement Savings Investment Behaviours: Theory and Evidence". CSIRO-Monash Superannuation Research Cluster Project 3: Better Superannuation Outcomes, Working Paper.

Davies, G, 2017. "New vistas in risk profiling." CFA Institute Research Foundation Briefs (3), 1-23.

Financial Services Authority, 2011. "Assessing suitability: establishing the risk a customer is willing and able to take and making a suitable investment selection." Finalised guidance.

Gigerenzer, G, 2015. "Risk savvy". Penguin. London.

Kahneman, D, 2011. "Thinking fast and slow." Penguin Books. London. (Chapter 13)

Kahneman, D & Riepe, M, 1998. "Aspects of investor psychology". Journal of Portfolio Management, 24 (4), 52-65.

Russell, S, 2017. "Can you spot the difference?" LinkedIn.

Sheedy, E, 2017. "Senior female bankers don't conform to stereotypes and are just as ready to take risks". The Conversation.

Weber, E & Klement, J, 2018. "Risk tolerance and circumstances". CFA Institute Research Foundation Briefs, 4 (2).

CHAPTER 3: HAPPINESS, MOTIVATION & FUTURE GOALS

Notes

1.   Kahneman (2011).

2.   Kahneman (2011) reports that the emotional experience of American women of the time spent with their children was slightly less enjoyable than doing housework.

3.   High incomes can still lead to greater satisfaction when people reflect on their lives.

4.   Baker & Ricciardi (2014).

5.   Albeit it tends to take 5-7 years before people fully adapt to their higher incomes (Baker & Ricciardi, 2014).

6.   Subsequently studies have failed to replicate this original finding but have supported the different types of thinking used by silver and bronze medallists, *'with silver medallists being more preoccupied by thoughts of how things could have been better'* (Busch, 2019).

7.   Stephens-Davidowitz (2017).

8.   Dunn et al. (2011).

9.   Ariely (2010).

10. Whillans (2019).

11. This is just one definition of 'purpose'; researchers use a range of others.

12. Rainey (2014).

13. Rainey (2014).

14. Baker & Ricciardi (2014).

15. Dunn et al (2011).

16. Locke & Latham (2016).

17. Kahneman (2011).

18. Brooks et al (2015).

19. Brooks et al (2015).

20. However, research shows that people are more likely to save for retirement when their retirement is expressed as a precise date, rather than as a vague range (Ariely & Kreisler, 2017). This suggests that a financial plan that is based on achieving fuzzy goals might best be communicated with some precision. For example: *'your goal is to retire on your 60th birthday, being 2 July 2034, but you are happy to work a couple of years longer if needed'*.

21. Brooks et al (2015).

22. A similar quote has also been (incorrectly, it appears) attributed to Keynes.

23. Dunn et al (2011). In relation to savouring the good things in life, I try to do this by closing my eyes while I consume good food and good music, in an attempt to overcome the dominance of visual processing and focus on other relevant sensory inputs. I also explicitly (verbally) note when I experience a warm sunny day, in an attempt to focus my attention on it. Subjectively, both strategies seem to be effective at lifting my mood and enjoyment of the moment.

References and further reading

Ariely, D, 2010. "The upside of irrationality." HarperCollins. New York. (Chapters 2 & 6)

Ariely, D, & Kreisler, J, 2017. "Dollars and sense." HarperCollins. New York.

Baker, H & Ricciardi, V. (eds), 2014. "Investor Behavior." Wiley. New Jersey. (Chapters 9 & 10)

Brooks P, Davies, G & Smith, R, 2015. "A behavioral perspective on goal-based investing." Investment & Wealth Monitor, 16-37.

Busch, B, 2019. "Are bronze medallists really happier than silver medallists? New insights from the 2016 Olympics". The British Psychological Society.

Dunn, E, Gilbert D & Wilson, T, 2011. "If money doesn't make you happy, then you probably aren't spending it right." Journal of Consumer Psychology, 21(2), 115-125.

Gilbert, D, & Wilson, T, 2000. "Miswanting: Some problems in the forecasting of future affective states." In Thinking and feeling: The role of affect in social cognition, edited by Forgas, J, 178-197. Cambridge University Press, Cambridge.

Holmes, C, 2018. "What kind of happiness do people value most." Harvard Business Review.

Kahneman, D, 2011. "Thinking fast and slow." Penguin Books. London. (Chapters 35-38)

Locke, E & Latham, G, 2016. "New directions in goal setting theory." Current Directions in Psychological Science, 15 (5), 265-268.

Rainey, L, 2014. "The search for purpose in life: an exploration of purpose, the search process, and purpose anxiety." University of Pennsylvania.

Stephens-Davidowitz, S, 2017. "Everybody lies". Boomsbury Publishing. London.

Whillans, A, 2019. "Time for happiness: why the pursuit of money isn't bringing you happiness – and what will". Harvard Business Review.

CHAPTER 4: THE (OFTEN OVERSTATED) ROLE OF FINANCIAL LITERACY

Notes

1.   Willis (2008). Other reviews of the relevant literature have similarly concluded that the evidence is mixed at best.

2.   For example, ASIC (2014) defines financial literacy as: *'a combination of financial knowledge, skills, attitudes and behaviours necessary to make sound financial decisions, based on personal circumstances, to improve financial wellbeing.'*

3.   ANZ (2015).

4.   Wilkins & Lass (2018).

5.   Baker & Ricciardi (2014).

6.   See Agarwal et al (2009), and the associated discussion in Hastings et al (2013). Also, in an Australian context, Wilkins & Lass (2018).

7.   See Baker & Ricciardi (2014).

8.   Fernandes et al (2013).

9.   ANZ (2018).

10. Fernandes et al (2013).

11. Fernandes et al (2013).

12. Boser (2017).

13. Baker & Ricciardi (2014).

14. Benartzi (2012).

15. Benartzi (2012), Pink (2018).

16. Pink (2018), who in turn quoted Dai, Milkman & Riis.

17. Hastings et al (2013).

18. Hira (2010).

References and further reading

Agarwal, S, Driscoll, J, Gabaix, X & Laibson, D, 2009. "The age of reason: financial decisions over the life-cycle with implications for regulation." Brookings Papers on Economic Activity, 2, 51-117.

ANZ, 2015. "ANZ survey of adult financial literacy in Australia". The Social Research Centre.

ANZ, 2018. "Financial wellbeing: a survey of adults in Australia".

ASIC, 2011. "Financial literacy and behaviour change." Report 230.

ASIC, 2014. "National financial literacy strategy, 2014-2017". Report 403.

Baker, H & Ricciardi, V. (eds), 2014. "Investor Behavior." Wiley. New Jersey. (Chapter 4)

Benartzi, S, 2012. "Save more tomorrow." Penguin. New York.

Boser, U, 2017. "Learn better". Rodale Books, Pennsylvannia.

Clark, G, Duong, H, Gerrans, P, Lajbcygier, P, Moulang, C, Strydom, M, Vaz, J & Wickramanayake, J, 2013. "A review of retirement savings investment behaviours: theory and evidence". CSIRO-Monash Superannuation Research Cluster Project 3: Better Superannuation Outcomes, Working Paper.

Fernandes, D, Lynch, J & Netemeyer, R, 2013. "Financial literacy, financial education and downstream financial behaviors." Management Science.

Hastings, J, Madrian, B & Skimmyhorn, W, 2013. "Financial literacy, financial education, and economic outcomes." Annual Review of Economics, 5, 347-373

Hira, T, 2010. "The NEFE quarter century project: implications for researchers, educators, policy makers from a quarter century of financial education". National Endowment for Financial Education.

Pink, D, 2018. "When: the scientific secrets of perfect timing". The Text Publishing Company, Melbourne.

Wilkins, R & Lass, I, 2018. "The household, income and labour dynamics in Australia survey: selected findings from waves 1 to 16." Melbourne Institute.

Willis, L, 2008. "Evidence and ideology in assessing the effectiveness of financial literacy education". University of Pennsylvania Law School, Faculty Scholarship, Paper 197.

CHAPTER 5: MARKET CYCLES & THE BEHAVIOURAL ROLLER-COASTER

Notes

1. Baker & Ricciardi (2014).

2. But people don't respond to all losses in this way. In fact, in some cases investors who suffer losses become more risk-seeking rather than risk-averse. This could occur, for example, when an investor purchases a share that declines in value. In this case, the prospect of recovering the losses and breaking even tends to hold more psychological weight than the potential for further losses.

3. See Kahneman (2011) for a good review of subconscious emotional effects on decision-making.

4. Baker & Ricciardi (2014).

5. See 'Applying Behavioural Finance in Australia' (Russell, 2016) for a more detailed discussion on why the DCA strategy tends not to be profitable.

6. Benartzi (2012).

7. For a discussion, see Cabinet Office (2010).

References and further reading

Baker, H & Ricciardi, V. (eds), 2014. "Investor Behavior." Wiley. New Jersey. (Chapters 15, 19 & 24)

Benartzi, S, 2012. "Save more tomorrow." Penguin. New York.

Benartzi, S & Thaler, R, 1995. "Myopic loss aversion and the equity premium puzzle." Quarterly Journal of Economics, February.

Cabinet Office, 2010. "MINDSPACE: influencing behaviour through public policy". Discussion document.

Crosby, D, 2016. "The laws of wealth: psychology and the secret to investing success". Harriman House, Hampshire, UK.

Russell, S, 2016. "Applying Behavioural Finance in Australia." Publicious. Melbourne. (Chapters 7 & 11)

Russell, S, 2018. "A very simple thing some investment professionals are not doing". LinkedIn.

CHAPTER 6: EXPLOITING BEHAVIOURAL BIASES IN MARKETS

Notes

1. Basu (1977).

2. The forecasts used in this analysis were the sell-side EPS forecasts for companies listed on the ASX. These companies were split into cohorts based on their historical EPS growth rates. Companies in the cohorts with the highest historical EPS growth rates experienced the greatest gap between their (lower than historically achieved) forecast EPS growth, and the subsequently realised (even lower) actual EPS growth for the same periods. This is as expected, as more extreme events are likely to be more greatly influenced by mean reversion.

3. Of course, one of the uncertainties that is relevant for value stocks is whether they will be 'disrupted' by, say, competitors using new technologies or new business models. See Russell (2018) for a discussion of why the often-quoted expectations of revered tech-industry heavy-weights are likely to be wrong.

4. Kahneman (2011). Investors are particularly likely to overreact to low probability events that have high salience (ie that are highly imaginable, vivid and tangible) and that are emotionally engaging.

5. Kahneman (2011).

6. See Russell (2016) for a more detailed discussion of the disposition effect and how it drives short-term momentum.

7. For relevant empirical research, see Russell (2016).

8. Blitz et al (2014).

9. It isn't as important for sell-decisions because when it comes to selling, unless they are taking short positions, most investors' attention is necessarily focused on the typically much more limited pool of stocks in their portfolio.

10. Malmendier and Tate (2008).

11. Some investors already appear to be interpreting management signals in this way. For example, Malmendier and Tate (2008) find that investors are more sceptical about bid announcements made by optimistic CEOs.

12. The analysis can be extended further. A third-order thinker would choose two thirds of 22, and so on. This reasoning can be taken to its logical conclusion, where each investor chooses tinier and tinier fractions, ultimately approaching zero. But when people are given this exercise the results show that few provide an answer of zero. Many stop at one or two orders of thinking. And if some investors stop at these levels, it pays for other investors to stop before zero too, even if they have considered the logicality of the infinite regress. For a discussion, see Montier (2007).

13. Frazzini, Kabiller & Pedersen (2013).

14. Bender et al (2013)

15. This might not necessarily be the case, however. Momentum strategies tend to hold stocks that are going up and sell those that are going down, meaning that transactions might create a tax advantage for clients by bringing forward the realisation of capital losses and deferring capital gains. The tax outcome will also depend on clients' tax position and investment structure.

References and further reading

Baker, H & Ricciardi, V. (eds), 2014. "Investor Behavior." Wiley. New Jersey. (Chapters 15, 20 & 27)

Basu, A & O'Shea, L, 2014. "The predictive ability of P/E ratio: evidence from Australia and New Zealand." 2014 Financial Markets & Corporate Governance Conference.

Basu, S, 1977. "Investment performance of common stocks in relation to the price-earnings ratios: a test of the efficient markets hypothesis". Journal of Finance, Vol 32, No.3. 663-682.

Bender, J, Briand, R, Melas, D & Subramanian, R, 2013. "Foundations of factor investing". MSCI Research Insight.

Blitz, D, Falkenstein, E & Van Vliet, P, 2014. "Explanations for the volatility effect: an overview based on the CAPM assumptions." The Journal of Portfolio Management, Spring, 61-76.

Frazzini, A, Kabiller, D & Pedersen, L, 2013. "Buffett's alpha". AQR Capital Management.

Malmendier, U, & Tate, G, 2008. "Who makes acquisitions? CEO overconfidence and the market's reaction". Journal of Financial Economics, 89, 20–43

Montier, J, 2007. "Behavioural investing." Wiley Finance. West Sussex. England.

Russell, S, 2016. "Applying Behavioural Finance in Australia." Publicious. Melbourne. (Chapters 1, 4, 5, 7 & 12)

Russell, S, 2017. "What investment puzzle is hidden in your pizza?" LinkedIn.

Russell, S, 2017b. "How to spot the subconscious CEO." LinkedIn

Russell, S, 2018. "Why Bill Gates is (probably) wrong". LinkedIn.

CHAPTER 7: MISSING A FREE LUNCH? BIASES IN DIVERSIFICATION & ASSET ALLOCATION

Notes

1. Foad (2010).

2. A caution here is that some evidence suggests that, for Australian investors at least, the currency exposure associated with international equities can actually reduce the volatility of investment returns. This is because the Australian dollar tends to correlate with international equity markets, thereby dampening the volatility of investors' returns in Australian dollar-terms. However, this conclusion doesn't necessarily hold for other classes of international investments, such as bonds. Considering currency risk in isolation from these broader investment considerations is another example of how 'narrow framing' can sometimes lead investors to the wrong conclusions.

3. Having a strategic asset allocation target for each country would, of course, be unwieldy. Once established, the results could be aggregated for practical purposes.

4. Melas, Briand and Urwin (2011) comment on how these risk factors are often overlooked: 'the institutional asset allocation process continues to focus more heavily on the selection of active managers than the selection and combination of risk premia, despite growing evidence that risk premia contribute more to the long-term performance of the portfolio.'

5. Although, of course, they may also hold other investments that provide diversification. Investment Trends (2015).

6. When I started giving people this question, I noticed that a small number of them chose a range of 1 metre to a billion light years, or similar. They appeared to believe that they had outsmarted the question and were assuredly correct. In response I have since added a clarification that their range should not be so wide that it captures every possibility, as that would equate to a 100% confidence range, rather than 90%. In effect, the person who sets the bottom of their range at 1 metre is suggesting that they believe there is a 5% chance that the moon is less than 1 metre away from the earth. They should make sure to duck as it zooms overhead! At the other extreme I had a participant who said that she didn't need to give me a range because she knew the correct answer. She was an amateur astronomer, she informed me. She knew that the moon was one light-second away from the earth and that distance light travels in a second is 300,000kms. I asked her to humour me nonetheless, and to give me a range. She relented, and provided a range of 290,000 to 310,000kms. The actual answer is approximately 384,000kms.

7. De Bondt (1998).

8. Wilkins & Lass (2018).

9. This was the case for 89% De Bondt's investors and 67% of a group of Australian investors studied by Durand et al (2008).

10.   De Bondt (1998). This also suggests why factors other than beta have been found to predict investment returns. Despite its theoretical primacy in portfolio construction, clearly some investors are not focused on beta as a key measure of risk.

11.   While this suggests that most people need not worry about the correlation of their employment income with their investment returns, for some clients the correlation might be particularly relevant. People working in, say, the wealth management, investment management or real estate industries should expect a higher than average correlation. As advisers would be aware, there can also be cause for concern when employees make disproportionately large equity investments in their employer. While the US pension system differs from the Australian model, high profile cases from the US, such as Enron employees investing their retirement savings in Enron shares, have highlighted this risk.

12.   Benatzi & Thaler (2001). However, while naïve diversification can sometimes result in poor client outcomes, decision-making research shows that simplified decision-making rules are not always inferior. For example, when constructing share portfolios, the 1/n heuristic can create a superior risk/return combination than traditional approaches, such as using market capitalisation weighting.

13.   He has reportedly changed his approach since that time, stating that *'now I don't do that ... I split my money among asset classes, like efficient portfolios I have seen.'* (http://jasonzweig.com/what-harry-markowitz-meant/)

14.   Those who allocate 0% typically refer to the fact that Bob already has a large allocation to growth assets as a result of his property ownership. The median allocation to growth is typically around 65%.

15.   The difference between advisers and non-advisers is consistent with research that shows that a person's knowledge has a mediating effect on their sense of cognitive overload, and therefore on their use of mental shortcuts.

References and further reading

Baker, H & Nofsinger, J (eds), 2010. "Behavioral Finance: investors, corporations and markets". John Wiley & Sons, New Jersey. (Chapter 15)

Baker, H & Ricciardi, V. (eds), 2014. "Investor Behavior." Wiley. New Jersey. (Chapter 22)

Benartzi, S & Thaler, R, 2001. "Naive diversification strategies in defined contribution saving plans." The American Economic Review, 91 (1), 79-98

De Bondt, W, 1998. "A portrait of the individual investor". European Economic Review, 42, 831-844.

Durand, R, Newby, R & Sanghani, J, 2008. "An intimate portrait of the individual investor". Journal of Behavioral Finance, 9 (4), 193-208.

Foad, H, 2010. "Familiarity bias", in "Behavioral Finance: investors, corporations and markets". (Baker & Nofsinger eds). John Wiley & Sons, New Jersey.

Foerster, S, Linnainmaa, J, Melzer, B & Previtero, A, 2014. "Retail financial advice: does one size fit all?" National Bureau of Economic Research. Working Paper 20712.

Ibbotson, R, Milevsky, M, Chen, P & Zhu, K, 2007. "Lifetime financial advice: human capital, asset allocation, and insurance." Research Foundation of CFA Institute.

Kahneman, D, 2011. "Thinking fast and slow." Penguin Books. London. (Chapter 5)

Investment Trends, 2015. "2015 Self Managed Super Fund Survey".

Melas, D, Briand, R, Urwin, R, 2011. "Harvesting risk premia with strategy indices – from today's alpha to tomorrow's beta". MSCI Research Insights.

Russell, S, 2016. "Applying Behavioural Finance in Australia." Publicious. Melbourne. (Chapter 6)

Wilkins, R & Lass, I, 2018. "The household, income and labour dynamics in Australia survey: selected findings from waves 1 to 16." Melbourne Institute.

CHAPTER 8: ADVISING OVERCONFIDENT INVESTORS

Notes

1. Plous (1993).

2. Klein & Helweg-Larsen (2002).

3. Dunning et al (2004).

4. Ariely (2010).

5. Moore, et al (2016).

6. It is actually logically possible that 80% of people are above average at something. One of my favourite examples is that the vast majority of people have an above average number of legs; most people have 2, a few have 1 or zero, making the average something slightly less than 2. However, for this to apply, it relies on there being a negatively skewed distribution of outcomes. In contrast, arguably the distribution of investment skill is positively skewed (ie lots of people with low skills and only a small number with high skills). In contrast to the example with the number of legs, this means that a large majority of investors could actually be below average.

7. Source: Jonathan Scholes, financial adviser, personal communication.

8. Kahneman & Klein (2009).

9. Kahneman (2011).

10. For example: Barber & Odean (2001).

11. Moore et al. (2016).

12. At the time of writing investors were able to claim a 50% reduction in their capital gains tax if they held a stock for more than 12 months. Additional costs were not included in these calculations, such as the compounded effect of bringing forward tax payments, any potential loss of franking credits from more frequent trading, as well the impact of additional transaction costs and buy-sell spreads.

13. Actually, this wider range may still under-estimate uncertainty. Research shows that in some cases the appropriate ranges for share market estimates need to be 4 times wider than people expect.

14. For example, Goyal and Wahal (2008) found that pension funds hire investment managers after those investment managers achieve large positive excess returns, but that this return-chasing behaviour does not deliver positive excess returns thereafter. Similar evidence exists for retail investors.

15. Kahneman (2011).

16. Baker & Ricciardi (2014).

17. Sharpe (1975).

18. Campbell & Shiller (1998).

19. Tetlock (2005), and Tetlock & Gardner (2015).

20. Ptak (2012).

21. In some cases, taking a longer view can increase the probability of being correct. For example, it's easier to forecast the average annual return for equity markets over the next 10 years, than it is over the following 12 months. However, because of the effects of compounding and the sensitivity to the rate of return, it is still difficult to predict the dollar outcome from a portfolio in 10 years-time. It is even more difficult over the longer periods that advisers face when working with clients about their long-term financial objectives. For example, increasing the return from 8% to 9% makes little difference over 5 years ($100 turns into $147, versus $154, ie a 5% difference), but over 30 years the difference becomes much larger ($1,006 versus $1,327, ie a 32% difference). As a demonstration of the difficulty of making these types of long-term estimates, I asked a group of about 30 mostly financial advisers and asset managers to create a 90% confidence interval for a problem that required them estimating a long-term compounded financial outcome. Theoretically 27 people (90% of 30 people) should have found the answer fell within their 90% confidence range. However, not a single person did. No-one was even close! Estimating long-term non-linear outcomes is difficult for clients, but also not easy for advisers.

22. Kinniry et al (2015).

References and further reading

Ariely, D, 2010. "The upside of irrationality." HarperCollins. New York. (Chapters 3 & 4)

Baker, H & Ricciardi, V. (eds), 2014. "Investor Behavior." Wiley. New Jersey. (Chapter 25)

Barber, B & Odean, T, 2001. "Boys will be boys: gender, overconfidence, and common stock investment." Quarterly Journal of Economics, 116 (1), 261-292.

Campbell, J, & Shiller, R, 1988, "Stock Prices, Earnings, and Expected Dividends". Journal of Finance, 43(3), 661–676.

Dunning, D, Heath, C & Suls, J, 2004. "Flawed self-assessments". Psychological Science in the Public Interest, 5 (3), 69-106.

Goyal, A & Wahal, S, 2008. "The selection and termination of investment management firms by plan sponsors". The Journal of Finance, 63 (4), 1805-1847.

Kahneman, D, 2011. "Thinking fast and slow." Penguin Books. London. (Part 3)

Kahneman, D & Riepe, M, 1998. "Aspects of investor psychology". Journal of Portfolio Management, 24 (4), 52-65.

Kahneman, D & Klein, G, 2009. "Conditions for intuitive expertise: a failure to disagree". American Psychologist, 64 (6), 515-526.

Kinniry, F, Jaconetti, C, Chin, P, Polanco, F & Zilbering, Y, 2015."Putting a value on your value: Quantifying Vanguard Adviser's Alpha". Vanguard Research

Klein, C & Helweg-Larsen, M, 2002. "Perceived control and the optimistic bias: a meta-analytic review." Psychology and Health, 17 (4), 437-446.

Moore, D & Healy, P, 2008. "The trouble with overconfidence". Psychological Review, 115 (2), 502-517.

Moore, D, Tenney, E & Haran, U, 2016. "Overprecision in judgment" in "The Wiley Blackwell Handbook of Judgment and Decision Making", Keren, G & Wu, G (eds). Wiley-Blackwell. New Jersey.

Montier, J, 2007. "Behavioural investing." Wiley Finance. West Sussex. England.

Ptak, J, 2012. "In practice: tactical funds miss their chance." Morningstar.

Plous, S, 1993. "The Psychology of Judgment and Decision Making". McGraw-Hill, New York.

Russell, S, 2016. "Applying Behavioural Finance in Australia." Publicious. Melbourne. (Chapters 2, 3 & 8)

Sharpe, W, 1975. "Likely gains from market timing." Financial Analysts Journal, 31 (2), 60-69.

Silver, N, 2012. "The signal and the noise: why most predictions fail – but some don't." Penguin, London.

Tetlock, P, 2005. "Expert political judgment." Princeton University Press. New Jersey.

Tetlock, P & Gardner, D, 2015. "Superforecasting: the art and science of prediction." Random House Books. London.

CHAPTER 9: RESIDENTIAL REAL ESTATE; THE MOST BIASED ASSET CLASS?

Notes

1. For example, in a report for the Reserve Bank of Australia, Fox & Tulip (2014) found that *'if real house prices grow at their historical average pace, then owning a home is about as expensive as renting,'* but that *'if prices grow more slowly … the average home buyer would be financially better off renting.'* These results are an average, with individual differences creating further complexities: *'a household expecting historically average capital appreciation will be better off owning than renting if it values home ownership for non-financial reasons, if it expects to remain in the house for longer than average, or if it has substantial financial savings that it cannot profitably invest elsewhere.'*

2. Fagundes (2017).

3. Gilbert & Wilson (2000).

4. Christian & Griffiths (2016).

5. Ignoring all of the complexities that are normally associated with recruitment.

6. Peng (2013).

7. Morgan et al (2018).

8. Cialdini (1984).

9. The anchoring effect didn't work entirely in favour of the auctioneer. As the bidding progressed, the bids themselves created lower anchors. To ensure that bidders weren't distracted by these lower anchors, part way though the auction the auctioneer reminded bidders of the $2 million figure. One way to overcome the effects of a low anchor is with the use of a high one.

10. Northcraft & Neale (1987).

11. The auctioneer used other aspects of social influence well too. For example, he nodded and smiled as he asked for higher bids. Because people's *'mirror neurones'* reflect the actions of others, it is almost as if bidders were smiling and nodding in response. From smiling and nodding, it is just a short step to bidding.

12. See Thaler (1998).

13. Brain imaging studies also show that selling goods that one would normally use activates regions of the brain that are associated with disgust and pain (Kahneman, 2011).

14. Gilbert & Wilson (2000).

15. Kahneman (2011).

16. Baker & Ricciardi (2014).

17. Baker & Ricciardi (2014).

References and further reading

Baker, H & Ricciardi, V. (eds), 2014. "Investor Behavior." Wiley. New Jersey. (Chapter 30)

Christian, B & Griffiths, T, 2016. "Algorithms to live by: the computer science of human decisions." Henry Holt, New York.

Cialdini, R, 1984. "Influence." HarperCollins. New York.

Fagundes, D, 2017. "Buying Happiness: Property, Acquisition, and Subjective Well-Being," 58 Wm. & Mary L. Rev. 1851

Fox, R & Tulip, P, 2014. "Is housing overvalued". Reserve Bank of Australia, Research Discussion Paper, RDP 2014-06.

Genesove, D & Mayer, C, 2010. "Loss aversion and seller behavior: evidence from the housing market", Quarterly Journal of Economics 116, 1233-60.

Gilbert, D, & Wilson, T, 2000. "Miswanting: Some problems in the forecasting of future affective states." In Thinking and feeling: The role of affect in social cognition, edited by Forgas, J, 178-197. Cambridge University Press, Cambridge.

Kahneman, D, 2011. "Thinking fast and slow." Penguin Books. London. (Chapters 11 & 13)

Morgan, V, Bates, C & Russell S, 2018. "The elephant in the room property podcast: Episode 1 – who is really making the decisions when you bid at auction."

Northcraft, G & Neale, M, 1987. "Experts, amateurs, and real estate: an anchoring-and-adjustment perspective on property pricing decisions." Organizational Behavior and Human Decision Processes, 39, 84-97.

Peng, S, 2013. "Maximizing and satificing in decision-making dyads". Wharton Research Scholars, 98.

Thaler, R, 1998. "Anomalies: the winner's curse". The Journal of Economic Perspectives, 2 (1), 191-202.

Thaler, R, 1999. "Mental accounting matters". Journal of Behavioral Decision Making, 12, 183-206.

CHAPTER 10: THE PSYCHOLOGY OF SAVING & RETIREMENT PLANNING

Notes

1. For example, in one US study employers offering to match every dollar that their employees contributed to their retirement account with an additional contribution of $1.50 (rather than with just 25c), raised average contributions by only 0.2 to 0.3% of income. This is despite the arrangement providing investors with an immediate guaranteed 150% return on their investment, as well as the long-term benefits of compounded investment returns thereafter (Choi et al, 2017).

2. Dunn et al (2011).

3. Benartzi (2010).

4. Thaler (1999).

5. Such a budget might also make the amount spent in each category more salient, facilitating trade-offs being made between broad expenditure categories.

6. Benartzi (2012).

7. Benartzi (2012).

8. Martin et al (2014).

9. Dunn et al (2011).

10. Benartzi (2012).

11. Ariely & Kreisler (2018).

12. The salience of insurance premiums is likely to be reduced in some cases, such as where they are automatically deducted from a client's superannuation.

13. An obvious exception is the insurance that some people receive by default through their superannuation, although the amount received in this way is likely to be inadequate to cover some clients' requirements.

14. Brooks et al (2015).

15. Mitchell & Utkus (2003).

16. Benartzi (2010).

17. Benartzi (2010), Agarwal et al (2009).

18. Agarwal et al (2009).

19. Benartzi (2010).

20. Williams (2017)

21. Quoidbach et al, (2013).

22. Dunning et al, (2004).

23. Mitchell & Utkus (2003).

References and further reading

Agarwal, S, Driscoll, J, Gabaix, X & Laibson, D, 2009. "The age of reason: financial decisions over the life-cycle with implications for regulation." Brookings Papers on Economic Activity, 2, 51-117.

Ariely, D & Kreisler, J, 2018. "Dollars and sense: how we misthink money and how to spend smarter." Harper Collins, New York.

Baker, H & Ricciardi, V. (eds), 2014. "Investor Behavior." Wiley. New Jersey. (Chapter 16)

Behavioural Insights Team., 2012. "EAST: four simple ways to apply behavioural insights". Discussion document.

Benartzi, S, 2010. "Behavioral finance and the post-retirement crisis". A Response to the Department of the Treasury/Department of Labor request for information regarding lifetime income options for participants and beneficiaries in retirement plans.

Benartzi, S, 2012. "Save more tomorrow." Penguin. New York.

Brooks P, Davies, G & Smith, R, 2015. "A behavioral perspective on goal-based investing." Investment & Wealth Monitor, 16-37.

Cabinet Office, 2010. "MINDSPACE: influencing behaviour through public policy". Discussion document.

Choi, J, Haisley, E, Kurkoski, J & Massey, C, 2017. "Small cues change savings choices". Journal of Economic Behavior & Organization, 142, 378-395.

Collins, N & Miller, L, 1994. "Self-disclosure and liking: a meta-analytic review." Psychological Bulletin, 116 (3), 457-475.

Cronqvist, H & Siegel, S, 2015. "The origins of savings behavior". Journal of Political Economy, 123 (1), 123-169.

Dunn, E, Gilbert D & Wilson, T, 2011. "If money doesn't make you happy, then you probably aren't spending it right." Journal of Consumer Psychology, 21(2), 115-125.

Dunning, D, Heath, C & Suls, J, 2004. "Flawed self-assessments". Psychological Science in the Public Interest, 5 (3), 69-106.

Ibbotson, R, Milevsky, M, Chen, P & Zhu, K, 2007. "Lifetime financial advice: human capital, asset allocation, and insurance." Research Foundation of CFA Institute.

Irving, K, 2009. "Overcoming short-termism: mental time travel, delayed gratification and how not to discount the future." Australian Accounting Review, 51 (19).

Kidd, S, 2009. "Determinants of annuity demand: a literature survey". Challenger's third submission to the Review of Australia's Future Tax System.

Martin, S, Goldstein, N & Cialdini, R, 2014. "The small big: small changes that spark big influence." Grand Central Publishing. New York.

Mitchell, O & Utkus, S, 2003. "Lessons from behavioral finance for retirement plan design." Pension Research Council Working Paper, Wharton.

Quoidbach, J, Gilbert, D & Wilson, T, 2013. "The end of history illusion". Science, 339, 96.

Russell, S, 2015. "How time travel can help you save." LinkedIn.

Russell, S, 2015b. "How your brain may prevent you making good retirement choices." LinkedIn.

Thaler, R, 1999. "Mental accounting matters". Journal of Behavioral Decision Making, 12, 183-206.

Williams, B, 2017. "The ageing brain: the impact of ageing on financial decisions." State Street Global Advisors.

CHAPTER 11: CLIENT ENGAGEMENT & INFLUENCE

Notes

1.   Boser (2017).

2.   Assuming that there is one right option and 9 wrong ones, and ignoring combinations of different options.

3.   Benartzi (2012).

4.   Mitchell & Utkus (2003).

5.   Baker & Ricciardi (2014).

6.   Hunt, Brimble & Freudenberg (2011)

7.   ASIC (2012).

8.   Todorov (2017).

9.   Cialdini (1984).

10.   Boser (2017).

11.   Hunt et al (2011).

12.   Choi et al (2017).

13.   Hunt et al (2011).

14.   Ariely (2010).

15.   Goldstein & Cialdini (2014).

16.   Cabinet Office (2010).

17.   Cialdini (2017).

18.   Collins & Miller (1994).

19.   Epley (2014).

20.   Moore et al (1999).

21.   Moore et al (1999).

22.   ASIC (2012).

23.   Ariely & Kreisler (2017).

24.   Buell (2019).

25.   Ariely (2008).

26. Although, as a result of the consistency effect, the very act of the adviser soliciting and recording their client's intentions might make their client more likely to stick with those intentions than they otherwise would have.

27. Russell (2016).

28. Davies & Brooks (2017).

29. Epley (2014).

30. Epley (2014).

31. Martin et al (2014).

32. Cialdini (1984).

References and further reading

ASIC, 2012. "Shadow shopping study of retirement advice". Report 279.

Ariely, D, 2008. "Predictably irrational." HarperCollins. New York.

Ariely, D, 2010. "The upside of irrationality." HarperCollins. New York.

Ariely, D, & Kreisler, J, 2017. "Dollars and sense." HarperCollins. New York.

Auh, S, Bell, S, McLeod, C & Shih, E, 2007. "Co-production and customer loyalty in financial services." Journal of Retailing, 83 (3), 359-370.

Baker, H & Ricciardi, V. (eds), 2014. "Investor Behavior." Wiley. New Jersey. (Chapter 11)

Behavioural Insights Team., 2012. "EAST: four simple ways to apply behavioural insights". Discussion document.

Benartzi, S, 2012. "Save more tomorrow." Penguin. New York.

Blunden, H, Wood Brooks, A, Gino, F, Logg, J & John, L, 2018. "Seeker beware: the interpersonal costs of ignoring advice." Working Paper 18-084, Harvard Business School.

Boser, U, 2017. "Learn better". Rodale Books, New York.

Buell, R, 2019. "Operational transparency." Harvard Business Review, March-April 2019.

Cabinet Office, 2010. "MINDSPACE: influencing behaviour through public policy". Discussion document.

Carey, B, 2015. "How we learn". Random House, New York.

Choi, J, Haisley, E, Kurkoski, J & Massey, C, 2017. "Small cues change savings choices". Journal of Economic Behavior & Organization, 142, 378-395.

Cialdini, R, 1984. "Influence." HarperCollins. New York.

Cialdini, R, 2017. "Pre-suasion." Cornerstone. London.

Collins, N, 1994. "Self-disclosure and liking: a meta-analytic review." Psychological Bulletin, 116 (3), 457-475.

Davies, G, & Brooks, P, 2017. "Practical challenges of implementing behavioral finance: reflections from the field." In "Financial behavior: players, services, products, and markets." H. Kent Baker, Greg Filbeck, and Victor Ricciardi, (editors), 542-560, Oxford University Press, New York.

Epley, N, 2014. "Mindwise: how we understand what other think, believe, feel and want." Penguin Books.

Gino, F, 2008. "Do we listen to advice just because we paid for it? The impact of advice cost on its use." Organizational Behavior and Human Decision Processes, 107, 234-245.

Harvey, N & Fischer, I, 1997. "Taking advice: accepting help, improving judgment, and sharing responsibility." Organizational Behavior and Human Decision Processes, 70 (2), 117-133.

Hunt, K, Brimble, M & Freudenberg, B, 2011. "Determinants of client-professional relationship quality in the financial planning setting". Australasian Accounting, Business and Finance Journal, 5 (2), 69-99.

Martin, S, Goldstein, N & Cialdini, R, 2014. "The small big: small changes that spark big influence." Grand Central Publishing. New York.

Mitchell, O & Utkus, S, 2003. "Lessons from behavioral finance for retirement plan design." Pension Research Council Working Paper, Wharton.

Moore, D, Kurtzberg, T, Thompson, L & Morris, M, 1999. "Long and short routes to success in electronically mediated negotiations: group affiliations and good vibrations". Organizational Behavior and Human Decision Processes, 77 (1), 22-43.

Russell, S, 2015. "Limiting choice – why less is more for clients and advisers". LinkedIn.

Russell, S, 2016. "Applying Behavioural Finance in Australia." Publicious. Melbourne. (Chapters 13 &14)

Russell, S, 2017. "A beginner's guide to behavioural fintech for super funds." LinkedIn.

Russell, S, 2018. "The psychology behind why some client-centric strategies don't translate into good client outcomes." LinkedIn.

Todorov, A, 2017. "Face value: the irresistible influence of first impressions". Princeton University Press, New Jersey.

CHAPTER 12: TOPICAL ISSUES: ETHICS, TECHNOLOGY & COGNITIVE DIVERSITY

Notes

1. Sah (2018).

2. Montier (2009).

3. Russell (2016).

4. Blunden et al (2018).

5. Ariely (2013).

6. Moore et al (2010).

7. Russell (2018).

8. Sah (2018).

9. Sunstein & Hastie (2015).

10. Russell (2018b).

11. For example, Tetlock & Gardner (2015).

12. Asch (1951).

13. Page (2007).

14. Parasuraman & Bazerman (2010).

References and further reading

Ariely, D, 2013. "The (honest) truth about dishonesty." HarperCollins. New York.

Asch, S, 1951. "Effects of group pressure upon the modification and distortion of judgments." Groups, Leadership, and Men, 222-236.

ASIC, 2012. "Shadow shopping study of retirement advice". Report 279.

Baker, H & Ricciardi, V. (eds), 2014. "Investor behavior." Wiley. New Jersey. (Chapter 28)

Davies, G, 2016. "Shiny new toys: does wealth management need AI?" Cognitive Finance Paper.

Davies, G, & Brooks, P, 2017. "Practical challenges of implementing behavioral finance: reflections from the field." In "Financial behavior: players, services, products, and markets." H. Kent Baker, Greg Filbeck, and Victor Ricciardi, (editors), 542-560, Oxford University Press, New York.

Linnainmaa, J, Melzer, B & Previtero, A, 2018. "The misguided beliefs of financial advisors". Kelley School of Business Research Paper No. 18-9.

Montier, J, 2009. "Value investing: tools and techniques for intelligent investment." John Wiley & Sons, UK.

Moore, D, Tanlu, L & Bazerman, M, 2010. "Conflicts of interest and the intrusion of bias". Judgment and Decision Making, 5 (1), 37-53.

Page, S, 2007. "The difference: how the power of diversity creates better groups, firms, schools, and societies". Princeton University Press, New Jersey.

Parasuraman, R & Manzey, D, 2010. "Complacency and bias in human use of automation: an attentional integration". Human Factors, 52 (3), 381-410.

Russell, S, 2014. "What behavioural finance can tell us about life insurance advice and commissions." Professional Planner.

Russell, S, 2016. "Applying Behavioural Finance in Australia." Publicious. Melbourne. (Chapter 10)

Russell, S, 2016b. "How to capture the benefits of diverse thinking in asset management." LinkedIn

Russell, S, 2017. "Cyborg: how to optimally integrate human and machine investment decision-making". Publicious. Melbourne.

Russell, S, 2018. "Conflicts of interest – just another bias?" LinkedIn.

Russell, S, 2018b. "The human psychology at the centre of the CBA machine." LinkedIn.

Russell, S, 2018c. "The psychology of financial automation: 7 strategies". LinkedIn.

Russell, S, 2018d. "Who wins when a human, an algorithm and a cyborg drive to the airport?". LinkedIn.

Russell, S, 2018e. "To leverage your knowledge and expertise in an increasingly digital financial world, don't learn to code. Learn to ask these 7 questions instead." LinkedIn.

Russell, S, 2018f. "Why Bill Gates in probably wrong." LinkedIn.

Sah, S, 2018. "Conflicts of interest and disclosure". Research Paper. Royal commission into misconduct in the banking, superannuation and financial services industry.

Sunstein, C & Hastie, R, 2015. "Wiser." Harvard Business Review Press. USA.

Tetlock, P & Gardner, D, 2015. "Superforecasting: the art and science of prediction." Random House Books. London.

Thompson, C, 2014. "Smarter than you think." HarperCollins. London.

CHAPTER 13: CONCLUSIONS & PRACTICAL CHALLENGES

Notes

1. Davies & Brooks (2017).

2. Davies & Brooks (2017).

References and further reading

Davies, G, & Brooks, P, 2017. "Practical challenges of implementing behavioral finance: reflections from the field." In "Financial behavior: players, services, products, and markets." H. Kent Baker, Greg Filbeck, and Victor Ricciardi, (editors), 542-560, Oxford University Press, New York.

Martin, S, Goldstein, N & Cialdini, R, 2014. "The small big: small changes that spark big influence." Grand Central Publishing. New York.

Russell, S, 2018. "8 gaps in the way asset managers use behavioural finance." LinkedIn.

ACKNOWLEDGEMENTS

My thanks to my father, Emeritus Professor Alan Russell, and to David Bywater for their editorial comments. Without their input the concepts discussed in this book would be less well developed and articulated, and the book would contain many more typos. Any errors that remain are my own.

www.ingramcontent.com/pod-product-compliance
Lightning Source LLC
Chambersburg PA
CBHW061141220326
41599CB00025B/4313